Cybersecurity and Local Government

Cybersecurity and Local Government

Donald F. Norris

Laura K. Mateczun

Richard F. Forno

Registered Offices
John Wiley & Sons, Inc., 111 River Street, Hoboken, NJ 07030, USA
John Wiley & Sons Ltd, The Atrium, Southern Gate, Chichester, West Sussex, PO19 8SQ, UK

Editorial Office
The Atrium, Southern Gate, Chichester, West Sussex, PO19 8SQ, UK

For details of our global editorial offices, customer services, and more information about Wiley products visit us at www.wiley.com.

Wiley also publishes its books in a variety of electronic formats and by print-on-demand. Some content that appears in standard print versions of this book may not be available in other formats.

Library of Congress Cataloging-in-Publication Data
Names: Norris, Donald F., author. | Mateczun, Laura, author. | Forno, Richard, author.
Title: Cybersecurity and local government / Donald F. Norris, Laura Mateczun, Richard F. Forno.
Description: Hoboken, NJ : John Wiley & Sons, 2022. | Includes bibliographical references and index. |
    Contents: Why local government cybersecurity? -- What is cybersecurity? -- Cybersecurity 101 for local
    governments -- What the literature tells us about local government cybersecurity -- Cyberattacks on local
    government -- Managing local government cybersecurity -- Cybersecurity policies local governments
    should adopt -- People: The root of the problem -- The NIST Framework demystified -- Cybersecurity
    law -- Important questions to ask -- The future of local government cybersecurity -- Summary and
    recommendations.
Identifiers: LCCN 2022004676 (print) | LCCN 2022004677 (ebook) | ISBN 9781119788287 (hardback) |
    ISBN 9781119788294 (pdf) | ISBN 9781119788300 (epub) | ISBN 9781119788317 (ebook)
Subjects: LCSH: Local government--United States. | Computer security--United States.
Classification: LCC JS331 .N65 2022 (print) | LCC JS331 (ebook) | DDC 320.8/50973--dc23/eng/20220213
LC record available at https://lccn.loc.gov/2022004676
LC ebook record available at https://lccn.loc.gov/2022004677

Cover image: Images courtesy of Siemens Energy
Cover design by Wiley

Set in 9.5/12.5pt STIXTwoText by Integra Software Services Pvt. Ltd, Pondicherry, India
Printed and bound by CPI Group (UK) Ltd, Croydon, CR0 4YY

C9781119788287_210322

Dedication

This book is dedicated to the officials, staff, and volunteers working cybersecurity in local governments across the USA and around the world. Theirs is one of the most important jobs in local government (really, in almost all organizations) today. And in their case, it's often a thankless task played out in an especially challenging environment. They have our deepest appreciation, respect, and thanks!

Contents

Preface

The highest purpose of any government is to ensure the safety, security, and well-being of its citizens. From providing day-to-day services like business licenses, utilities, emergency services, and processing tax payments, to ensuring an effective response to weather events, disasters, or (hopefully) one-off existential events like the COVID-19 pandemic, local governments truly are at the center of it all. So the old adage that "all politics is local" certainly rings true.

The innovations and conveniences of internet technologies, along with the evolving expectations of a networked society and workplace since the 1990s, has led to a reliance on information technology in nearly every facet of modern life. These tools and platforms have permeated our society, including how local governments operate internally and provide external services to their communities. Yet hardly a day goes by without news reports about how local governments were victimized, if not crippled, by cyberattacks launched by criminals or international adversaries. Therefore, ensuring the ability of government to function and deliver services to its citizens in an available, secure, and trusted manner is more important than ever. In other words, regardless of whether you're an elected leader, senior manager, or rank-and-file employee within local government, the importance of implementing and maintaining strong cybersecurity measures and practices within your purview cannot be overstated.

But providing effective cybersecurity isn't an easy task for any type of organization, and local governments, as political creatures, have unique attributes that can make this process even more challenging. *Cybersecurity and Local Government* is intended to help these often beleaguered local government officials enhance, or in some cases, *establish*, the necessary measures to protect their information systems and preserve their ability to continue delivering services to their communities.

To accomplish this, we begin by discussing the need for cybersecurity and why it's a particularly important concern for local governments. While ongoing news headlines about cities held hostage by ransomware are easy to point at to illustrate the severity of this issue and need for strong local government cybersecurity, as researchers we are required to base analysis upon data and other reputable evidence. Thus, much of *Cybersecurity and Local Government* centers around the findings of two separate nationwide surveys (conducted in 2016 and 2020) of local government IT and cybersecurity leaders. This deep-dive into America's grassroots provided a useful and realistic understanding of America's local government cybersecurity – or lack thereof – upon which we could then base recommendations on. **Sadly, in several ways, it's not a pretty picture.**

After confirming the tenuous state of local government cybersecurity in the US, the logical follow-on question is: what can be done to improve things? We answer that by offering multiple recommendations based on current and time-proven industry best practices for local government officials to consider implementing. In doing so, we emphasize that from budgets, staffing, and political considerations to policies, procedures, and training, local government cybersecurity is a complex and nuanced issue and one that technology alone can't remedy. Indeed, we devote an entire chapter presenting people as the root of most cybersecurity problems.

While much of the book tends to be retrospective and focuses on things from the past, we conclude *Cybersecurity and Local Government* by looking into the future. What are the trends in technology most likely to present cybersecurity concerns for networked organizations like local governments? How will the threat landscape change? And of course, how can local governments adapt their cybersecurity thinking to reflect shifts in society due to COVID-19, such as remote work and providing expanded online citizen services? While we certainly don't claim to have all the answers – or indeed know all the questions – we are convinced that *Cybersecurity and Local Government* provides local government readers a solid resource to consult when they are looking to establish or enhance their respective cybersecurity programs.

Twenty years after the internet revolutionized the world, it's unfortunate that any modern organization – and especially local governments – still needs to be advised about implementing effective cybersecurity. While cybersecurity professionals may find this a distressing reality, upon closer reflection, this itself may be a useful lesson in cybersecurity for everyone: no matter how fast the world moves, or how complex the issues at hand, the protection of information and information resources is a necessary enabler of modern society. This is especially true for local governments and their ability to provide trusted services to their local communities.

- Don, Laura, and Rick

About the Authors

Donald F. Norris, PhD, is Professor Emeritus of Public Policy at the University of Maryland, Baltimore County. He retired from UMBC in 2017 after serving twenty-seven years as Director of the Maryland Institute for Policy Analysis and Research and ten years as Director of the UMBC School of Public Policy. His fields of study include: (1) public management, where he specializes in information technology in governmental organizations, including e-government and cybersecurity; and (2) urban affairs broadly, but with specific attention to metropolitan governance. Dr. Norris has published seven books, thirty-seven articles in refereed journals, twenty-five chapters in books, and four-teen papers in refereed conference proceedings. His most recent scholarly works appeared in *Public Administration Review* in 2019 and the *Journal of Urban Affairs* in 2020 (online) and 2021 (in print). The data for these papers came from the first nation-wide survey of local government cybersecurity and was conducted by UMBC scholars in partnership with the International City/County Management Association (ICMA). Dr. Norris received a BS in history from the University of Memphis and an MA and a PhD in political science from University of Virginia. He can be reached at: norris@umbc.edu.

Laura K. Mateczun, JD, is a PhD student in the School of Public Policy at the University of Maryland, Baltimore County where she is writing her dissertation on local govern-ment cybersecurity. She received a Graduate Certificate in Cybersecurity Strategy and Policy from UMBC in 2021. She has also co-authored four peer-reviewed articles based on the results of the first-ever nationwide survey on local government cybersecurity. Her policy interests are interdisciplinary in nature and span fields from public management to criminal justice and cybersecurity. She is a 2014 graduate of the University of Maryland, Francis King Carey School of Law and is a member of the Maryland Bar. Laura received a BA in public policy and political science from St. Mary's College of Maryland in 2011. She can be reached at: lam6@umbc.edu.

Richard F. Forno, PhD, is a principal lecturer in the UMBC Department of Computer Science and Electrical Engineering, where he directs the UMBC Graduate Cybersecurity Program and serves as the assistant director of UMBC's Center for Cybersecurity. His twenty-year career in operational cybersecurity before academia spans the government, military, and private sectors in both technical and management roles, including helping to build a formal cybersecurity program for the US House of Representatives, serving as the first Chief Security Officer for Network Solutions (then, the global center of the internet DNS system), consulting to Fortune 100 companies, and more. Dr. Forno holds degrees in international relations from American University and Salve Regina University, and is a graduate of Valley Forge Military College and the United States Naval War College. His doctoral research at Curtin University of Technology explored the complex nature of security informatics and risk communication for internet-based organizations, and as one of the early thought leaders on cyberwarfare, he continues to research, write, and speak about resiliency and the influence of internet technology upon global society. He can be reached at: rforno@umbc.edu.

1

Why Local Government Cybersecurity?

This book begins with a simple question: why examine cybersecurity among America's local (or grassroots) governments? What's so special about these organizations that they deserve scrutiny? They are, after all, just organizations, and most, if not all organizations have certain similarities, especially the need to maintain effective levels of cybersecurity.

The need for cybersecurity is demonstrated every day and is a common staple in the popular media. And local governments do not differ much, if any, in the need for cybersecurity from organizations such as Microsoft, Target, Home Depot, JPMorgan Chase, the White House, or many others. The similarity to which readers should be aware is that *all* of these organizations have been successfully hacked...as has a growing number of local governments.

1.1 Most Important Reason

Perhaps the most important reason that cybersecurity among local governments warrants our attention is that these governments are increasingly targets of cybercriminals and are under constant, or nearly constant, attack (Norris et al., 2018, 2019, 2020). Moreover, aside from relatively few studies, little is known about the specific vulnerabilities, exposures, practices, and shortcoming of local governments in this matter – yet every local government cybersecurity official who one of the authors (Norris) helped interview in 2013 agreed that their governments were under constant attack. Among local governments responding to a survey that two of the authors (Norris and Mateczun) helped conduct in 2016, 28 percent reported being attacked at least hourly or more frequently, and 19 percent said at least once a day (for a total of 47 percent of all respondents). What is really troubling, however, is that more than a quarter (nearly 28 percent) said that they *did not know how frequently they were being attacked* (Norris et al., 2019).

Among local government Chief Information Security Officers (CISOs) responding to a 2020 survey of mainly large US local governments, 57 percent said that they were under attack constantly, 29 percent said at least hourly, and 14 percent said daily (Norris, 2021). Last, the frequency and severity of cyberattacks against local governments is expected to continue to grow, not to abate, because these governments have become favorite targets of cybercriminals. A reason for this undesirable outcome is that while many

Cybersecurity and Local Government, First Edition. Donald F. Norris, Laura K. Mateczun and Richard F. Forno.
© 2022 John Wiley & Sons Ltd. Published 2022 by John Wiley & Sons Ltd.

organizations, on average, typically do a poor job with cybersecurity, local governments do it even more poorly.

1.2 Additional Reasons

There are other reasons to be concerned about cybersecurity among local governments. The first is the sheer number of American local governments. As of the 2017 Census of Governments, there were 90,074 units of local government, of which 38,779 are general purpose governments, including 3031 counties, 19,519 municipalities and 16,360 towns and townships. There were also 38,542 special districts, most of which are single purpose districts providing such services as fire protection (5975), potable water (3593), drainage/flood control (3344), etc. Last, there were 12,754 independent public school districts (US Census Bureau, 2017). Taken together, this represents a *lot* of governments, especially considering that there are only 50 states and one federal government in the US.

A related point is that most general purpose (municipalities, counties, townships) local governments in the US are small. Around three-quarters of the nation's incorporated places had fewer than 5000 residents in 2020 (Toukabri and Medina, 2020). Moreover, the great majority of American cities (78 percent) have populations of 10,000 or less (ICMA, 2013). This does not include the 12,801 municipalities with populations of less than 2500, which constituted 47 percent of all cities in 2017 (Miller, 2018; see also Chapter 13). And, because of their size, small local governments are faced with budgetary constraints not typically experienced by large local governments like those of big cities and counties. This is one reason smaller local governments are unable to to fund adequate levels of cybersecurity. See Table 1.1 that shows the dramatic differences in municipalities by population, with the vast majority (80 percent) having populations of 10,000 or less, not including the number with fewer than 2500 inhabitants (ICMA, 2015). The distribution of county governments is somewhat similar, although not quite as skewed toward those with very small populations.

Except for the smallest among them, local governments operate information technology (IT) systems that are critical to their ability to function and to provide services to their residents. Cumulatively, they spend billions of dollars each year to support their IT systems. One estimate placed state and local government spending on information technology at over $109 billion per year (GovDataDownload, 2019).

Second, local governments provide essential, often critical public services to their residents and visitors. Consider the following and their importance to the daily lives of everyone involved: public safety (police and fire especially), the courts, election systems, emergency medical services, water provision and wastewater collection and treatment, and emergency and disaster management. Disrupting any of these services or shutting them down altogether would produce serious consequences for local governments. Modern cybercriminals know this and target local governments to steal from them and/or impede their ability to function. As of this book's writing, September of 2021,[1] the

Table 1.1 Cumulative distribution of US municipalities (over 2500) and counties (all).

Municipalities		Counties	
Over 1 Million	9	Over 1 Million	33
500,000 to 1 Million	25	500,000 to 1 Million	73
250,000 to 499,999	42	250,000 to 499,999	124
100,000 to 249,999	208	100,000 to 249,999	296
50,000 to 99,999	486	50,000 to 99,999	390
25,000 to 49,999	888	25,000 to 49,999	614
10,000 to 24,999	1939	10,000 to 24,999	828
5,000 to 9,999	1934	5000 to 9999	379
2500 to 4,999	1993	2500 to 4999	164
		Under 2500	130
Total	7524		3031

Source: ICMA (2013). The Municipal Yearbook 2013. Tables 2 and 3, pp. xii and xv.

most recent trend in cyberattacks against local governments involves ransomware. Such attacks are when a cybercriminal obtains access to a local government IT system, locks it down, encrypts its data, and demands payment (ransom, often in the form of cryptocurrency) for the promised return the IT system and its data to the local government unharmed.[2]

In 2018 and 2019, respectively, Atlanta, Georgia and Baltimore, Maryland were victims of ransomware attacks that, among other things, caused considerable disruption of their ability to perform basic functions and provide public services. (Brief discussions of the incidents in Atlanta and Baltimore appear later in this chapter.)

A third reason to examine cybersecurity among America's local governments is that they receive, utilize, and store volumes of sensitive information, especially personally identifiable information (PII) such as names, addresses, drivers' license numbers, credit card numbers, social security numbers, tax records, and medical information. Such information is valuable to cybercriminals and obtaining it is often the purpose of cyberattacks. In fact, over the past few years, numerous local governments have reported that they lost at least some of their PII as a result of data breaches and subsequent information exfiltration. In some cases, they were threatened with the data being released (or destroyed) unless they paid a ransom.

As noted earlier, in many ways local governments are quite similar to other types of organizations in both the public and private sectors. True enough, but they also have characteristics that set them apart in ways that challenge their ability to provide high levels of cybersecurity. This represents the fourth reason for this book's direct focus on local government cybersecurity.

These characteristics include but are not limited to the fact that local governments are *public* entities that provide *public* services; they are subject to politics in ways that private sector entities are not; their structure is often federated; there is never enough money in a local government's budget to cover all needs (real and perceived); and finally their residents are essentially their owners. We will address each of these characteristics briefly below.

Local governments are *public* entities that provide *public* services. This means that the "bottom line" is not quarterly or annual profits and maximizing shareholder returns, but rather the delivery of a wide variety of services such as those noted above and others. Few private sector businesses have as wide a span of responsibilities. And, within local governments, each separate function or service competes with all the rest for attention, funding, and cybersecurity.

This is where politics (both the good, the bad, and the ugly) comes in. Decision-making in local governments involves small "p" politics (so to speak) in the sense of choosing among available and fundable alternatives. One hopes that such decision-making is a more or less rational process, and that it is driven by evidence and objective analysis. Unfortunately, decisions in local government are often also driven by large "P" politics. Here, the interests of the chief elected officials and the elected councilors may clash because of political party, ideology, or electoral interests, having little to do with what is best for the city or county at that moment or in the future. Certainly, there is politics in private firms, but at the end of the day firms measure success by the financial bottom line. Local governments have no such simple metric, and each official has his or her own view of success, often involving what is politically convenient for the official. This means that the calculations made by officials when choosing among alternatives (small "p") are often colored by large "P" factors.

The structure of local governments is typically federated among executive, legislative, and judicial branches (although courts play a more limited role in local government administration than at the state and federal levels). In a private business, what the CEO, board chairman, or owner of a firm decides is final and employees must abide by that decision or policy. This not to say that there may be spirited discussion and debate within the organization, but it is those leaders' sole responsibility to make the decision. By contrast, in local governments, even those with structurally powerful elected executives, decisions often are made by parties in least two different and often competing branches of government (and a third if the courts are involved). In mayor-council cities, these are the mayor and city council. In council-manager cities, the chief decision-maker for city administration is the city manager, but he or she must act within the bounds of policy adopted by the city council. And council members often have differing views regarding alternative policies and courses of administration. This makes for a decision-making process in the public sector that is very different from that of the private sector (e.g., Allison, 1983).

Additionally, there is never enough money in a local government's budget to cover all needs (real and perceived) throughout the organization. Indeed, lack of adequate funding is nearly always the number one complaint heard from Chief Information Officers (CIOs) and CISOs (Norris et al., 2019, 2020). This is almost certainly true of many private sector businesses as well, but few of them have as many different and competing functions to perform and services to provide as local government. To give a perhaps overly simplistic example, General Motors builds cars, and GM dealerships sell cars and repair cars. Yet both singularly focus all of their efforts on cars.

Cumulatively, these characteristics mean that providing high levels of cybersecurity in local governments is more complex and more difficult than in private sector organizations. They also provide good reasons to closely examine local government cybersecurity and to provide recommendations to help improve it (as this book does).

Fifth, cybercriminals have become increasingly successful in hacking both private and public sector organizations in recent years. Among many others, these have included in the private sector: Home Depot, Target, JPMorgan Chase, AT&T, Yahoo, eBay, Google, Anthem, Equifax, SolarWinds, Microsoft, and others. In the federal government: the Office of Personnel Management (OPM), US Central Command, the US Postal Service, the White House, the National Oceanic and Atmospheric Administration (NOAA), and others. Among local governments: the cities of Atlanta, Baltimore, Dallas, and New Orleans, the city and county governments of Durham, NC, and many more. A simple scan of daily headlines continues to demonstrate that all types of organizations from the government and private sector remain under active cyberattack.

Sixth, cyberattacks are deployed not only by individuals and organizations, but also by nation-states and their surrogates and by transnational, non-state actors such as terrorists. One of the clearest and most frightening examples is the ongoing "meddling" in US elections by the Russian government. Here, American intelligence agencies have unanimously concluded that hackers under the control and by the direction of the Russian government interfered in the 2016 American presidential election with the intent of helping Donald Trump, the Republican nominee, become president. Indeed, since 2016, American intelligence agencies continue to identify active Russian efforts to use cyberattacks (e.g., hacking) in supporting traditional influence activities such as misinformation and disinformation intended to interfere with America's domestic elections.

Hacking by nation-states also reaches down to the local government level. In the ransomware attack in March of 2020 against the city and county governments of Durham, NC, cybercriminals deployed malware of Russian origin. According to the North Carolina State Bureau of Investigations, the attack was the work of Russian hackers using the Ryuk malware delivered via phishing emails (Ropek, 2020). This is the same malware that took down the City of New Orleans IT system in 2019.

Seventh, cyberattacks are very costly to the US and world economies. Cybersecurity Ventures estimates that by 2025 the annual cost of data breaches will reach $10.5 trillion worldwide, up from $3 trillion in 2015, and would represent the greatest transfer of economic wealth in history (Morgan, 2020). As discussed below, the attacks on Atlanta and Baltimore cost those cities at least $17 and $18 million, respectively, not including the cost of lost productivity. These are only two of many local governments that have experienced breaches recently. Expect more to be similarly impacted in coming years.

Eighth, The Internet of Things (IoT), also called "cyber-physical systems," is a rapidly expanding phenomenon that introduces new vulnerabilities and risks for local governments. In many cases, this is evidenced through initiatives aimed at creating "smart cities" that deploy internet-connected devices to sense, collect, and share data and in some cases, directly control physical systems, for improved monitoring and management of assets and resources. To provide a sense of the enormity of the IoT, the research firm Statistica estimated that there would be 13.8 billion IoT and non-IoT devices connected to the internet in 2021. This was expected to more than double to

30.9 billion by 2025 (2021). By contrast, just a few years ago, a typical US household with broadband internet service had one or two computers connected. According to one source, in 2020 such homes had a Wi-Fi router connecting 12 devices that include computers, televisions, thermostats and smoke alarms, security cameras and smart speakers like Amazon Echo, which is expected to increase to 20 by 2025 (Parks Associates, 2020).

Local governments increasingly use IoT devices to better support their services, such as monitoring traffic and parking, detecting rubbish levels in trash receptacles, smart meters, and security cameras. Moreover, as they increasingly manage "smart" cyber-physical systems, such as wastewater, electricity, etc., the consequences of poor defense are more than just data breaches or system failures – they now include physical harm and damage to the community.

For local governments, the spread of IoT devices greatly increases the "attack surface" that makes them vulnerable to cybersecurity threats.[3] This attack surface was expanded significantly with local government employees working from home during the COVID-19 pandemic of 2020–2022. Moreover, the set of IoT devices and cyber-physical systems may be large and very heterogeneous, with different manufacturers, capabilities, and interfaces. The result is an environment that is inherently difficult to monitor and update as new security vulnerabilities are discovered.

One prominent risk is that some IoT devices could be infected and used to launch Distributed Denial of Service (DDoS) attacks on internet services and sites. For example, in 2016 the Mirai Botnet compromised as many as 600,000 IoT devices and used these to attack and disable several popular internet sites (Antonakakis et al., 2017). Other risks are that such devices can be disabled, have their sensor data stolen or modified, or have their activator functions used inappropriately that could result in damage. Before incorporating IoT technologies, local governments must understand and plan for the additional security risks they introduce by developing and supporting policies that will protect them from current and future threats.[4]

Ninth, the expanded attack surface arising from the shift to working from home is yet another reason local government cybersecurity warrants attention. Working from home strains computer networks and poses additional risks such as the use of insecure Wi-Fi networks and the use of personal devices when working with sensitive information. COVID-19 and other disasters bring a surge of phishing attacks, often bearing ransomware, and these only become worse with the enlarged attack surface from working at home. Cybercriminals take advantage of both the trends of the day and the human element of cybersecurity.

Cybersecurity officials are mission enablers regardless of the type of organization for which they work. For local governments in times of disaster, this means cyber staff must preserve the use of technology, protect the organization's information assets wherever they might be located, and help to provide the continuous operational capability for the many critical functions of the organization that rely on technology. Their focus also needs to be on resilience during disaster, which means not only the ability to prevent a cyberattack and, if necessary, to stop a successful one, but also to recover from it while continuing critical operations in as normal a manner as possible.

Finally, as discussed elsewhere in this book, there is an enormous gap in the scholarly and professional publications on the subject of local government cybersecurity. Indeed, the extensive literature review conducted in preparation for this book identified only 14 articles about local government cybersecurity in peer-reviewed journals in the social sciences and computer science between 2000 and summer 2021 – a problem that may begin to be at least partly rectified with this book (Appendix 1.1). Likewise, this search found very few works in the professional literature directly discussing local government cybersecurity. This said, many works from the professional world are relevant to local governments, especially those that discuss common cybersecurity problems and best cybersecurity practices.

1.3 Case Studies

This chapter next examines two cases of notable instances of local governments that were successfully hacked, including Baltimore, MD and Atlanta, GA. These examples were selected to demonstrate the current state of local government cybersecurity and the impact that a successful cyberattack can have upon local communities that are not properly prepared for them.

Case 1.1 Atlanta and the Two Iranians

Atlanta, GA, a city with a population of nearly 500,000 in a metropolitan area of almost 6 million has the distinction of being hacked, according to the US Justice Department which indicted them, by two Iranians (Deere, 2018c). Although the nationality of the hackers mattered little to Atlanta officials and residents at the time, that the city's computer system had been taken down in a ransomware attack mattered significantly. The attack occurred, or rather, was discovered, on March 22, 2018, although it could have been going on much longer.

Atlanta's attackers used a ransomware known as SamSam in a "brute force" attack against the city's IT system (Colorado Computer Support (CCS), 2018). In such an attack, the attacker repeatedly runs passwords against elements of an IT system until it finds a match and, upon successfully logging into the network, inserts the malware into the system. These attacks can occur over weeks or even months. Unfortunately, whatever method is employed, attackers often succeed, get into a target's system, remain there doing their damage until detected and removed.

The city initially reported that the attack had taken down the municipal court system, the city's email, water, and traffic ticket payment systems, and Wi-Fi at Hartsfield-Jackson International Airport (Blinder and Perlroth, 2018). Dashboard camera videos from police cars were destroyed (Freed, 2019). Later, officials discovered that financial, customer relationship management, and service desk systems were affected along with the data associated with them, and several years' worth of officials' and employees' correspondence had been lost (Freed, 2019). The attackers demanded a ransom in Bitcoin equal to about $51,000, but the city chose not to pay and instead began to remove the malware and get their systems back up and running again. No small task, it turned out.

In April, the city paid $2.7 million for contracts with cybersecurity and communications firms to assist in their recovery efforts (Deere, 2018a). Over time, the city's estimated recovery costs were $9.5 million (Kearney, 2018), and, later still, the full cost of the recovery, not including lost city productivity, was estimated to be $17 million (Deere, 2018b). However, by June of 2018, about one-third of software programs the city relied on still were partly or completely unusable. And, as much as a year later, the city's systems were not fully restored, and the city was still in the process of improving its cybersecurity program (Freed, 2019).

What went so wrong in Atlanta? The answer appears to be at once simple and complex. The simple part is found in three reports on the city IT system from the city auditor. These reports, dated 2010, 2014, and 2018, found numerous weaknesses and vulnerabilities in Atlanta's IT system, including up to 2000 "severe vulnerabilities" discovered by monthly vulnerability scans. Many of the vulnerabilities identified were *over a year old* and the report found "no evidence of mitigation of the underlying issues" (Deere, 2018b). The final report also found evidence of "ad hoc and undocumented [security] processes," and almost 100 servers using a version of Windows that Microsoft no longer supported (Freed, 2019). These findings are damning and strongly suggest that Atlanta's IT department was guilty of both IT and cybersecurity malpractice. Indeed, one cybersecurity expert suggested as much by saying that negligence was likely involved (Deere & Klepal, 2018)

The complex part, which at least partially excuses the IT department, is found in the then new mayor's acknowledgement that cybersecurity had not been a city priority. Clearly, the auditor's reports had not gained traction with city elected officials and top management or their findings would have been taken seriously and efforts necessary to fix a demonstrably broken and vulnerable IT system would have been underway. Making such efforts, however, is not simple for local governments. Cybersecurity is expensive and competes with many other needs, both real and perceived. To complicate matters, local governments never have enough money to meet all needs and must choose which ones are funded, especially in times of severe economic downturns (such as the great recession of 2007–2009 and the brief COVID-19 recession of 2020). This is where politics (or making choices in order to govern) gets involved and often makes a complex situation even more confusing. Not to mention, politicians almost always favor funding of highly visible things like education, public safety, and other needs than things like cybersecurity that no one ever sees; that is, until there is a cybersecurity incident with its corresponding cost, chaos, and adverse media publicity.

Case 1.2 Baltimore and Robbinhood

Baltimore, MD, a city with a population of 600,000 residents in a metropolitan area of 2.7 million, has the distinctly undesirable reputation of having been successfully attacked twice in as many years, 2018 and 2019. The 2018 incident occurred on March 25 and involved a ransomware attack on and takedown of the city's Computer Assisted Dispatch (CAD) system that supports Baltimore's 911 emergency dispatch and 311 non-emergency phone systems. During this incident, city IT and cybersecurity staff were able to identify the problem quickly and, according to the city's CIO, Frank Johnson, "isolate and take offline the affected server, thus mitigating the threat" (Rector, 2018a). The system was restored in less than 24 hours. The city later revealed that the incident occurred because staff were working on part of the IT system and had misconfigured a firewall accidentally and exposed a port (an opening to the internet) for 24 hours. Consequently, the attackers found the opening they needed and managed to enter the city's network (Rector, 2018b).

Apparently, however, Baltimore did not learn much from this experience – or, at least, did not learn enough from it – because on May 7, 2019, the city was attacked again and with far greater consequence and cost. Baltimore's IT system was attacked by as yet unknown cybercriminals using the Robbinhood ransomware, which had successfully penetrated the city of Greenville, NC, a month earlier (Duncan and Zhang, 2019).

This time, the attackers took over and encrypted nearly all of Baltimore's data infrastructure, demanded a ransom of 13 Bitcoin (at the time, around $76,000) to release the hostage's systems and data. The city refused to negotiate, and it took months before their systems were fully up and running again. During this time, several city services were either fully or partially disabled, including water billing (which was not fully functional for several months), property tax collection, parking ticket payments, and the city's government email and voice mail systems. Real property sales were interrupted for several weeks because the system that handled property transfers was offline as well (Chokshi, 2019; Gallagher, 2019)

Of course, as with any high-profile cybersecurity incident, there is the embarrassment factor to contend with. How could this attack have occurred just after the one in 2018? Were no lessons learned? It turns out that apparently few if any were. For example, Baltimore had a great opportunity to buy cybersecurity insurance in the aftermath of the 911 attack. It did not. This is unfortunate for at least two reasons. First, in the process of applying for cybersecurity insurance, the city almost certainly would have had to conduct a vulnerability analysis to qualify for coverage. Such an analysis might have found the exact weakness that permitted the attack to succeed. According to cybersecurity expert Herb Lin of Stanford University, if Baltimore had installed a simple patch for Windows that Microsoft made available in 2017, this entire episode could have been prevented (Ropek, 2019). Second, the cyber insurance could have covered at least some of the estimated $18 million that the attack cost the city.

What enabled this attack to be successful? First, for years the city had underinvested in cybersecurity. The CIO had warned city officials months earlier to purchase cybersecurity insurance and also that its IT system was essentially a disaster waiting to happen due to a lack of adequate funding and lack of cybersecurity training of employees (Duncan and Zhang, 2019; Gallagher, 2019). Of course, the CIO was placed "on leave" (or fired), some think, made a scapegoat over this incident since someone had to be publicly held responsible and it certainly couldn't be any of the city's elected officials.

Next, Baltimore's IT system consisted largely of old technology that was improperly managed and underfunded. According to a knowledgeable local observer, technology writer Sean Gallagher, Baltimore's IT system consisted of "a dangerously ill-prepared, kludged together municipal IT system" with a "chaotic jumble of operating systems," whose IT staff were "overworked, underpaid…[and] dramatically underfunded" (Shen, 2019). Gallagher also noted that the "city does not have a full handle on its vulnerability management and patch management and keeping up to date with things." There were also reports about how Baltimore needed to send IT staff personally to each computer because the city had no way of providing updates to systems from a central location (Duncan & Zhang, 2018). If these observations are true, and there is little reason to believe otherwise, then it was only a matter of time before a serious incident occurred.

Case 2.1 Lessons from Atlanta and Baltimore: In retrospect, successful cyberattacks like these are not terribly surprising. This is, in part, because many, if not most local government officials do not fully or even substantially understand the need for cybersecurity. Nor do these officials provide adequate funding for cybersecurity (Norris et al., 2020). This seems to have been abundantly true in Atlanta and Baltimore: both cities experienced ransomware attacks, both attacks took down important city services, both were costly in terms of recovery, both cities had a history of under-investing in already vulnerable IT systems, and both attacks brought considerable municipal embarrassment.

The primary lessons that should be drawn here are that local government officials must fully understand the need for and provide adequate direction and funding for high levels of cybersecurity. Failure to do so will result in similar outcomes just about every time.

1.4 Conclusion

In addition to the reasons discussed earlier in this chapter, the Atlanta and Baltimore examples should demonstrate clearly why it is crucial that local governments and the officials leading them understand the many cybersecurity issues they face. Failure to do so places their communities at increased risk of experiencing likely preventable cybersecurity problems.

This understanding should, at a minimum, encompass the cyberthreats that these governments face, the actions they should take to protect their information assets from attack, and to mitigate the damage after successful attacks, the gap between those actions and the need for high levels of cybersecurity at the grassroots and, finally, the barriers that these governments encounter when deploying cybersecurity. Understanding these issues will enable local officials not only to see why cybersecurity is crucial to their governments' digital well-being but will help ensure that cybersecurity has their full support and is adequately funded and properly managed.

Appendix 1.1   Local Government Cybersecurity Articles in Peer-Reviewed Journals from 2000 to mid-2021

Article	Topic
Surveys and Focus Groups	
(Hatcher et al., 2020)	Survey of public officials in US cities of cybersecurity strategic plans, support for those plans, types of cybersecurity policies implemented, and resources needed for cybersecurity planning
(Norris et al., 2020)[2]	Nationwide survey of US local government cybersecurity management
(Norris et al., 2019)[2]	Nationwide survey of cyberattacks against US local governments
(Norris et al., 2018)	Focus group of local government IT and cybersecurity leaders in one US state on cyberattacks and cybersecurity management
(Caruson et al., 2012)	Survey of local government officials in Florida, examining the relationship between agency size and various cybersecurity issues
(MacManus et al., 2012)	Survey of local government officials in Florida, measuring cross-pressure between transparency and privacy
Smart Cities	
(Ali et al., 2020)	Exploration of critical factors of information security requirements of cloud services within the Australian regional and local government context
(Habibzadeh et al., 2019)	A survey of cybersecurity, data privacy, and policy issues in cyber-physical system deployments in smart cities
(Vitunskaite et al., 2019)[1]	A comparative case study of Barcelona, Singapore, and London smart cities governance models, security measures, technical standards, and third party management based on 93 security standards and guidance
Case Study	
(Phin et al., 2020)[1]	Case study evaluation of a Malaysian local government organization for the physical security components of its IT department

(Continued)

Article	Topic
Frameworks	
(Falco et al., 2019)	A cyber negotiation framework to help defend urban critical infrastructure against cyber risks and bolster resilience
(Ibrahim et al., 2018)[1]	Case study evaluation of a local government organization in Western Australia using the NIST Cybersecurity Framework
Economic Techniques	
(Kesan & Zhang, 2019)[1]	Uses linear models to understand the relationship between local government budgets, IT expenditures, and cyber losses
(Li & Liao, 2018)	Study of alternative economic solutions to the cybersecurity threat of smart cities

[1]Indicates article was published in a computer science journal.
[2]Indicates article is discussed in depth in Chapters 5, and 6.

Notes

1 The authors completed the manuscript for this book at the end of September 2021. All further references to when the book will simply state: "As of this writing." to mean that date.
2 Promises that are not always kept!
3 For cybersecurity purposes, an attack surface consists of the totality of the points in an information system that is vulnerable to attack.
4 Many thanks to our UMBC colleague Professor Tim Finin, who wrote this section on the IoT for a paper he and Professor Anupam Joshi co-authored with two of the co-authors of this book (Norris and Mateczun).

References

Ali, O., Shrestha, A., Chatfield, A., and Murray, P. (2020). Assessing information security risks in the cloud: A case study of Australian local government authorities. *Government Information Quarterly*, 37(1), https://www.sciencedirect.com/science/article/pii/S0740624X19300231

Allison, G.T. (1983). Public and private management: Are they fundamentally alike in all unimportant respects? In J.M. Shafritz and A.C. Hyde (Eds.) *Classics of Public Administration*. Wadsworth Cengage Learning.

Antonakakis, M., April, T., Bailey, M., et al., (2017). *Understanding the Mirai Botnet*. A paper included in the Proceedings of the 26th USENIX Security Symposium August 16–18, Vancouver, BC, Canada.

Blinder, A. and Perlroth, N. (2018, March 27). *Cyberattack Hobbles Atlanta, and Security Experts Shudder*. New York Times. https://www.nytimes.com/2018/03/27/us/cyberattack-atlanta-ransomware.html

Caruson, K., MacManus, S.A., and McPhee, B.D. (2012). Cybersecurity policy-making at the local government level: An analysis of threats, preparedness, and bureaucratic roadblocks to success. *Homeland Security & Emergency Management*, 9(2), 1–22. https://www.degruyter.com/document/doi/10.1515/jhsem-2012-0003/html

Chokshi, N. (2019, May 22). *Hackers are holding Baltimore hostage: How they struck an what's next.* New York Times. https://www.nytimes.com/2019/05/22/us/baltimore-ransomware.html

Colorado Computer Support (CCS) (2018). *The City of Atlanta held hostage by cybercriminals.* https://www.coloradosupport.com/the-city-of-atlanta-held-hostage-by-cybercriminals

Deere, S. (2018a, April 12). *Cost of City of Atlanta's cyber attack: 2.7 million and rising.* Atlanta Journal-Constitution. (Accessed March 20, 2020). https://www.ajc.com/news/cost-city-atlanta-cyber-attack-million-and-rising/nABZ3K1AXQYvY0vxqfO1FI

Deere, S. (2018b, August 1). *Confidential report: Atlanta's cyber attack could cost taxpayers $17 million.* Atlanta Journal-Constitution. https://www.ajc.com/news/confidential-report-atlanta-cyber-attack-could-hit-million/GAljmndAF3EQdVWlMcXS0K

Deere, S. (2018c, November 28). *Feds: Iranians let cyberattack against Atlanta, other US entities.* Atlanta Journal-Constitution. https://www.ajc.com/news/local-govt–politics/feds-iranians-led-cyberattack-against-atlanta-other-entities/xrLAyAwDroBvVGhp9bODyO

Deere, S. and Klepal, D. (2018, March 29). *Emails show Atlanta received multiple alerts about cyber threats.* Atlanta Journal-Constitution. https://www.ajc.com/news/local-govt–politics/emails-show-atlanta-received-multiple-alerts-about-cyber-threats/xbFP3eVt3Eq72lw5UqjIFP

Duncan, I., and Zhang, C. (2018, May 17). *Analysis of ransomware used in Baltimore attack indicates hackers needed "unfettered access" to city computers.* Baltimore Sun. https://www.baltimoresun.com/politics/bs-md-ci-ransomware-attack-20190517-story.html

Duncan, I. and Zhang, C. (2019, May 17). *Analysis of ransomware used in Baltimore attack indicates hackers needed "unfettered access" to city computers.* Baltimore Sun. https://www.baltimoresun.com/politics/bs-md-ci-ransomware-attack-20190517-story.html

Falco, G., Noriega, A., and Susskind, L. (2019). Cyber negotiation: A cyber risk management approach to defend urban critical infrastructure from cyberattacks. *Journal of Cyber Policy*, 4(1), https://doi.org/10.1080/23738871.2019.1586969

Freed, B. (2019, March 22). *One year after Atlanta's ransomware attack, the city says it's transforming its technology.* Statescoop. (Accessed April 15, 2020). https://statescoop.com/one-year-after-atlantas-ransomware-attack-the-city-says-its-transforming-its-technology

Gallagher, S. (2019, May 20). *Baltimore ransomware nightmare could last weeks more, with big consequences.* Ars Technica. https://arstechnica.com/information-technology/2019/05/baltimore-ransomware-nightmare-could-last-weeks-more-with-big-consequences

GovDataDownload (2019, March 26). *State and local government sees an uptick in IT spending; Cybersecurity remains top focus.* https://govdatadownload.netapp.com/2019/03/state-local-government-sees-uptick-it-spending-cybersecurity-remains-top-focus/#.YVJQWNNKjOQ

Habibzadeh, H., Nussbaum, B.H., Anjomshoa, F., et al., (2019). A survey on cybersecurity, data privacy, and policy issues in cyber-physical system deployments in smart cities.

Sustainable Cities and Society, 50. https://www.sciencedirect.com/science/article/pii/
S2210670718316883

Hatcher, W., Meares, W.L., and Heslen, J. (2020). The cybersecurity of municipalities in the
United States: An exploratory survey of policies and practices. *Journal of Cyber Policy*.
https://doi.org/10.1080/23738871.2020.1792956

Ibrahim, A., Valli, C., McAteer, I., and Chaudhry, J. (2018). A security review of local
government using NIST CSF: A case study. *The Journal of Supercomputing*, 74. https://
link.springer.com/article/10.1007/s11227-018-2479-2

International City/County Management Association (ICMA) (2013). *The municipal yearbook
2013*. International City/County Management Association. Washington, DC: Author.

Kearney, L. (2018, June 6). *Atlanta officials reveal worsening effects of cyber attack*. Reuters.
https://www.reuters.com/article/us-usa-cyber-atlanta-budget/
atlanta-officials-reveal-worsening-effects-of-cyber-attack-idUSKCN1J231M

Kesan, J.P., and Zhang, L. (2019). An empirical investigation of the relationship between
local government budgets, IT expenditures, and cyber losses. *IEEE Transactions on
Emerging Topics in Computing*, 9(2), Advance online publication. https://doi.org/10.1109/
TETC.2019.2915098

Li, Z. and Liao, Q. (2018). Economic solutions to improve cybersecurity of governments and
smart cities via vulnerability markets. *Government Information Quarterly*, 35(1), 151–160.
https://www.sciencedirect.com/science/article/abs/pii/S0740624X16302155

MacManus, S.A., Caruson, K., and McPhee, B.D. (2012). Cybersecurity at the local
government level: balancing demands for transparency and privacy rights. *Journal of
Urban Affairs*, 35(4), 451–470. https://www.tandfonline.com/doi/
full/10.1111/j.1467-9906.2012.00640.x

Miller, B. (2018, December 3). *Nearly half of U.S. cities have fewer than 1,000 residents*.
Government Technology. https://www.govtech.com/data/nearly-half-of-us-cities-have-
fewer-than-1000-residents.html

Morgan, S. (2020, November 13). *Cybercrime to cost the world $10.5 trillion annually by 2025*.
Cybersecurity Ventures. https://cybersecurityventures.com/
hackerpocalypse-cybercrime-report-2016

Norris, D.F. (2021, July 14). *A new look at local government cybersecurity: Recommendations
for staying vigilant against persistent cyber threats*. Local Government Review/Public
Management. Washington, DC: International City/County Management Association.
https://icma.org/sites/default/files/2021-07/PM%20%2B%20LGR%20July%202021%20
LOW-RES.pdf

Norris, D.F., Mateczun, L., Joshi, A., and Finin, T. (2018). Cyber-security at the grassroots:
American local governments and the challenges of internet security. *Journal of Homeland
Security and Emergency Management*. 15(3), https://www.degruyter.com/document/
doi/10.1515/jhsem-2017-0048/html

Norris, D.F., Mateczun, L., Joshi, A., and Finin, T. (2019). Cyberattacks at the grassroots:
American local governments and the need for high levels of cybersecurity. *Public
Administration Review*, 79(6), https://onlinelibrary.wiley.com/doi/abs/10.1111/puar.13028

Norris, D.F., Mateczun, L., Joshi, A., and Finin, T. (2020). Managing cybersecurity at the
grassroots: Evidence from the first nationwide survey of local government cybersecurity.

Journal of Urban Affairs, 43(8), Published online April 17, 2020. https://www.tandfonline.com/doi/full/10.1080/07352166.2020.1727295

Parks Associates (2020, August 20). *Broadband difficulties driving demand for value added services*. https://www.parksassociates.com/blog/article/broadband-difficulties-driving-demand-for-value-added-services

Phin, P.A., Abbas, H., and Kamaruddin, N. (2020). Physical security problems in local governments: A survey. *Journal of Environmental Treatment Techniques*, 8(2), 679–686. http://www.jett.dormaj.com/docs/Volume8/Issue%202/Physical%20Security%20Problems%20in%20Local%20Governments%20A%20Survey.pdf

Rector, K. (2018a, March 27). *Baltimore 911 Dispatch System hacked, investigation underway, officials confirm*. Baltimore Sun. https://www.baltimoresun.com/news/crime/bs-md-ci-911-hacked-20180327-story.html

Rector, K. (2018b, March 28). *Hack of Baltimore's 911 dispatch system was ransomware attack, city officials say*. Baltimore Sun. https://www.baltimoresun.com/news/crime/bs-md-ci-hack-folo-20180328-story.html

Ropek, L. (2019, June 14). *Over a month on, Baltimore still grappling with hack fallout*. Government Technology. https://www.govtech.com/security/over-a-month-on-baltimore-still-grappling-with-hack-fallout.html

Ropek, L. (2020, March 11). *Ransomware attach hits Durham, N.C.* Government Technology. https://www.govtech.com/security/ransomware-attack-hits-north-carolina-city-county-governments.html

Shen, F. (2019, May 21). *Baltimore's out-of-date and underfunded IT system was ripe for ransomware attack*. Baltimore Brew. (Accessed March 29, 2020). https://baltimorebrew.com/2019/05/21/baltimores-out-of-date-and-underfunded-it-system-was-ripe-for-a-ransomware-attack

Statistica (2021). *Internet of Things (iot) and non-iot active device connections worldwide from 2010 to 2025*. https://www.statista.com/statistics/1101442/iot-number-of-connected-devices-worldwide/#:~:text=The%20total%20installed%20base%20of,that%20are%20expected%20in%202021

Toutabri, A. and Mediona L. (2020, May 21). *Latest City and Town Population Estimates of the Decade Show Three-Fourths of the Nation's Incorporated Places Have Fewer Than 5,000 People*. Washington, DC: Census Library, U.S. Census Bureau. https://www.census.gov/library/stories/2020/05/america-a-nation-of-small-towns.html

US Census Bureau (2017). *2017 Census of Governments*. https://www.census.gov/data/tables/2017/econ/gus/2017-governments.html

Vitunskaite, M., He, Y., Brandstetter, T., and Janicke, H. (2019). Smart cities and cyber security: Are we there yet? A comparative study on the role of standards, third party risk management and security ownership. *Computers & Security*, 83, 313–331. URL is:https://dergipark.org.tr/en/download/article-file/876546

2

What is Cybersecurity?

2.1 Introduction

This chapter begins with a brief description of cybersecurity, followed by a definition of the term itself. Next, it discusses the three "dimensions" of cybersecurity or the "cybersecurity cube." Third, it introduces the five functions of cybersecurity as laid out by the National Institute of Standards and Technology (NIST) Cybersecurity Framework. Finally, it concludes with a brief history of the origin of the internet and e-government.

Cybersecurity can be considered "good health care" for local governments and society at large. In fact, the term "cyber-hygiene" has been applied to the implementation of routine cybersecurity measures. In today's world and probably for a long time into the future, cybersecurity is essential. This is because society has grown dependent on computing and the internet to structure daily lives and corporate or government operations which increasingly rely on information and information resources. Therefore, a simple interpretation of cybersecurity is the protection of information technology systems such as computers and mobile devices in organizations (and homes) and the data that they collect, manipulate, store, and transmit.

By extension, information transferred over networks, the networks themselves, and the software, hardware, and other devices involved must all be secured and protected. In some cases, such as with laptops or mobile devices, these information resources do not necessarily need to be connected to the internet in order for cybersecurity to be a concern. Cybersecurity also extends to the physical security of the hardware, devices, and data in an organization, as well as underlying physical infrastructure such as fiber optic cables and the electricity or water necessary to power and/or cool it all.

2.2 Cybersecurity Defined

Perhaps the best definition of cybersecurity comes from the Department of Homeland Security's (DHS) Cybersecurity Infrastructure and Security Agency (CISA). "Cybersecurity is the art of protecting networks, devices, and data from unauthorized access or criminal use and the practice of ensuring confidentiality, integrity, and

Cybersecurity and Local Government, First Edition. Donald F. Norris, Laura K. Mateczun and Richard F. Forno.
© 2022 John Wiley & Sons Ltd. Published 2022 by John Wiley & Sons Ltd.

availability of information" (CISA, 2019). However, to ensure that all readers have the same understanding of the terms used in this definition this section briefly explains them.

Networks are groups of computers and other electronic devices that are connected together and able to communicate with one another. Many homes today have wireless networks that allow families to surf the web, stream TV and movies, communicate with others, engage in commercial transactions, and more. During the COVID-19 pandemic, these home networks and the devices associated with them allowed children to go to school virtually and parents to go to work remotely. Businesses and local governments across the nation have computer networks of all sizes that are essential to them being able to conduct business and provide services to customers and residents. The internet is the largest computer network in the world with literally billions of devices connected to it (13.8 billion expected in 2021, and 30.9 billion by 2025), many more devices than people living on the planet (Statista, 2020).

Hardware includes the physical connections that make up networks. In addition to computers, tablets, cellphones, routers, and more, devices also include items considered part of the "Internet of Things" (IoT) like printers, smart speakers, home assistants (e.g., from Amazon and Google), smart locks, video cameras, security systems, access card systems, thermostats, air quality controllers, HVAC controls, smoke alarms, lights, parking lot gates, traffic monitoring systems, and more. See Chapter 12 for a more detailed discussion of the IoT.

Data represents the information stored in IT systems and communicated over networks. Data exists in three states: 1) at rest or in storage; 2) in transit; and 3) in use. Accordingly, data needs to be protected while in each state: when it is stable, when it is traveling over networks, and when it is being used. Examples of data commonly stored, communicated, and used by local governments might include financial records including billing and tax records, budgets and budgetary documents, personally identifiable information (PII) such as names, addresses, social security numbers and driver's license or ID numbers, records of various kinds including student, medical, police, planning, and meeting records, and assorted internal and external communication among others.

The networks, devices, and data used by local governments require appropriate, if not in many cases, very high levels of cybersecurity because the entire operation of a local government can be severely damaged or rendered inoperable by a successful cyberattack. This is certainly what happened to Atlanta and Baltimore when they experienced successful cyberattacks (see Chapter 1).

The second part of CISA's definition of cybersecurity addresses how local government networks, devices, and data are secured. Specifically, this relates to how maintaining the confidentiality, integrity, and availability of an organization's information helps protect it from unauthorized and criminal use. In the cybersecurity discipline, this is known as the CIA triad and has served as one of the bedrock principles of the field since the early 1970s (Fruhlinger, 2020). In short, **confidentiality** means that information is accessible only to parties with proper authorization. **Integrity** means that the information has not been improperly altered and can be trusted by users. **Availability** means that people can access the information when needed. Steps taken to ensure the confidentiality and integrity of information can overlap and reinforce one another but care must be taken to balance those requirements by also ensuring that information remains available as intended.

Confidentiality of data and information is made possible by emphasizing the concepts of authentication and authorization when accessing a local government's information resources. Authentication is the process of determining that users are indeed who they say they are and can be accomplished by using strong passwords or newer forms of authentication such as biometrics, like facial recognition, or multi-factor authentication, in which two or more pieces of evidence authenticate a user such as a randomly generated set of numbers. Authorization means that the authenticated users have the authority to access the information relevant to their job duties and are not authorized to access information outside the scope of their responsibilities. Information can also be kept confidential through encryption and/or by physical security controls that restrict who can access that information. In other words, confidentiality means that only authorized users, who have been properly authenticated, can access a local government's systems and information. This is important to remember because if users have access to everything that is considered sensitive or confidential, then nothing really can be considered sensitive or confidential.

Integrity means protecting information against unwanted alteration and ensuring it can be trusted by users. This includes not only the malicious altering of information but also unintentional accidents, human errors and mistakes, malfunctions and/or physical corruption caused by hardware or software problems. Integrity means the information is accurate and complete in its original form, as long as it is trustworthy. Data corruption can occur during the processes of writing, reading, collecting, storing, and transmitting the information. Accidents happen, and data can be corrupted due to ignorance or negligence. Physical corruption of hardware can happen naturally over time, especially if exposed to too much heat or through prolonged use, such as a server's hard drive.

To help ensure integrity of information resources, in addition to applying technical controls to prevent or report unauthorized modification to information resources, audits and checkups are helpful to detect either accidental or malicious alteration. For example, a regular audit would have immediately recognized the impact of the virus created by the disgruntled software employees in the 1999 cult film classic *Office Space* (Judge, 1999). There, the employees developed a faulty virus to siphon fractions of a penny from each of the company's transactions into a separate bank account, which allowed them to steal hundreds of thousands of dollars in only a few days. Similarly, a manual examination of system anomalies (as in the movie) – such as a seventy-five cent accounting error – is what led Berkeley astronomer-turned-hacker-tracker Cliff Stoll to uncover a prominent Soviet cyber-espionage plot against the United States in the 1980s as chronicled in *The Cuckoo's Egg* (1989).

Availability means information is accessible to users when they need it. In order to ensure availability, information systems must operate correctly. For example, if a local government stores data on the cloud (or, with an outside organization) and does not have the necessary internet bandwidth (speed and capacity) to access the information during times of high traffic, the information may not be available, and the local government may not be able to complete tasks efficiently, if at all. Ensuring this principle of availability, at least within the cybersecurity sense, requires close coordination between the local government's cybersecurity team and IT department, since the latter is responsible for network administration and availability.

2.3   Dimensions of Cybersecurity

Organizational cybersecurity involves more than the specific technologies utilized by a local government. Indeed, it can be perceived as a cube: one dimension is the three principles of security (protecting the confidentiality, integrity, and availability of information); the second dimension is the three states of data (at rest, in transit, and in use); and the third dimension involves the three ways of ensuring the CIA of information in its three states, through technology, policies, and practices and people (Figure 2.1).

John McCumber, a retired Air Force officer and former Cryptologic Fellow at the NSA, developed the cube of information security for a paper he presented at conference in 1991. The intent of the cube is to establish a "comprehensive model for understanding the threat to our automated information systems...This model not only addresses the threat, it functions as an assessment, systems development, and evaluation tool" (McCumber, 1991, p. 328).

So far, this chapter has discussed the CIA triad and the three states of data in the previous section. It also discussed technology, including the devices, hardware, and software involved in protecting the cybersecurity of a local government. The remaining aspects of cybersecurity safeguards include policies and practices, and people. These policies, procedures, and practices enable local governments to use information technologies to

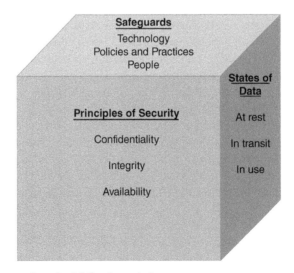

Figure 2.1   Cybersecurity cube (McCumber cube).

protect the CIA of information in its three states. Policies include the written measures that local governments implement through various practices and procedures, which may or may not be specifically established by policy.

People develop policies, procedures, and practices, and people use technologies (although, certain if not many of these can be automated). In his initial writing, McCumber described this third cybersecurity safeguard as "education, training, and awareness" (McCumber, 1991, p. 333). Without cybersecurity education, training, and awareness among staff and officials, it would be impossible for local governments to protect the security of their information resources. All local government employees and officials, whether elected or appointed, must be trained in basic cybersecurity awareness. The five functions of cybersecurity also address how people are involved in successful cybersecurity operations.

The cybersecurity cube provides a succinct model for understanding how to address local government cybersecurity. All three dimensions, and each aspect of the three dimensions, must be considered when developing and implementing a comprehensive cybersecurity policy. The NIST Cybersecurity Framework, first published in 2014, mentioned throughout this book, provides the methodology for doing so.

2.4 The Five Functions of Cybersecurity

The five functions of cybersecurity found in the NIST Cybersecurity Framework form a cycle through which local governments can help protect the confidentiality, integrity, and availability of their information resources by organizing how to accomplish these goals through technology, policies and practices, and people (see also Chapter 9). These functions are: Identify, Protect, Detect, Respond, and Recover, and they work together in a continuous cycle with each function reinforcing the other (see Figure 2.1). These functions can be found in the NIST Cybersecurity Framework Version 1.1, which is discussed in greater detail in Chapter 9 (NIST, 2018). As a local government moves through the framework, it can assess its current cybersecurity posture and identify how to improve its cybersecurity and reach its desired level of performance.

The framework puts forth flexible standards and guidelines that can be applied differently depending on the critical infrastructure sector in which the organization operates, as shown in Table 2.1.

Depending on their local geography, the functions they perform and the services they provide, local governments likely will be interested in the cybersecurity issues facing several of these sectors. In many cases, these governments will share common concerns with sectors like emergency services, government facilities, healthcare, power, and water/wastewater systems.

The **Identify** function involves "develop[ing] an organizational understanding" of the particular cybersecurity risks facing the local government (2018, p. 7). Assessing a local government's cybersecurity posture involves identifying which "systems, people, assets, data, and capabilities" are involved in supporting critical functions and services (2018, p. 7). A local government must understand the hardware and software it is using before its

Table 2.1 NIST critical infrastructure sectors.

Chemical	Commercial Facilities	Communications	Critical Manufacturing
Dams	Defense Industrial	Emergency Services	Energy
Financial Services	Food and Agriculture	Government Facilities	Healthcare and Public Health
Information Technology	Nuclear Reactors, Materials and Waste	Transportation Systems	Water and Wastewater Systems

Source: NIST (2021).

systems can be protected. It must also develop risk assessment and risk management plans, such as presented in the NIST Risk Management Framework (NIST, n.d.). The Identify function goes beyond identifying how the local government currently governs cybersecurity and involves identifying all of the stakeholders and the objectives specific to the local government's overall operations. Ultimately, however, local governments must first identify risks in order to protect against them.

Protect, the second function of cybersecurity, means "develop[ing] and implement[ing] appropriate safeguards to ensure delivery of critical services" (2018, p. 7). Local governments must aim to protect the confidentiality, integrity, and accessibility of their information resources. Accordingly, this function involves protecting local government assets identified in the previous function to prevent adverse cybersecurity events and limit the effects of successful cybersecurity attacks. Access management (authentication and authorization) and regular maintenance are examples of basic protocols under the Protect function. Maintenance should occur regularly and according to policy. Cybersecurity awareness training for all system users is also essential to protecting local government information systems. Protect also involves the more technical functions such as logs of audits and system changes and system back-ups. With protection systems and polices in place, the occurrence and impact of cybersecurity events can be mitigated. Even if local government information systems are protected with high levels of cybersecurity, they are also under constant or nearly constant attack, which can result in cybersecurity incidents and breaches. As a result, these systems must be properly staffed, equipped, and managed to perform the Detect function.

Detect means "develop[ing] and implement[ing] appropriate activities to identify the occurrence of a cybersecurity event" (2018, p. 7). The time it takes to discover a breach can exponentially increase the amount of damage inflicted. According to IBM, in 2021 it took organizations an average of 287 days to identify that a cybersecurity breach occurred (IBM, 2021). Anomalous activity on a local government's information systems should be detected through continuous monitoring of the network, the physical environment, and employee activity. Once a baseline of network activity is understood, incident alert thresholds can be established, and events can be analyzed for attack targets and methods. These detection methods can be improved with regular testing. The detection of emergent threats, such as Zero-Day vulnerabilities discussed in Chapter 3, represents a growing problem for cybersecurity officials since the very nature of these vulnerabilities means that defenders cannot defend against or remediate them because they are unknown.

> Zero day attacks target vulnerabilities so new that people aren't aware of them and defensive measures aren't available to fix them yet.

The **Respond** function involves instituting "appropriate activities to take action regarding a detected cybersecurity incident" (2018, p. 8). Response planning, external and internal communications, analysis, mitigation, and improvement are all aspects of this function. Once a cybersecurity incident has been detected, the response plan needs to be executed and procedures followed. Local governments should develop and implement clear personnel roles and responsibilities in order to ensure quick and effective response. Event analysis is essential to understanding the incident's full impact. This includes performing digital forensics and addressing the vulnerabilities found, as well as properly collecting and preparing evidence for a possible legal action. After action reports and lessons learned help build institutional memory and improve a local government's overall cybersecurity posture.

Finally, the **Recover** function entails utilizing "appropriate activities to maintain plans for resilience and to restore any capabilities or services that were impaired due to a cybersecurity incident" (2018, p. 8). Local governments should maintain resiliency plans for when events do occur and update them with lessons learned. The goal is to return to normal operations as quickly as possible, and to improve the systems in place. Similar to the Respond function, communications and public relations is a critical aspect of recovery (Figure 2.2).

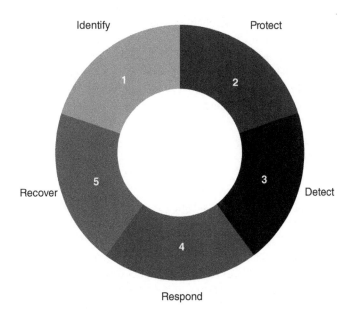

Figure 2.2 NIST five functions of cybersecurity.

2.5 Origin of the Internet and E-government

This section presents a brief history of the formation of the internet, because regardless of its many benefits the internet has opened organizations to unprecedented risks from cyberattacks. Unfortunately, the way the internet was developed has security ramifications to this day and likely well into the future. In the late 1960s and early 1970s the Defense Advanced Research Projects Agency established the precursor to the internet (ARPANET) as a way of developing a resilient communications medium that could survive the effects of a nuclear war. At the time, the ARPANET connected only a handful of research institutions and universities in the United States (McKenzie, 2009). By 1981 the network had grown to 213 hosts, including some international organizations (Norman, n.d.). Unfortunately, those developing ARPANET did not consider the security of the network when building it, because trusted parties like academic and research institutions, were its only users (Timberg, 2015) and its future evolution into the global public internet was never considered. Hence, no one understood or could foresee why security would be so important.

Moving forward to the 1990s and the early 2000s and the advent of e-government (also known as electronic government or digital government), there was a growing movement and interest in shifting the delivery of government services online as much as possible. This evolution of online service delivery continues to this day, especially as local governments have witnessed the conveniences and cost savings from it. Starting with the federal government in the 1990s, state and local level e-government did not gain significant traction until the mid-2000s. Similar to how the internet was developed, initial e-government efforts focused little on the security of websites and how to place information and services online except for posting privacy and security policies (West, 2008). The security of local governments' systems themselves was not as high a priority. As more and more local governments became digitally enabled, the number of (often successful) attacks against them has increased, thus increasing attention to the need for strong cybersecurity on these systems. As mentioned earlier, this is necessary to ensure the confidentiality, integrity, and availability of the information stored on them and to enable those governments to continue providing public services even when being attacked and, especially when these systems are breached.

2.6 Conclusion

Cybersecurity involves three dimensions: the three principles of information security; the three states of data; and the three safeguards of cybersecurity. Protecting the confidentiality, integrity, and availability of information is the ultimate goal of an effective cybersecurity program. This information must be protected in all three of its states: at rest, in transit, and in use. The best way to accomplish these goals is to enable a robust cybersecurity program that involves technology, policies, procedures, practices, and people. As a reliable starting point, local governments should follow the NIST Cybersecurity Framework and the five functions of cybersecurity to institute the highest levels of cybersecurity possible for their organizations.

References

Cybersecurity Infrastructure and Security Agency (CISA), US Department of Homeland Security (2019, November 14). *Security Tip (ST04-001) What is cybersecurity?* https://us-cert.cisa.gov/ncas/tips/ST04-001

Fruhlinger, J. (2020, February 10). *The CIA triad: Definition, components and examples.* CSO Magazine. https://www.csoonline.com/article/3519908/the-cia-triad-definition-components-and-examples.html

IBM (2021). *Cost of a data breach report 2021.* https://www.ibm.com/downloads/cas/OJDVQGRY

Judge, M. (Director). (1999). *Office Space* [film]. 20th Century Studios.

McCumber, J. (1991). Information systems security: A comprehensive model. 14th National Computer Security Conference (pp. 328–337). National Institute of Standards and Technology/National Computer Security Center.

McKenzie, A. (2009, December 4). *Early sketch of ARPANET's first four nodes.* Scientific American. https://www.scientificamerican.com/gallery/early-sketch-of-arpanets-first-four-nodes

Norman, J. (n.d.). *There are 213 hosts on Arpanet.* HistoryOfInformation.com. https://www.historyofinformation.com/detail.php?id=98#:~:text=In%201981%20there%20were%20213,added%20approximately%20every%2020%20days

Statista (2020, November). *Internet of Things (IoT) and non-IoT active device connections worldwide from 2010 to 2025.* https://www.statista.com/statistics/1101442/iot-number-of-connected-devices-worldwide

Stoll, C. (1989). *The Cuckoo's Egg.* Doubleday.

Timberg, C. (2015, May 30). *A flaw in the design.* The Washington Post. https://www.washingtonpost.com/sf/business/2015/05/30/net-of-insecurity-part-1

U.S. National Institute of Standards and Technology (2018, April 16). *Framework for improving critical infrastructure cybersecurity: Version 1.1.* https://nvlpubs.nist.gov/nistpubs/CSWP/NIST.CSWP.04162018.pdf

U.S. National Institute of Standards and Technology (2021, June 03). *Critical infrastructure resources.* https://www.nist.gov/cyberframework/critical-infrastructure-resources

U.S. National Institute of Standards and Technology (n.d.). *Risk management framework.* https://csrc.nist.gov/Projects/risk-management

West, D.M. (2008). *State and federal electronic government in the United States, 2008.* Brookings Institution. https://www.brookings.edu/wp-content/uploads/2012/04/0826_egovernment_west.pdf

3

Cybersecurity 101 for Local Governments

3.1 Introduction

The purpose of this chapter is to acquaint elected officials and top managers of local governments with the basics of cybersecurity and to provide them with an overview of what they should know about this subject, especially if they are not cyber savvy or fluent. The chapter is not technology heavy, but rather addresses cybersecurity fundamentals in lay terms in order to ensure that local officials understand the fundamentals of cybersecurity and why it is important.

The chapter begins with perhaps the most important thing that local officials must fully grasp – cyberattacks. This is followed in order by discussions of cybersecurity vulnerabilities, cybersecurity administration and, finally, non-technical actions to take to ensure high levels of cybersecurity in local governments.

The book also includes a White Paper developed in 2020 by two of the book's authors at the request of the Coalition of City CISOs (https://cityciso.org) about what local officials should know and should do about cybersecurity. Although the White Paper covers only 10 points and this chapter has covered 20, it is included here because it remains highly relevant and covers some of the most important information about cybersecurity that all local officials, regardless of title, should know. It is also available in an easy-to-follow format as a power point presentation. The White Paper can be downloaded from: https://publicpolicy.umbc.edu/research/white-papers.

3.2 Attacks

This section addresses cyberattacks, their frequency and likelihood of success, types of attacks, and types of attackers.

3.2.1 Under Constant Attack

Local governments are under constant attack or nearly constant cyberattack. More than one-quarter of the respondents to our 2016 survey (27 percent) said that they were attacked hourly and 19 percent said at least daily (totaling 47 percent). Unfortunately,

Cybersecurity and Local Government, First Edition. Donald F. Norris, Laura K. Mateczun and Richard F. Forno.
© 2022 John Wiley & Sons Ltd. Published 2022 by John Wiley & Sons Ltd.

nearly one in three (29 percent) said that they did not know how frequently their governments were under cyberattack (Norris et al., 2019). Over half (57 percent) of respondents to the 2020 survey said constantly, followed by 29 percent who said hourly, totaling 89 percent (Norris, 2021). So, all local government officials should assume that their information systems are under constant attack. As a result, these officials must make cybersecurity a high priority, fund cybersecurity adequately, and ensure their cybersecurity technology, policies, practices, and personnel are prepared to identify and repel attacks.

3.2.2 Attacks Will Succeed

Inevitably, some attacks will succeed. There is a saying in the field that it is not *if* an organization will be breached, but *when*, and the saying is largely true. It is also true that organizations frequently do not know if they had been breached. In the 2016 survey, 62 percent said they did not know if they had been breached. Half of the governments in the 2020 survey had been breached at least once in the previous year and of those, 21 percent had been breached more than once (7 percent more than three times).

> All data breaches are cybersecurity incidents, but not all cybersecurity incidents are breaches.

The news media frequently report major cybersecurity incidents, and this is where ordinary Americans get most of their information about successful attacks, largely because there are few federal or state requirements for organizations to publicly report being breached. The biggest report in 2020 concerned the Russian hack in late December of the software company SolarWinds. That incident affected the company's customers around the globe including several federal agencies. Similarly, in 2021 a different group of Russian hackers breached the software firm Kaseya and between 1000 and 1500 customers were affected.

Breaches are increasingly common, even breaches of what are thought to be well-protected organizations. So, all local government officials should assume that at some point their governments will be breached and should make sure that they have up-to-date plans to deal with the breach, to ensure the continuity of essential operations during the breach, and to recover from it.

3.2.3 Types of Attacks

Local government officials should be aware of the principal types of cyberattacks that they are likely to face. Although there are numerous types of cyberattacks, this chapter discusses eight of the more common types of attacks.

Malware: Malware is not a type of attack but it is often something that attackers use once they have penetrated a victim's IT system. They install malware. Malware is malicious software (hence, malware) that can do one of several things (all bad) such as encrypting data and files, blocking user access to systems or components of systems, exfiltrating data and files, and more. Fileless malware makes it possible to deliver malware through legitimate programs in order to infect a computer (McAfee, n.d.). Ransomware is a form of malware that is increasingly used in cyberattacks. Significant local government examples include Atlanta, Georgia, and Baltimore, Maryland, as discussed in Chapter 1.

Ransomware: Ransomware is an especially nefarious form of malware. It is typically delivered via social engineering, most often in phishing or spear phishing emails. Once the malware has penetrated an organization's IT system, the objective is to find and encrypt sensitive data and files and lock down or seriously degrade an organization's entire IT infrastructure – thus likely paralyzing and preventing it from conducting its regular business. In the case of local governments, ransomware prevents them from providing essential services to their residents and businesses. The cybercriminals then demand a ransom, usually in the form of Bitcoin or some other cryptocurrency to release the system and its files and data. The threat is that if the organization does not pay the ransom, the cybercriminal will leave the data and files encrypted or the entire system locked down, or in some cases publicly release the information. The FBI received 2474 complaints about ransomware attacks in 2020 costing an estimated $29 million in losses (Riley, 2021).

> "Social engineering is a manipulation technique that exploits human error to gain private information, access, or valuables. In cybercrime, these 'human hacking' scams tend to lure unsuspecting users into exposing data, spreading malware infections, or giving access to restricted systems" (Kaspersky, 2021). Here is a real-life example of social engineering:
>
> A few years ago, Don received a suspicious email from a trusted source. He contacted the source who said she had been hacked and not to trust or accept any emails from that email address. This went on for a couple of years before the attacker finally gave up. Don's personal rule is never open an attachment or click on a URL that he is not 100 percent certain is legitimate. Don and his son have a code word that they use when sending emails to one another that contain attachments or URLs. If the code word appears in the email, they know that the material is safe and legitimate, otherwise it isn't.

In the early years of ransomware attacks, many organizations paid the ransom to get their systems back because paying ransom is considerably cheaper than paying to restore an IT system. The consensus on whether to pay ransomware has shifted in recent years, although not totally, and organizations increasingly refuse to pay ransom. Today, it is commonly thought that paying ransom is a bad idea because it compensates cybercriminals for their criminality and encourages them to continue ransomware attacks. An article in ProPublica argued that paying ransom "fuels the rise in ransomware attacks" (Dudley, 2019). Also, if these attacks work, as demonstrated by ransom payments, and profit cybercriminals, the criminals will continue attacking.

At its annual meeting in 2019 and, at the urging of then Mayor Jack Young of Baltimore (see Chapter 1) the US Conference of Mayors adopted a resolution urging their members not to pay ransom if their IT systems were victims of a ransomware attack (Duncan, 2019). Also, the US Treasury Department now advises that, under some circumstances, organizations that pay ransom could face major legal penalties. Certainly, federal law enforcement advises against and frowns on paying, and this is increasingly true of state and local law enforcement.

It is never clear that paying ransom will actually result in the cybercriminal releasing the system. Nor is it clear that the criminal won't change their name and/or IP address and re-attack after payment, since the criminal already know the organization's vulnerability and willingness to pay. Hence, paying ransom entails some risk, not in the least because in some circumstances, paying ransom can be punished with steep fines (e.g., CISOMAG, 2020; KrebsOnSecurity, 2020).

Some, however, still think it is best to pay the ransom. In the short run and for purely financial reasons, this may appear to be the best choice. But paying ransom must also be understood as very short-sighted and selfish. Yes, paying ransom is cheaper, but the harm it causes by incentivizing cybercriminals is undeniable. Today, the best advice to local governments is DON'T pay ransom. Use the money that you would have paid (and more if needed) to further enhance organizational cybersecurity.

Nevertheless, and against this advice, organizations sometimes feel that there is no choice but to pay the ransom. In May of 2021, the company Colonial Pipeline, which supplies gasoline to much of the US east coast, fell victim to a ransomware attack. Because of the damage that the attack would have caused to the US economy, Colonial paid $4.4 million in ransom. The company's CEO, Joseph Blount, said that he made the decision to pay for the good of the country. As a result the gasoline shortage lasted days instead of weeks or longer had the cybercriminals made good on their threat and kept Colonial's data and systems locked up. Still, in Blount's own words, the decision was "highly controversial" (Bogage, 2021).

Following the Colonial Pipeline hack by just over a month, the software company Kaseya reported that it had been hit by a major ransomware attack, one that resulted from a zero day vulnerability. The attackers demanded $70 million in ransom to release systems and files that they had locked up. Kaseya provides software to about 40,000 customers and, at the time of this writing, it appears that between 1000 and 1500 customers were affected. Kaseya immediately informed its customers of the attack and advised them to disconnect from any Kaseya software they were using (Lerman and De Vynck, 2021).

To prevent ransomware attacks from crippling their IT systems, local governments should, among other things, continually scan their systems for malware, train their employees to never open suspicious emails, and regularly back-up their systems (see Back-up and Restore in Section 3.3.4).

Phishing: Phishing is a form of social engineering in which cybercriminals "go fishing" for victims by sending emails, seemingly from trusted parties, with promises, opportunities, or threats the attackers hope victims will fall for. A common phishing attack, which many people have received (and which dates to the late 1990s) is an email from someone in Nigeria promising the targeted party (aka potential victim or victim) a large amount of money. The attacker asks the victim for their bank account details so that the attacker can transfer the money. Of course, the transfer never happens, and the scammer later steals funds from the victim's account. There are variations of this attack, some including URLs or attachments in the email that, if the victim clicks on or opens, will give the attacker access to the victim's computer and all of the information in it.

Spear phishing: Spear phishing is a more sophisticated form of phishing in which the cybercriminal uses just enough information to make the victim believe the email came from someone known to the victim or other trusted source. For example, if the victim follows baseball and is a fan of the Baltimore Orioles baseball team, he or she might receive an email that reads something like: "Hey Don (or Laura or Rick)! Have you seen the latest about the Orioles pitching staff? You'll want to read this" and includes an attachment or a URL for the recipient to open or click on. The email may also come from what is or looks like a trusted source's (friend or associate) email address. Given this scenario, many a victim has been tricked into opening the attachment or clicking on the URL. The same result occurs as with phishing – the victim's computer and all of the information in it are wide open to the attacker. In the 2020 survey, responding CISOs said that phishing and spear phishing were the most common attacks that they experienced.

Brute force: Brute force is not so much an attack as it is a method that cybercriminals use to break into IT systems. The term brute force refers to the way an attacker "bangs away" at a victim's computer, network, or IT system using specifically designed software to try to guess a password that will enable them to penetrate the system. Once penetration has been achieved, the attacker can then install malware. It was a brute force attack that resulted in the 2018 Atlanta, Georgia breach and the installation of ransomware.

Zero-day: Like brute force, a zero-day exploit is not an attack, but rather an attacker's identification of a weakness in a network or IT system (typically a previously unknown defect in software that had not been found and patched, such as the Log4Shell vulnerability, identified in late 2021, in the Apache Log4j 2 library, which is used ubiquitously by many applications and platforms). Once the weakness has been identified, the attacker uses it to break into the system and install malware. Zero-day attacks worry cybersecurity teams a great deal because defenses against them have not yet developed yet.

Denial of Service (DoS): A DoS attack occurs when an attacker sends massive volumes of traffic to an organization's website or server – so much so that the website or server cannot handle the traffic, essentially shutting the server or website down so no one can use it. Sometimes, this can happen for purely innocent reasons, such as when the University of Maryland Baltimore County's (UMBC) website crashed because of a traffic overload that occurred when its president was interviewed in the CBS news magazine *60 Minutes*. DoS attacks can also be totally malicious, for example, to disrupt normal business operations or extort a fee from the victim to stop the attack.

Distributed Denial of Service (DDoS): A DDoS attack is a DoS attack on steroids. It is an attack on a server or website by many different computers simultaneously for the purpose of shutting it down. According to Bloomberg News, the US Department of Health and Human Services was hit by a DDoS attack in March of 2020 and was "part of what people familiar with the incident called a campaign of disruption and disinformation that was aimed at undermining the [HHS] response to the coronavirus pandemic and may have been the work of a foreign actor" (Stein and Jacobs, 2020).

3.2.4 Typical Attackers

There are several common types of cyberattackers. According to the 2016 survey, 71 percent of local governments experienced attacks from external actors-organizations, 60 percent from external actors-individuals, 29 percent from state actors (nations) and 13 percent from malicious insiders. Just over one-third (36 percent) of respondents to the 2020 survey said they had been attacked by external actors-organizations, 14 percent said by external actors/individuals, and 22 percent said by hactivists/spammers. A Ponemon Institute survey of small- and medium-size businesses found that 60 percent of breaches were caused by employee or contractor negligence (2018). Typically, this means lack of malice on the part of employees and contractors, although Verizon found that 34 percent of breaches "involved internal actors," suggesting actual malice (Verizon, 2019).

Moschovitis lists the following as typical attackers or, in his words, "threat actors" and their motives (Moschovitis, 2018) (see Table 3.1).

Twenty-one years prior to Moschovitis' table, in October 1997, the President's Commission on Critical Infrastructure issued a report entitled "Critical Foundations: Protecting America's Infrastructures." It contained a graphic that described the threat spectrum from that era. It is included here because comparing the two suggests that the cyber threat landscape has not much has changed in the past two decades. Information warriors of 1997 are little different from cyberspies and cyberterrorists in 2018; terrorists of 1997 are little different from cyberterrorists; institutional hackers of 1997 are little different from online social hackers of 2018; recreational hackers of 1997 are little different from hactivists of 2018; and so on (see Table 3.2).

Table 3.1 Threat actors and motives.

Actor	Motive
Cybercriminals	Money
Online social hackers	Money
Cyberspies	Espionage
Hactivists	Activism
Cyberfighters	Patriotism
Cyberterrorists	Terrorism
Script kiddies	Curiosity, thrill, fame, money

Source: Moschovitis (2018), Table 3.1, p. 99.

Table 3.2. Threat spectrum.

National Security Threats	Information Warrior	Reduce US Decision Space, Strategic Advantage, Chaos, Target Damage
	National Intelligence	Information for Political, Military, Economic Advantage
Shared Threats	Terrorist	Visibility, Publicity, Chaos, Political Change
	Industrial Espionage	Competitive Advantage
	Organized Crime	Revenge, Retribution, Financial Gain, Institutional Change
Local Threats	Institutional Hacker	Monetary Gain, Thrill, Challenge, Prestige
	Recreational Hacker	Thrill, Challenge

(For all threat types, the attacker may be external or internal to the victim or target.)

Source: President's Commission on Critical Infrastructure (1997).

3.3   Vulnerabilities

This section examines cybersecurity vulnerabilities in general and several of the more prominent ones of recent years. What this chapter presents is at a relatively high level because most of the vulnerabilities considered here are addressed in greater detail in Chapter 7. Additionally, when local government policies (such as email, social media, and internet usage policies), are recommended in this chapter, Chapter 7 provides examples of and links to such policies.

3.3.1   Potential Vulnerabilities

According to Whitman and Mattord, a vulnerability on a computer system is: "A weakness or fault in the system or protection mechanism that opens it up to attack or damage" (2014, p. 13). NIST defines vulnerability as: "Weakness in an information system, system security procedures, internal controls, or implementation that could be exploited or triggered by a threat source" (NIST, n.d.). Whatever the definition, it is clear that computer systems have vulnerabilities that open them to attack. According to Moschovitis, vulnerabilities are numerous, especially in hardware, software and operating systems. But "a vast number of technical vulnerabilities are known and technical fixes (patches) exist for them. Unfortunately, in many cases these patches have not been applied, rendering systems open to attack" (2018, pp. 33–34). According to one knowledgeable source, there are six categories of vulnerabilities: 1) hardware; 2) software; 3) networks; 4) personnel – e.g., people are the weakest link; 5) physical – e.g., security, power source, natural disaster, etc.; and 6) organizational – e.g., lack of needed plans and policies (Tunggal, 2021).

> Even simpler, cybersecurity can be seen as a suite of three interlinked components: the "hardware" (devices), the "software" (programs and user data), and the "wetware" (human beings.) But unfortunately while the human brain – e.g., the "wetware" – is the most complicated computer in the world, it's also the most vulnerable and easiest for adversaries to exploit."
> Richard Forno speaking at the "The Dark Side of Data: When Information is Weaponized" panel at the SAP NS2 Summit in Tysons Corner, VA (2018).

It is not necessary that local officials know the technology underlying either vulnerabilities themselves or vulnerability management. These officials should however know that vulnerabilities exist (most who know say they are plentiful) and that processes exist for vulnerability management. The first step in vulnerability management is for the cybersecurity staff to create an accurate inventory of information assets. That is, identify every hardware and software element that is part of or connected to the information technology system or that is likely to be connected to it and create a map of the network including all devices. Next, the cybersecurity staff should identify the principal threats to each information asset and create a document that can be considered a Threats-Vulnerabilities-Assets (TVA) worksheet. Then they should conduct a thorough risk assessment (Whitman and Mattord, 2010). Cybersecurity staff should periodically brief top officials on their local government's vulnerabilities and recommend actions to mitigate as many as possible. Then, with the approval of those officials, take those actions. Needless to say, this is an ongoing process that must be regularly conducted and kept up-to-date.

3.3.2 Email Usage

Today, most organizations use email for both internal and external communication, and many employees at all levels use their organization's email for personal communication. A 2020 survey, for example, found that about 80 percent of respondents used their employers' email systems to send and respond to personal emails (Proofpoint, 2020).

As a result, it is important that local governments develop and enforce written policies about the proper use of their email systems (email usage policies), train officials and employees in these policies, and hold all end users, regardless of rank or position, accountable for their email usage. Local governments should also train all officials and staff to understand what they *should not do* when using email. They should not: open attachments in or click on links provided in emails that are not 100 percent trustworthy; share sensitive information online with anyone; share passwords; allow anyone else to use their email accounts; remain logged in to email, especially when leaving their desktops or laptops unattended; and visit unsecure, disreputable, or unsafe websites.

It is important that software patches be applied to email servers as soon as they are available. Failure to patch vulnerabilities explains the huge breach of the Equifax system in 2017 in which 143 million records were compromised. It was the same story at JPMorgan Chase in 2014, where 43 million records were compromised. And the story goes on. Keeping abreast of events and security solutions such as these is an essential aspect of cybersecurity management.

3.3.3 Social Media Usage

The use of social media by Americans today is widespread. According to the Pew Research Center, large portions of Americans regularly use social media, with 73 percent using YouTube and 69 percent using Facebook (2019). At the same time, however, only about half of businesses have formal social media policies (Digital Information World, 2018). Sometimes people, including local government officials and staff, abuse social media and do so to the detriment of their governments and themselves. Because of the possibility of misuse of social media and to protect themselves from potential consequences of such behavior, local governments need to adopt and strictly implement social media use policies. A key element of social media use policies is accountability. Should end users (regardless of position or title) misuse social media, local governments must have the ability, within the limits of applicable laws, to take action to, for example, retrain such personnel, take away their personal social media privileges at work, and take action up to and including terminating their employment.

3.3.4   Internet Usage

Internet use is even more ubiquitous than social media use (which also constitutes internet use). As a result, local governments should adopt internet usage or acceptable use policies. Alternatively, local governments could combine their internet use policies into their general acceptable use policies.

3.3.5   Passwords

There are a few, rather simple, rules about passwords. The first subsumes all the rest. Make passwords strong. Longer and more complex passwords using letters, numbers, and perhaps special characters are better still. Do not use simple passwords like "password" or "123456" because it is ridiculously easy for the bad guys to crack them. It takes only a few minutes. A 14-digit password consisting of letters only (not in alphabetical order – "dogeatscatfine"), on the other hand, will take a computer 249,000 years to crack. Add more years, many more, if you use letters (lowercase and capital), numbers and symbols. A supercomputer can crack the 14-digit password in just seven days, but to use it will cost you $100,000 to buy the time on the supercomputer (Larg*Net, 2019).

Do not use personal information, such as your spouse or children's names, your birthplace or birthday, personally important dates, address, high school or college, and names of relatives and pets as passwords. Do not write passwords on a piece of paper that is kept in plain sight or in a desk drawer because it is too easy for someone to view or steal. Instead, and if permitted, use a reputable password manager such as Keeper, LastPass, Dashlane, or Bitwarden to generate and store effective passwords. See (Rubenking and Moore, 2021), for *PC Magazine's* top 11 password managers.

Finally, note that NIST has changed its guidance regarding changing passwords. Initially, the agency recommended periodic password changes. However, while many organizations continue to do so as a matter of established practice or tradition, NIST no longer recommends frequent or scheduled password changes because these actions can cause more harm than good over time (Horowitz, 2020).

3.3.6   Telework

This book was written during the very height of the COVID-19 pandemic (winter and spring 2021) when organizations of many kinds, including local governments, had moved from in-person attendance for most or all employees to a regime of mostly telework; that is, some to many if not all employees working from home or other remote locations. According to the Canada Centre for Cyber Security [*sic*], telework poses several cybersecurity risks including:

- Physical access to your computer by unauthorized users which could lead to tampering, breakage, or theft.
- Malicious code being inserted into your device.
- Social engineering whereby threat actors trick you into sharing information or granting access to your device.

- Compromised login credentials, forgetting your password, weak security, etc.
- Compromised communication links through: Eavesdropping – an attacker listens to Wi-Fi or network or records online activity...Theft of service – where an attacker tries to use a teleworker's internet service or processing power for their own purposes... (Canada Center for Cyber Security, 2019, verbatim)

To address these and other potential cybersecurity risks that arise from telework, local governments should identify all risks that telework poses, address those risks, and also adopt clear policies that govern all aspects of telework.

3.3.7 Personal Devices

It is quite common today for employees to bring their own electronic devices to work (aka, BYOD or bring your own device). These include flash drives, external hard drives, laptops, tablets, cell phones, etc. Employees may bring them for personal use (e.g., listen to music, watch videos, view social media, contact others by phone, email, and text and more). They may also use their personal devices to connect to their employers' IT systems. A 2020 survey found that 95 percent of organizations let employees use personal devices at work and that two-thirds of employees used their own devices without regard to company policy (Brook, 2020).

Therefore, it is important that local governments, adopt clear BYOD policies. However, there two are main issues regarding the use of personal devices in the workplace. The first is the use of personal devices for personal use, and the second is whether and how officials and staff may (or may not) connect personal devices to the local government's IT system. In both cases, local governments need to provide clear rules regulating the use of these devices.

The first issue is rather straightforward. As long as using personal devices for non-work-related activity does not interfere with an official or staff member's ability to perform the functions under his or her responsibility, arguably this use should be permitted within the local government's rules. However, use of these devices in ways that materially interfere with one's job performance or reduces one's efficiency and effectiveness on the job should probably not be permitted. Whatever the case, local governments should develop rules so all officials and staff know what is permitted and what is not.

3.3.8 The Internet of Things

As discussed in Chapter 1, the Internet of Things (IoT) adds considerably to cybersecurity risks faced by local governments. The more devices that local governments and their officials and employees connect to the internet, especially from their local governments' IT systems, the greater is their exposure to cyberattack. Hence, local governments should carefully examine this exposure and develop policies to govern which devices, owned by both the local government and its officials and employees, and under what conditions or circumstances, will be allowed to be connected to its IT system and through that connection to the internet.

3.4   Administering Cybersecurity

This section addresses several aspects of cybersecurity administration, including local government cybersecurity budgets, whether cybersecurity is centrally managed or is decentralized, performing regular back-ups, cybersecurity insurance, and cybersecurity awareness training and cybersecurity accountability.

3.4.1   Cybersecurity Budgets

As this book has already shown, it is very important that local elected and appointed officials provide sufficient funding for cybersecurity, especially for hardware, software, policies, procedures, practices, personnel, and training. Previous research has uncovered a number of barriers to local government achievement of high levels of cybersecurity. For example, the 2016 survey found that the top four barriers were: 1) inability to pay competitive salaries (59 percent); 2) insufficient number of staff (53 percent); 3) lack of funds (53 percent); and 4) lack of adequately trained staff (46 percent). Notably, all of these barriers are somewhat or totally related to funding. The results of the 2020 survey are reasonably consistent with those of the 2016 survey in that the two top barriers were lack of funds (79 percent) and lack of adequate/adequately trained staff (71 percent).

Both surveys asked what three things local governments needed to do or possess to be able to achieve the highest levels of cybersecurity. The top three needs identified in the 2016 survey were: 1) greater funding (55 percent); 2) better cybersecurity policies (38 percent); and 3) greater cybersecurity awareness among local government employees (35 percent). Respondents to the 2020 survey listed funding (57 percent) and staffing (50 percent) as the top two needs, followed by leadership buy-in (29 percent). The lack of leadership buy-in and support is a common complaint among IT cybersecurity officials, and we return to it later in this chapter.

The 2020 Deloitte-National Association of State Chief Information Officers (NASCIO) Cybersecurity Study (based on a survey of state CISOs) produced similar findings among state governments (Deloitte-NASCIO, 2020). Three of the top five barriers involved funding: lack of funding, lack of cybersecurity staff, and lack of dedicated budget. Lack of dedicated cybersecurity budgets is also a problem for too many local governments, and local officials should remedy it as soon as possible.

Also, according to the 2020 Deloitte-NASCIO report, most states spend under 3 percent of their IT budgets on cybersecurity, which is far less than financial institutions and federal agencies. By contrast, according to Gartner, average spending by US businesses on cyber across sectors is between 5 and 8 percent of their IT budgets (Nash, 2019, citing a Gartner study). Moreover, only about 36 percent of states have formally established cybersecurity budgets (Deloitte-NASCIO, 2020).

Among the local governments in the 2020 survey, the average spending was 4 percent of the IT budget, and the range was between zero and 10 percent. Fifty-seven percent of these governments spent less on cybersecurity (as a percent of their IT budgets) than Gartner found among US businesses, while 36 percent were within or greater than Gartner's estimate (Nash, 2019). Forty-three percent spent less than NASCIO found among state governments while 57 percent spent more. These data tend to confirm that funding for cybersecurity is inadequate for at least some (if not most) local governments. This is not surprising because studies of IT and government, e-government, and cybersecurity among local governments have consistently produced similar results.

As local governments across the nation have learned the hard way, inadequate spending on cybersecurity often results in the predictable – breaches and worse. Until local governments affirmatively address these and perhaps other barriers, but especially funding, they cannot expect to improve their cybersecurity outcomes or more effectively protect their information assets.

3.4.2 Centralized v. Decentralized Cybersecurity

If they have not already done so, another way that local governments can reduce their vulnerabilities and improve overall cybersecurity is to consider centralizing their IT systems within a single IT department with a single Chief Information Officer (CIO) and a single Chief Information Security Officer (CISO). The CISO should have responsibility for cyber throughout the organization, and all officials and employees should come under the CISOs purview. However, in some, perhaps many local governments, IT and cybersecurity are decentralized or fragmented (some call this federated) among numerous departments and agencies. The 2020 survey found that nearly two-thirds of responding governments said the CISO had total responsibility for cybersecurity while just over one-third said it was divided (Norris, 2021). One CISO reported that cybersecurity in his local government was divided among more than *fifty* different departments and agencies.

Under centralized cybersecurity management, cybersecurity in all departments and among all personnel is the responsibility of the CISO. As a result, all personnel receive the same training, operate under and must follow the same rules and policies, and are held accountable for their cyber-hygiene under the same regime. Centralization provides top officials and cyber leaders with a better overall view of the cyber strengths of and challenges to the organization. Centralization is also more efficient because it reduces unnecessary duplication, reduces the number of staff required, and resources can be prioritized more efficiently and effectively across the entire organization. Additionally, centralized procurement means that technology can be standardized and purchasing can benefit from quantity, all of which help to reduce costs and technological and operational complexity. According to a recent Deloitte-NASCIO survey, most state CISOs agreed that centralization will improve cybersecurity. Centralization can also lead to greater agility and efficiency in cybersecurity resource deployment (Deloitte-NASCIO, 2020).

Conversely, decentralized cybersecurity management means that there is likely to be considerable diversity among departments in cyber technology, policies, practices, rules, regulations, and training. This diversity may be thought of as a strength by the diverse units because it grants them a degree (often a large degree) of autonomy. From the perspective of cybersecurity management, however, decentralization also leads to inefficiencies, higher costs, and communication difficulties. Different units may have different levels of risk tolerance and risk management. Decentralization can also result in greater levels of cybersecurity staffing and cost.

There are, of course, local governments in which decentralization is not only the norm but is nearly or completely unavoidable. This is particularly true where there is a high degree of federation within those governments. County commission or supervisor governments are good examples of federated governments because of the number of independently elected officials and thus, departments in them. In Ohio for example, counties have 11 independently elected officials: three county commissioners, an auditor, treasurer, prosecuting attorney, clerk of courts of common pleas, engineer, coroner, recorder, and sheriff. In such governmental structures, each elected official possesses some degree of independence and executive authority, and there is no chief executive officer for the entire government. This makes centralized IT and cybersecurity difficult and may produce inefficiencies, unnecessary duplication, and additional costs.

Although there are pros and cons to fragmented cybersecurity management in local governments, on balance centralization is preferable from the standpoints of control, standardization, efficiency, effectiveness, and cost. Thus, wherever possible, local governments should endeavor to place cybersecurity in the hands of a single CISO who has full responsibility for this function across all departments, officials, and employees.

3.4.3 Cybersecurity Insurance

Adoption of cybersecurity insurance, commonly known as cyber insurance, among organizations, including local governments, is growing in the face of unprecedented numbers of ransomware attacks. The 2016 survey found that less than half (45 percent) of local governments had purchased cybersecurity insurance, although only slightly more than one in four (27 percent) had full coverage. This compares well with a 2018 survey of organizations in North America and Europe that found that 38 percent of organizations had purchased cybersecurity insurance. Nearly half (45 percent) had done so within the past two years (Spiceworks, 2019). In 2019, the Federal Reserve Bank of Chicago reported that 58 percent of large businesses had cyber insurance compared to just 21 percent of small businesses (Granato and Polacek, 2019).

If insuring against ransomware attacks is not enough of a reason for local governments to consider purchasing cybersecurity insurance, there are other benefits as well. For example, in the process of purchasing the insurance, local governments will almost certainly be required by potential insurers to conduct a vulnerability analysis to qualify for the insurance. Such an analysis, if conducted seriously, should help to identify weaknesses that, when corrected, will provide the insured with a stronger cyber defense. Second, cyber insurance will likely cover at least some of the costs of a breach, whether ransomware was involved or not.

Why else might local governments consider cybersecurity insurance? One survey found that 71 percent of respondents purchased cyber insurance as a precautionary measure; 44 percent because of an increased priority the organization placed on cybersecurity and 28 percent said industry regulations (Tsai, 2019). But there are cons as well as pros to buying cyber insurance. One view is that cyber insurance should be considered almost a must in today's threat environment. Organizations that choose to go without it would probably never go without liability insurance, fire insurance, flood insurance (if in flood-prone areas) and the like. Why would they go without cyber insurance since it provides so many benefits?

There are also downsides to cybersecurity insurance. Perhaps the most important of which is that having cybersecurity insurance provides a false sense of security. The fact of owning cyber insurance does not provide a shield against cyberattacks, but it may lower the bar of cybersecurity precautions. Because cyber insurance shifts financial risk for security events from organizations onto the insurers, it can foster a sense of complacency based on the spurious notion that there is no longer any financial risk to the local government. This is obviously not the case and local governments must continue to be vigilant and provide the highest levels of cybersecurity regardless of whether they have cyber insurance. A second potentially negative aspect of having cybersecurity insurance is that the cost of cyber insurance might be better spent on additional levels or measures of cybersecurity. And given the steady increase in ransomware attacks in the last few years, there is no guarantee that insurance companies will continue providing cybersecurity insurance policies that are affordable and/or do not contain significant exclusions to their coverage.

3.4.4   Back-up and Restore

One of the easiest, cheapest, and best ways that the cybersecurity staff can help protect a local government's information system from the results of a breach or other adverse cyber event is to conduct regular, complete back-ups of the system, store the back-ups off site, and keep several iterations of back-ups spanning weeks and preferably months. The latter is especially important because the malware may have been installed weeks or months before the breach is discovered and running back-ups with malware does not seem like a good idea under any circumstances. According to Verizon, in 2019, 56 percent of breaches "took months or longer to discover" (Verizon, 2019, p. 5). The now infamous SolarWinds breach occurred as much as nine months before it was found. Backing systems up these days is easier than ever with numerous vendors offering software for automatic back-ups. Chapter 7 discusses system back-ups in more detail.

3.4.5   Cybersecurity Awareness Training and Accountability

Cybersecurity awareness training is essential in all organizations, local governments included. Its purposes are: 1) to educate employees and officials at all levels about the need for high levels of cybersecurity; 2) to create a supportive environment for cybersecurity within the employees and across the organization; and 3) to teach them what to do and what not to do in their daily activities involving the organization's information technology system (that is commonly called cybersecurity hygiene).

Training alone, however, is not sufficient. It must be accompanied by accountability measures so that if any employee or official fails (intentionally or unintentionally) to follow the cybersecurity rules laid down by the organization (typically developed by the IT director or CISO) and approved by top officials, they will face consequences. Chapter 7 discusses training and accountability in greater detail.

3.5   Non-technical Ways to Improve Cybersecurity

This section addresses some common sense, non-technical actions that local governments can take to improve their ability to protect their information assets. These are mostly management, policy, and process-oriented measures that organizations committed to cybersecurity will implement.

3.5.1   Identify and Report

People, regardless of rank or title in local governments, are the biggest cybersecurity problem in organizations because of both human error (common mistakes) and malicious behavior. At the same time, people are important elements of a local government's cyber defense. This is true for at least two reasons. The first is when they use proper cyber hygiene and the second is when they are cyber alert and know how to identify suspicious cyber activity (e.g., phishing attacks and other scams) and report it. Hence, cybersecurity training needs to focus on both – proper hygiene and threat detection and reporting. What are the common threats, attacks, and attackers; what sorts of cyber activities should arouse end users' suspicion; what should they do when suspicion is aroused; what should they not do? When employees do not follow training, they are subject to discipline. Those who report suspicious activity should be rewarded, most likely in symbolic ways such as recognition, and other non-monetary rewards.

3.5.2   Cyber hygiene

Hygiene can be defined as: "conditions or practices conducive to maintaining health and preventing disease, especially through cleanliness" (Oxford Languages, 2021). So, staying clean through such things as hand washing, teeth brushing, and bathing promote good hygiene, which promotes good health. Cybersecurity hygiene (or cyber hygiene) is similar in that it promotes good cyber practice, which, in turn, can support high levels of cybersecurity. Good cyber hygiene can also help to inculcate a culture of cybersecurity into organizations. According to Norton: "Cyber-hygiene is about training yourself to think proactively about your cyber security — as you do with your daily personal hygiene — to resist cyber threats and online security issues" (Norton, 2021). And, just like cleanliness, cyber-hygiene should become a habit that stays with you forever. "It involves three basic principles: using products and tools that fit your hygiene needs, performing these hygienic tasks correctly, and establishing a routine" (Norton, 2021). Chapter 7 addresses cyber hygiene in more detail.

3.5.3   Leadership Buy-in and Support

In order for a culture of cybersecurity to develop and flourish within local governments, top leadership buy-in and support (and not just at a rhetorical level) are essential. Top leaders, meaning elected officials and top managers, must: understand that they have an active role to play in their government's cybersecurity; provide the funding needed for effective cybersecurity; practice proper cyber-hygiene; promote cybersecurity through-out the organization as Job One for everyone; and must insist that all parties are held appropriately accountable for their cyber actions. If top officials fail to insist on such a culture and/or fail to act appropriately in their own cyber responsibility, those under them will almost certainly think: "If they don't care about cyber, why should I?" Top leadership buy-in and support will make all parties in an organization understand the importance of cybersecurity and their own cyber responsibilities and will make it more likely that they will practice proper cyber-hygiene, thus improving cyber outcomes throughout the local government.

Unfortunately, a common complaint heard from too many cybersecurity and IT prac-titioners is that there is insufficient top leadership buy-in and support in their local gov-ernments. Think Atlanta and Baltimore. Data from the 2016 survey found that most top officials in local governments were not sufficiently aware of the need for cybersecurity, did not provide high levels of support for it, and believed that cyber was more the respon-sibility of technologists than theirs. Reported cybersecurity awareness improved some-what in the 2020 survey and support for cybersecurity improved even more. However, in the absence of nearly total cybersecurity awareness and support from these leaders, establishing and maintaining high levels of cybersecurity will be problematic at the least. Without these leaders' unreserved commitment, local governments are not likely to properly prioritize and adequately fund and staff cybersecurity. This is a common find-ing across organizations and must change if organizations hope to improve their cyber-security outcomes.

3.5.4 Culture of Cybersecurity

The concept of creating a culture of cybersecurity began to gain traction among practi-tioners within the past decade or so (e.g., Deloitte and NASCIO, 2010). Among other things, a culture of cybersecurity means that everyone, regardless of their place on an organization's hierarchy, is thoroughly committed to cybersecurity, understands the importance of cybersecurity in everything they do, and practices proper cyber-hygiene. They know that Cyber is Job One.

It also means that all parties in local governments fully embrace and support cyber-security, play important roles in it, including, but not limited to, practicing proper cyber-hygiene and insisting that others in their governments do so as well and hold-ing all accountable when they do not. In a fully developed culture of cybersecurity: cybersecurity overlaps all functions and positions in the organization; there is ongo-ing mandatory cybersecurity awareness training for everyone; all parties are periodi-cally tested for their cybersecurity hygiene (and retrained and retested as needed); all parties are held accountable for their cyber-hygiene; local governments provide incentives for proper cyber-hygiene and disincentives for its absence; they have strong cybersecurity policies; and security responsibility is written into all job descriptions. Until and unless local governments inculcate a culture of cybersecurity from the top to the bottom of their organizations, maintaining high levels of cybersecurity will be difficult to achieve.

3.6   Conclusion

Typically, the conclusion of a book chapter contains a summary of what has been presented in previous pages. This, however, is not a typical book chapter because its objective is to provide readers, mainly local government elected officials and top managers, with information that they need to know about cybersecurity. To summarize that information here would be redundant. However, if there is one take-away from this chapter, it is that local elected officials and top managers must understand the basics of cybersecurity, at least enough to be able to ask the right questions of their cybersecurity staff and to intelligently direct and supervise these staff in their work protecting the local government's information assets.

References

Bogage, J. (2021, May 19). *Colonial pipeline CEO says paying $4.4 million ransom was "the right thing to do for the country."* Washington Post. https://www.washingtonpost.com/buiness/2021/05/19/colonial-pipeline-ransom-joseph-blunt

Brook, C. (2020, November 24). *The ultimate guide to BYOD security: Overcoming challenges, creating effective policies, and mitigating risks to maximize benefits.* Data Insider. https://digitalguardian.com/blog/ultimate-guide-byod-security-overcoming-challenges-creating-effective-policies-and-mitigating

Canada Center for Cyber Security (2019, March). *Telework security issues.* https://cyber.gc.ca/sites/default/files/publications/itsap.10.016-eng.pdf

CISOMAG (2020, October 5). *Paying ransom is now illegal! US Dept of Treasury warns.* CISOMAG. https://cisomag.eccouncil.org/paying-ransom-is-now-illegal-u-s-dept-of-treasury-warns/#:~:text=U.S.%20Dept%20of%20Treasury%20Warns&text=The%20U.S.%20Department%20of%20the,to%20cybercriminals%20is%20now%20illegal.&text=Ransomware%20payments%20may%20also%20embolden,future%20attacks%2C%E2%80%9D%20OFAC%20said

Deloitte-NASCIO (2020). *States at risk: The cybersecurity imperative in uncertain times.* https://www2.deloitte.com/content/dam/insights/us/articles/6899_nascio/DI_NASCIO_interactive.pdf

Deloitte and NASCIO (2010). *State governments at risk: A call to secure citizen data and inspire public trust.* https://www.nascio.org/wp-content/uploads/2019/11/Deloitte-NASCIOCybersecurityStudy2010.pdf

Digital Information World (2018, September 7). *Social media use during work hours by employees.* https://www.digitalinformationworld.com/2018/09/problems-social-media-workplace.html

Dudley, R. (2019, August 17). *The extortion economy: How insurance companies are fueling a rise in ransomware attacks.* Pro Publica. https://www.propublica.org/article/the-extortion-economy-how-insurance-companies-are-fueling-a-rise-in-ransomware-attacks

Duncan, I. (2019, July 10). *US mayors group adopts resolution proposed by Baltimore, vowing not to pay ransoms to hackers.* Baltimore Sun. https://www.baltimoresun.com/politics/bs-md-ci-mayors-ransom-20190710-cznelxwcg5hiziiqmubtg2elju-story.html

Granato, A. and Polacek, A. (2019). *The growth and challenges of cyber insurance.* Chicago Fed Letter, No. 426, 2019. Chicago, IL: Federal Reserve Bank of Chicago.

Horwitz, J. (2020, July 13). *NIST password guidelines: What you need to know.* InfoSecurity Magazine. https://www.infosecurity-magazine.com/blogs/nist-password-guidelines

KrebsOnSecurity (2020, October 1). *Ransomware victims that pay up could incur steep fines from Uncle Sam.* https://krebsonsecurity.com/2020/10/ransomware-victims-that-pay-up-could-incur-steep-fines-from-uncle-sam

Larg*Net (2019, April 4). *Estimated time to crack password.* https://www.largnet.ca/largblog/2019/3/25/estimated-time-to-crack-password

Lerman, R. and De Vynck, G. (2021, July 3). *Widespread ransomware attack likely hit "thousands" of companies in the eve of long weekend.* Washington Post. https://www.washingtonpost.com/technology/2021/07/02/kaseya-ransomware-attack

Lerman, R. and De Vynck, G. (2021, July 5). *Hackers demand $70 million to unlock businesses hit by sprawling ransomware attack.* Washington Post. https://www.washingtonpost.com/technology/2021/07/05/kayesa-ransomware-70-million-fbi

McAfee (n.d.). *What is fileless malware?* https://www.mcafee.com/enterprise/en-us/security-awareness/ransomware/what-is-fileless-malware.html

Moschovitis, C. (2018). *Cybersecurity Program Development for Businesses: The Essential Planning Guide.* Wiley.

Nash, K.S. (2019, December 30). *Tech chiefs plan to boost cybersecurity spending.* Wall Street Journal. https://www.wsj.com/articles/tech-chiefs-plan-to-boost-cybersecurity-spending-11577701802

Norris, D.F. (2021, July 14). *A new look at local government cybersecurity: Recommendations for staying vigilant against persistent cyber threats.* Local Government Review/Public Management. Washington, DC: International City/County Management Association. https://icma.org/sites/default/files/2021-07/PM%20%2B%20LGR%20July%202021%20LOW-RES.pdf

Norris, D.F., Mateczun, L., Joshi, A., and Finin, T. (2019). Cyberattacks at the grassroots: American local governments and the need for high levels of cybersecurity. *Public Administration Review*, 76(6), 895–904. https://onlinelibrary.wiley.com/doi/abs/10.1111/puar.13028

Norton (2021). *Good cyber hygiene habits help stay safe online.* https://us.norton.com/internetsecurity-how-to-good-cyber-hygiene.html

Oxford Languages (2021). *Hygiene.* https://www.lexico.com/definition/hygiene

Pew Research Center (2019, June 15). *Social mediafFact sheet.* https://www.pewresearch.org/internet/fact-sheet/social-media

Ponemon Institute (2018). *State of cybersecurity in small and medium size businesses.* https://www.keepersecurity.com/assets/pdf/Keeper-2018-Ponemon-Report-Infographic.pdf

President's Commission on Critical Infrastructure Protection (1997). *Critical Foundations: Protecting America's Infrastructures.* https://sgp.fas.org/library/pccip.pdf

Proofpoint (2020). *User risk report: Exploring vulnerability and behavior in a people-centric threat landscape.* https://www.proofpoint.com/us/resources/white-papers/user-risk-report

Riley, T. (2021, March 23). *The Cybersecurity 202: DHS official promises help for states struggling with digital attacks on critical services.* Washington Post. https://www.washingtonpost.com/politics/2021/03/23/cybersecurity-202-dhs-official-promises-help-states-struggling-with-digital-attacks-critical-services

Rubenking, N.J., and Moore, B. (2021, January 15). *The best password managers for 2021.* PC Magazine. https://www.pcmag.com/picks/the-best-password-managers

Spiceworks (2019). *Spiceworks study reveals nearly 40 percent of organizations have an active cyber insurance policy.* https://www.spiceworks.com/press/releases/spiceworks-study-reveals-nearly-40-percent-of-organizations-have-an-active-cyber-insurance-policy

Stein, S. and Jacobs, J. (2020, March 16) *Cyber-attack hits US health agency amid covid-19 outbreak.* Bloomberg News. https://www.bloomberg.com/news/articles/2020-03-16/u-s-health-agency-suffers-cyber-attack-during-covid-19-response

Tsai, P. (2019, January 28). *Data snapshot: How common is cyber insurance in the workplace?* Spiceworks. https://community.spiceworks.com/blog/3166-data-snapshot-how-common-is-cyber-insurance-in-the-workplace

Tunggal, A.T. (2021, September 14). *What is a vulnerability?* Upguard. https://www.upguard.com/blog/vulnerability

U.S. National Institute of Standards and Technology (NIST) (n.d.). *Computer security resource center.* Glossary. https://csrc.nist.gov/glossary/term/vulnerability

Verizon (2019). *2019 Data breach investigations report.* https://enterprise.verizon.com/resources/reports/2019-data-breach-investigations-report.pdf

Whitman, M.E., and Mattord, H.J. (2010). *Management of information security* (5th ed.). Cengage Learning

Whitman, M.E. and Mattord, H.J. (2014). *Principles of information security* (5th ed.). Cengage Learning.

4

What the Literature Says About Local Government Cybersecurity

4.1 Introduction

A common refrain heard about the scholarly literature on local government cybersecurity is that there is relatively little of it (Hatcher et al., 2020; Norris et al., 2019, 2020; Pries and Susskind, 2020). Only 14 peer-reviewed articles published in academic journals that were directly relevant to local government cybersecurity were found in an extensive review of the literature conducted between 2000 and mid-2021 for this book. However, the number of professional works published by consulting firms, research centers and institutes, industry associations, private IT and cybersecurity firms, and others helps to make up for the lack of academic research on this topic.

This chapter first reviews the peer-reviewed research on local government cybersecurity. In light of the small number of scholarly articles on this subject, the search was specifically limited to research-based articles. Then, it presents an overview of a sampling of the literature from the profession on cybersecurity among local governments or that is otherwise relevant to local governments. Taken together, these works are valuable resources to local government officials who should not only be aware of them but actually review them periodically (or subscribe to or monitor them) in order to maintain an up-to-date understanding of cybersecurity threats and trends, particularly those facing the public sector.

4.2 Peer-reviewed Research

Among the 14 articles on local government cybersecurity found in scholarly journals (Table 4.1) most were published in social science journals (10) and the rest (4) were published in computer science and related journals (Table 4.1). The list in the table includes works by two of this book's authors and their colleagues (Norris, et al., 2019 and 2020) but they are not reviewed here because Chapters 5 and 6 explore their findings in some depth. This section, therefore, provides brief reviews of the principal findings of 12 of the articles found in the scholarly literature review. The articles are thematically organized into five categories: surveys and focus groups, case studies, smart cities, frameworks, and articles using economic techniques.

Cybersecurity and Local Government, First Edition. Donald F. Norris, Laura K. Mateczun and Richard F. Forno.
© 2022 John Wiley & Sons Ltd. Published 2022 by John Wiley & Sons Ltd.

Table 4.1 Local government cybersecurity articles in peer-reviewed journals.

Article	Topic
Surveys and Focus Groups	
(Hatcher et al., 2020)	Survey of public officials in US cities of cybersecurity strategic plans, support for those plans, types of cybersecurity policies implemented, and resources needed for cybersecurity planning
(Norris et al., 2020)[2]	Nationwide survey of US local government cybersecurity management
(Norris et al., 2019)[2]	Nationwide survey of cyberattacks against US local governments
(Norris et al., 2018)	Focus group of local government IT and cybersecurity leaders in one US state on cyberattacks and cybersecurity management
(Caruson et al., 2012)	Survey of local government officials in Florida, examining the relationship between agency size and various cybersecurity issues
(MacManus et al., 2012)	Survey of local government officials in Florida, measuring cross-pressure between transparency and privacy
Smart Cities	
(Ali et al., 2020)	Exploration of critical factors of information security requirements of cloud services within the Australian regional and local government context
(Habibzadeh et al., 2019)	A survey of cybersecurity, data privacy, and policy issues in cyber-physical system deployments in smart cities
(Vitunskaite et al., 2019)[1]	A comparative case study of Barcelona, Singapore, and London smart cities governance models, security measures, technical standards, and third party management based on 93 security standards and guidance
Case Studies	
(Phin et al., 2020)[1]	Case study evaluation of a Malaysian local government organization for the physical security components of its IT department
Frameworks	
(Falco et al., 2019)	A cyber negotiation framework to help defend urban critical infrastructure against cyber risks and bolster resilience
(Ibrahim et al., 2018)[1]	Case study evaluation of a local government organization in Western Australia using the NIST Cybersecurity Framework
Economic Techniques	
(Kesan and Zhang, 2019)[1]	Uses linear models to understand the relationship between local government budgets, IT expenditures, and cyber losses
(Li and Liao, 2018)	Study of alternative economic solutions to the cybersecurity threat of smart cities

[1]Indicates article was published in a computer science journal.
[2]Indicates article is discussed in depth in Chapters 5 and 6.

4.2.1 Surveys and Focus Groups

In 2018, Hatcher et al. (2020) conducted a survey of 168 US municipalities with populations of 10,000 or greater. The survey focused on whether cities had formal cybersecurity strategic plans in place, the level support received for cybersecurity planning, the types of cybersecurity policies implemented in cities, and the resources necessary for cybersecurity planning. All of the respondents indicated that their municipalities maintained a website, 82 percent of which were maintained in-house. Seventy-one percent of the respondents indicated that their city had a formal cybersecurity policy in place, and 77 percent of those without formal policies reported plans to draft one. The authors identified three areas that effective cybersecurity policies should address: information security access, information security education, and the use of information technology. Additionally, the authors found that the presence of a formal cybersecurity policy was significantly related to three results including a higher likelihood of having a termination process during which former employees no longer have access to facilities and information systems (and other processes around access), cataloguing attacks and conducting vulnerability scans, and penetration testing on a regular basis (and other processes around prevention and response), and providing cybersecurity training. Perhaps the most worrisome finding of the survey is that only 37 percent of respondents maintained a formal record of cybersecurity attacks they have experienced, and 41 percent did not provide ongoing training. Regarding cybersecurity improvements, the authors recommended "maintaining a log of cybersecurity attacks, working with outside auditors and professionals to review policies and practices on a regular basis, and making cybersecurity more of a management function" (Hatcher et al., 2020, p. 11). Finally, and consistent with other findings in the scholarly literature, respondents noted the need for additional funding to implement cybersecurity policies.

Focus group research is a method that provides opportunities to help gain an in-depth understanding of complex issues. Norris, et al. (2018) conducted a focus group of IT and cybersecurity professionals in one US state. The discussion in this focus group centered on the types and frequency of cyberattacks against local governments, barriers to implementing effective cybersecurity, and actions to be taken to improve cybersecurity in local governments. Perhaps the most important finding was that cyberattacks against these local government were constant and could number in up to tens of thousands daily. When asked about their leading cybersecurity problem, these officials said that they had the technology mostly under control and people were their weakest link (see also Chapter 8). The biggest barriers to effective cybersecurity were lack of adequate funding and staff, governance issues, and lack of appropriate cybersecurity policies and poor enforcement of them. These themes are regularly echoed throughout the research on local government cybersecurity.

Caruson et al. (2012) discussed data from a survey that they conducted among 466 local government officials in the state of Florida's 67 counties. Thirty-five percent of respondents were generalists (e.g., county manager, county attorneys, and management and budget officials), 38 percent were specialists (e.g., health and social services, human relations, and emergency management and public safety) and 27 percent were IT professionals. Among the principal findings of the article, just under a quarter (24 percent) of respondents knew whether their government had experienced a cyberattack in the previous year. Almost a third (31 percent) of respondents did not know if they had been breached. Fewer than half of respondents (48 percent) reported that their governments had adopted cybersecurity policies and standards countywide, had conducted a risk assessment (46 percent), or had a cyberattack response plan in place (22 percent). Respondents also reported a number of pressing cybersecurity needs, including better end user awareness and training (53 percent), better access controls (53 percent), and acceptable use policies for end users (51 percent). More than half (60 percent) said that the main barrier to achieving better cybersecurity was a lack of funding. Insufficient training came in second (43 percent), followed by the need for personnel with more expertise (37 percent). The article also examined aspects of cybersecurity management and the impact of agency size on various cybersecurity issues. A little more than half (54 percent) of respondents represented small agencies (750 employees with access to the computer network or less, which was the median number of employees in the respondents' respective agencies). Administrators from larger agencies were more likely to perceive malicious insider attacks, system penetration, DNS attacks, and phishing as major threats than administrators from smaller agencies

In a second article from the same survey, MacManus et al. (2012) measured whether and to what extent respondents felt cross-pressured about the simultaneous need to protect the values of transparency and privacy and which types of information were the most difficult for local governments to protect. Eighty-four percent of respondents indicated experiencing "some" or "a lot" of cross-pressure to protect PII (personal identiable information) and provide government transparency, including 59 percent of IT professionals who felt "a lot" of pressure. The most difficult types of citizen data to protect included: PII (69 percent responding "very" or "somewhat" difficult); medical records (57 percent); personal financial information (47 percent); court records (31 percent); juvenile court records (27 percent) and academic records (13 percent). The fact that only 13 percent of respondents found it difficult to protect academic records is interesting in light of the more recent onslaught of ransomware attacks against educational institutions, discussed briefly later in this chapter. The most difficult government employee data to protect were employee payroll (38 percent "very" or "somewhat" difficult), employee performance evaluations (34 percent), and employee disciplinary actions (31 percent).

The findings in Caruson et al. (2012), Hatcher et al. (2020), and MacManus et al. (2012) are all mirrored in the research presented in Chapters 5 and 6 of this book. Themes from the 2016 and 2020 surveys are echoed throughout this chapter, and in the surveys above, namely: lack of adequate cybersecurity funding, lack of adequate cybersecurity staff, lack of employee awareness and training, lack of managerial awareness and support for cybersecurity, lack of awareness of attacks and breaches, lack of funding, and more.

4.2.2 Smart Cities

This section discusses the available research pertaining to the cloud, smart cities, and the Internet of Things (IoT). First, Ali et al. (2020) examined the information security requirements of cloud service providers in the context of local government (see Chapter 11 for more about "the cloud"). Using both field interviews and a survey of 480 IT staff from 47 regional local governments in Australia, the authors identified seven themes regarding these security requirements that the respondents identified as essential to providing effective cybersecurity in the cloud: 1) data transmission; 2) trustworthiness; 3) data storage; 4) redundancy; 5) back-up; 6) data privacy; and 7) government regulation.

A strong majority of respondents (70 percent) supported the idea that "the cloud provides secure data transfer through the use of sophisticated encryption techniques" (2020, p. 6). Eighty-six percent of respondents agreed that cloud adoption was trustworthy. Seventy-seven percent of respondents agreed that cloud service providers provided greater information security in data storage. Forty-six percent believed the cloud provides effective redundancy and 75 percent said that cloud service providers had effective back-up systems. Finally, 63 percent of respondents believed that cloud service providers maintain the privacy of the local government's data.

Smart city initiatives help local governments automate and centralize the management of essential services such as traffic and parking, water filtration, and more. Smart city initiatives require implementing what can be described as "cyber-physical systems" that combine networked devices and critical infrastructure. Habibzadeh et al. (2019) presented an overview of the various issues facing local governments when deploying cyber-physical systems in smart cities. Specifically, their review examined the security and safety implications for critical infrastructure in smart cities, policy implications at the city, regional, national, and international levels, security implications of the smart city architecture, and the various domain-specific security challenges of smart city applications (Table 4.2). This paper outlined the sheer technological complexity in place when local governments utilize the IoT and smart city devices and applications in their critical infrastructure and service delivery and identifies many significant implementation and technological vulnerabilities that these devices and systems can have. These concerns should also be taken into consideration by local governments as they move farther into embracing the "smart" community concept.

The IoT is what makes smart cities possible (see Chapter 11 for more on the IoT). However, there remain few mandated security requirements for these devices or their

Table 4.2 Implications for cyber-physical system deployments in smart cities.

Security and Safety Implications for Critical Infrastructure in Smart Cities	Policy Implications	Security Implications in Smart City Architecture	Domain-Specific Security Challenges
Infrastructure risk	Smart city security: a key factor of governance	Physical level vulnerabilities	Smart health
Information security and operational security	Smart cities, federalism, and national security	Communications level vulnerabilities	Smart transportation
Financial impacts vs. operational and safety impacts		Data processing and storage level vulnerabilities	Smart grid
			Smart home
			Public safety and emergency management

Source: Habibzadeh et al. (2019).

manufacture. Vitunskaite et al. (2019) conducted a comprehensive review of 93 IoT security standards and related guidance. Of the 93 standards reviewed, only 13 included elements pertaining to cybersecurity, most of which are extremely technical in nature and would be of interest mainly to local government IT staff and cybersecurity officials. The authors then compared the smart city governance models, security measures, technical standards, and third party management of Barcelona, Spain, Singapore, and London, England to one another. These cities have been identified as "the most developed smart cities" (referencing Sorrel, 2016). Using publicly available information (e.g., academic articles, official websites, and news reports), Vitunskaite et al. identified and compared the cities in the categories listed above. They found that two factors, collaboration and data sharing, and security at all levels must be present to implement effective security in smart cities.

Finally, Vitunskaite et al. presented a framework that they developed for managing the security of smart cities. The framework prioritizes mandatory adoption of technical standards, including government input throughout so as to embed "security by design" principles and maintaining the ability to adapt in the times of a shifting regulatory environment. It is clear that local governments must consider the cybersecurity of any and all devices, especially those that are networked, that they choose to incorporate into their operations. However, in most situations this means relying on the third party application developers and device manufacturers who make the devices for the inherent cybersecurity of those devices.

4.2.3 Case Study

Case studies can provide in-depth explorations of a particular local government's cybersecurity program. Rather than examining the cybersecurity of multiple governments in a survey, case studies offer the ability to drill-down and intensively examine particular aspects of cybersecurity in the selected local government. Here, Phin et al. (2020) conducted a case study of the physical security components of the IT department in a Malaysian local government organization, the Kota Bharu Municipal Council (KBMC) Islamic City. The authors identified six physical security cybersecurity problems facing the council including the complete lack of a security awareness program, insufficient funds for the department, the absence of support from top management, IT peripherals were not properly monitored, onsite visitors were not being monitored, and that there were minimal, if any, access control to the facilities including the IT department itself.

First, the only security awareness program implemented by the council involved printing cybersecurity posters and handing them out to every department; but beyond that no formal employee training program existed. In terms of funding, the IT department's daily expenditures (e.g., salary, utility bills, subscription fees, and building wear and tear) made up the majority of the department's budget. Other IT peripherals and solutions were "only approved when there [was] a leftover from the [Management Services Department's] monthly expenses and no fund [was] allocated solely for IT expenses" (Phin et al., 2020, p. 683). Third, support from management was minimal as, "top management of KBMC does not consider physical security an important element [of cybersecurity] because it does not generate any income for the organization" which forces the IT department to prioritize asset purchasing and maintenance in order to minimize cost (Phin et al., 2020, p. 683). Fourth, IT peripherals like computers were not properly monitored – faulty items were stored in insecure locations and computers were transferred to new employees without checking for faults or reformatting. Fifth, visitors to the department were not monitored and at least two physical break-in attempts were successful, resulting in the theft of two computers. And finally, there was no CCTV monitoring in the facility itself and all windows could be opened after closing. Taken as a whole, the findings of this case study – especially the lack of training and awareness, funding, and of managerial support – echo the findings of the 2016 and 2020 surveys and sadly are not surprising.

4.2.4 Frameworks

Organizations and social scientists devise and use frameworks in order to better understand complex problems, among them cybersecurity. One possible frame through which to view cybersecurity is negotiation theory, which utilizes game theory, decision-making analysis, and other techniques to model the processes involved in negotiations. Ransomware attacks inherently involve a negotiation process between the victim and the perpetrator through the course of trying to resolve the situation. Falco et al. (2019) devised a cyber negotiation framework after conducting interviews with urban critical infrastructure operators and applied the framework to previous ransomware attacks (e.g., attacks against Uber and the UK's National Health Services). The authors used negotiation theory to organize how urban critical infrastructure operators manage the risk of ransomware in three periods of time: pre-attack, mid-attack, and post-attack (Table 4.3).

Falco et al. investigated non-technical risk mitigation strategies that can help address these cyberattacks. They determined that pre-attack awareness (in other words, preparation) of cybersecurity was essential to addressing ransomware attacks. Developing and instituting an incident response plan, formal communication channels, and external relationships were important pre-attack strategies in addition to using technical defenses. Post-attack strategies included post-mortem reports, information sharing, documenting

Table 4.3 Cyber negotiation process.

Pre-attack	Attack	Post-attack
Develop a cyber incident response plan	Convene the incident command structure	Develop a post-mortem attack report
Build awareness	Determine event severity	Share information
Deploy technical defenses	Consult the legal team	Document lessons learned
Formalize communication channels	Negotiate	Conduct external reputational damage control
Establish external organizational relationships		

Source: Falco et al. (2019).

lessons learned, and external damage control, which also reflect time-tested industry best practices.

NIST's Cybersecurity Framework is a helpful tool by which organizations of all types and sizes can understand and improve their cybersecurity (see Chapter 9 for more on the framework). Ibrahim et al. (2018) assessed the cybersecurity of a (unidentified) local government organization in Western Australia using the NIST Cybersecurity Framework. The authors conducted interviews with executive, management, and technical employees within the local government. Perhaps unsurprisingly, the local government did not fully comply with four of the five functions in the framework. The local government only fully complied with the Recover function (100 percent). The Western Australian local government organization complied with the remaining functions as follows: Protect (45 percent); Respond (38 percent); Identify (36 percent); and Detect (25 percent). Ibrahim et al. made recommendations for the local government to improve its cybersecurity for each specific function including a list of related cybersecurity frameworks and case studies to use in cybersecurity planning, many of which are discussed throughout this book. Local governments can conduct similar analyses on their own cybersecurity operations by implementing the framework themselves or working with a cybersecurity firm that can help them to do so.

4.2.5 Economic Techniques

Cybersecurity can also be modeled through the lens of economics-based research. Viewing the issue economically can reveal the unique pressures facing local governments in attempting to institute effective cybersecurity. Kesan and Zhang (2019) used linear models to examine the relationships between cyber losses, local government budgets, and IT expenditures. According to the cyber incident data analyzed by the authors, there were six types of cyber incidents common to local governments: data breaches, unintentional data disclosure, disruption, privacy violation, fraud/extortion, and IT error. The authors found a positive correlation between the amount of cyber loss and the local government's budget. However, they also found a negative correlation between the amount of loss and the local government's IT expenditures. This means smaller local governments, with less capacity to fund cybersecurity were in a comparatively worse off position than larger governments because the amount of cyber loss is relative to the size of their budgets.

Modeling cybersecurity economically can also allow for opportunities to understand the overall context of the cybersecurity market and how to influence it in ways that do not necessarily involve passing legislation to create a more advantageous cybersecurity environment for organizations like local governments. Li and Liao (2018) delved into potential alternative economic solutions to improve the cybersecurity of smart cities. They developed a model for smart city vulnerability, which includes the probability of attack as well as a game theory analysis of the various actors involved. They offered economic-based solutions to improve smart city cybersecurity such as correcting application or device vendor's disincentives by either rewarding the vendor for security enhancements or punishing the vendor when vulnerabilities are exploited, and acquiring vulnerabilities in the gray market (or, purchasing known vulnerabilities as a defensive buyer). They also recommended a government policy instrument design to help ensure smart cities are built securely from the beginning, regulating vendors, inter-governmental collaboration, and information sharing with vendors and other government agencies. As mentioned elsewhere in this book, local government reliance on third party developers, IT administrators, and cybersecurity staff can also mean shifting the ability to ensure cybersecurity preparedness (or response) partially or completely away from the local government's direct purview, potentially increasing its level of risk.

4.3 Literature from the Profession

A substantial number of works from the professional world provide high quality, up-to-date information on cybersecurity, and they are published more frequently than those published via the academic peer-review process. Thirteen works were identified in the review conducted for this book that are especially relevant to local government cybersecurity (Table 4.4). These represent a very small sample of the large number of publicly available works on cybersecurity from the profession such as books, articles, reports, white papers, presentations, blogs, and other forms of professional discussion. While many of these publications addressed cybersecurity in the public sector, only a handful addressed local government cybersecurity directly. This said, their results are valuable to local governments, especially in identifying cybersecurity threats and trends.

4.3.1 Annual/Biennial Surveys

The Multi-State Information Sharing & Analysis Center (MS-ISAC), which has many local government organizations as members, conducts the Nationwide Cybersecurity Review (NCSR) annually (MS-ISAC, n.d.). The NCSR is a self-assessment tool for state, local, tribal, and territorial (SLTT) governments to assess the cybersecurity programs of these organizations based on the NIST Cybersecurity Framework. The NCSR measures the maturity of the government's cybersecurity program against the functions and categories in the framework on a scale of one to seven, one meaning the function or category is "not preformed" and seven being that it is "optimized." The minimum recommended level for local governments is a five ("implementation in process"). Participating governments receive individual reports and metrics to compare their governments anonymously against peer SLTTs. MS-ISAC also provides a biennial report to Congress on the NCSR.

The most recent NCSR report, published in 2019, was based on responses from 3135 SLTT organizations (MS-ISAC, 2019). Local governments made up 80 percent of SLTT respondents. Yet of that report, not a single SLTT government had reached a maturity level of five, and responding local governments had an average score of 3.6 (meaning "formal cybersecurity policies [were] in place, but [local governments were] informally performing cybersecurity functions without documented standard operating procedures" (p. 10). Local governments came second to state governments that had an average score of 4.8 (meaning that states were "in the process of developing standards and procedures that would allow for consistent implementation of practices" (p. 9)). In terms of

Table 4.4 Cybersecurity works from the profession.

Report	Name	Description
Annual/Biennial Surveys		
(Multi-State Information Sharing & Analysis Center [MS-ISAC], 2019)	Nationwide Cybersecurity Review (NCSR) (Survey conducted annually since 2013 with results shared to Congress every other year)	Survey of state, local, tribal, and territorial governments' cybersecurity programs based on the NIST Cybersecurity Framework
(Public Technology Institute and the Computing Technology Industry Association [PTI/CompTIA], 2021)	State of City and County IT National Survey (published annually)	Survey of local government technology executives on current IT practices, technology priorities, budgets, investments, management and evaluation, cybersecurity, emerging technologies, personnel, and more
(PTI/CompTIA, 2020)	Public Technology Institute and Computing Technology Industry Association – National Survey of Local Government Programs (published annually since 2018)	Survey of local government IT executives on cybersecurity including management, practices, managerial support, budgets, policies, training, and more
(Deloitte-NASCIO, 2020)	Deloitte-NASCIO Cybersecurity Study (Published biennially since 2010)	Survey of 50 states and one territory on the role of the CISO, including budget, governance, reporting, workforce, and operations
(Heid, 2020)	SecurityScorecard – State of the States (published biennially)	Report reviewing and grading the cybersecurity posture of the 56 US states and territories
(Verizon, 2021)	Verizon Data Breach Investigations Report (Published annually since 2008)	Extensive report analyzing incidents and breaches from around the world for trends and provides break out sections for 11 sectors, including the public sector
(Lovejoy, 2021)	EY – Global Information Security Survey (Published annually since 1998)	Survey of C-suite and business leaders, including the government and public sector, on the role of the CISO in their organization's cybersecurity
Public Sector		
(IBM Security & The Harris Poll, 2020)	(IBM Security & The Harris Poll, 2020) – Public Sector Security Research	Survey of US state and local government employees on their government's cybersecurity
(Donald F. Norris, 2021).	Published by the International City/County Management Association	A survey of local government CISOs conducted in 2020

(Continued)

Table 4.4 (Continued)

Report	Name	Description
(Goel et al., 2018)	IBM Center for the Business of Government – Managing Cybersecurity Risk in Government: An Implementation Model (2018)	Report covering cybersecurity risk management, federal cybersecurity risk, and proposing a model for cybersecurity decision-making (PRISM)
Ransomware		
(Black Fog, 2021)	The State of Ransomware in 2021 (Published annually)	Tracks publicized ransomware attacks by industry, country and month
(Emsisoft Malware Lab, 2021)	The State of Ransomware in the US (Published annually since 2019)	Tracks ransomware attacks in federal, state and municipal governments; healthcare facilities; and schools, colleges, and universities
Costs		
(IBM Security, 2021)	Cost of a Data Breach Report (Published annually since 2004)	Annual report analyzing the cost of cybersecurity breaches from different countries and industries including the public sector
(Smith & Lostri, 2020)	McAfee – The Hidden Costs of Cybercrime (Smith & Lostri, 2020) (Published biennially since 2014)	Report covering the "hidden" costs of cybercrime (other than cash) in the government sector among others

local government peer groups, the highest scoring was public utilities (3.8), followed by city (3.7), finance/revenue departments, including taxation and gaming offices and insurance/pension funds (3.7), all local government respondents (3.6), and county/parish (3.6).

For the fifth consecutive year the top five security concerns facing SLTT governments remained the same: lack of sufficient funding, increasing sophistication of threats, lack of documented processes, emerging technologies, and an inadequate availability of cybersecurity professionals. These are very similar to the findings of the 2016 and 2020 surveys (see Chapter 6) and some of the academic surveys discussed above.

The Public Technology Institute and the Computing Technology Industry Association (PTI/CompTIA) annually publish what are perhaps the most targeted survey of local government IT and cybersecurity. The first examines city and county IT management more generally, and the second specifically surveys local government cybersecurity. PTI/CompTIA's State of City and County IT National Survey examines local government IT practices, budgeting, management, and more (2021). Sixty-five local government technology executives responded to the survey. These respondents reported that their highest priority over the two years following the survey was cybersecurity/data loss prevention (88 percent), followed by providing new or updating digital services (48 percent), innovation (47 percent), and modernizing outdated IT systems (47 percent). The highest rated cybersecurity priorities included: training for general staff (54 percent rated highest priority); modernizing defenses (47 percent); further establishing a security mindset (46 percent); adopting a cybersecurity framework based on national standards (46 percent); and training for existing IT staff (43 percent). The CIOs identified three areas to improve in order to help bridge the IT skills gap: cybersecurity, soft skills, and cloud adoption. Similar to the findings of the 2020 survey, 49 percent of the CIOs expected their IT budgets to increase in the next year (17 percent increasing by 5 percent or more and 32 percent increasing 1 to 4 percent). Twenty-eight percent of respondents did not expect any change to their budget.

PTI/CompTIA's National Survey of Local Government Cybersecurity Programs, last published in 2020, more narrowly focused on local government cybersecurity rather than IT departments at large (PTI/CompTIA, 2020). First and foremost, nearly 67 percent of the 95 respondents did not feel that their government's cybersecurity budget was adequate. Nearly nine in ten (87 percent) governments provided employee awareness training, 56 percent of which was ongoing and 33 percent was provided once a year. Fifteen percent of local governments exempted elected officials and their staff from cybersecurity awareness training. In terms of plans and policies, 82 percent stated their local government had a cybersecurity plan or strategy, 71 percent of which were reviewed within the past year. Fifty-six percent of these plans allowed for exceptions to be made to the policy, which anecdotally tended to be for elected officials and their staff. Slightly more than a majority, 55 percent, of governments had a mobile device management policy in place. Less than half (46 percent) had formal incident response plans and disaster recovery plans that were tested each year, but many local governments had undergone a network or security audit in the past year (62 percent). The respondents varied in terms of how engaged they perceived their elected officials were in cybersecurity: 54 percent said they were somewhat engaged; and 23 percent each said very engaged or not engaged. And finally, 78 percent of the respondents said their local government purchased cybersecurity insurance.

Deloitte and the National Association of State Chief Information Officers (NASCIO) have produced biennial reports on state government cybersecurity since 2010. While these reports do not address local governments directly, the results can help identify cybersecurity issues and trends that both state and local governments likely share. The most recent Deloitte-NASCIO report was published in 2020 and deals specifically with how the COVID-19 pandemic affected state cybersecurity (Deloitte-NASCIO, 2020). The report found that the top five barriers to effective cybersecurity were a lack of sufficient cybersecurity budget, inadequate cybersecurity staffing, legacy infrastructure and solutions to support emerging threats, lack of dedicated cybersecurity budget, and an inadequate availability of cybersecurity professionals. These findings are highly consistent with findings from the scholarly works discussed above, findings of the 2016 and 2020 surveys discussed in Chapters 5 and 6, and the industry publications considered in this section. Importantly, lack of adequate cybersecurity funding and staffing are constant and ongoing issues making it difficult for state and local governments to provide effective levels of cybersecurity to their organizations.

The Deloitte-NASCIO survey also found that most state governments, on average, spent anywhere from 1 to 3 percent of their IT budgets on cybersecurity compared to financial institutions that spent 11 percent of their IT budgets on cybersecurity and federal agencies that spent a little over 16 percent. In the 2020 survey discussed in Chapters 5 and 6, local governments spent an average of 4 percent of their IT budgets on cybersecurity, with total annual cybersecurity spending ranging from zero to 10 percent.

Similar to the Deloitte-NASCIO surveys, SecurityScorecard issues a biennial report grading the 56 US states and territories on their cybersecurity postures (Heid, 2020). The security of these organizations is graded on a scale of 0 ("F") to 100 ("A"). The most recent scorecard, published in 2020, found that 75 percent received a grade of "C" or below, with 35 percent having a "D" or below. "C" rated states were three times more likely to be breached compared to states that received an "A" ("D" states were five times more likely). The highest ranking states were Kansas (95), Kentucky (92) and Michigan (92), and the lowest ranking states were North Dakota (59), Illinois (60) and Oklahoma (60).

Another prominent, if not an annual must-read report is the Verizon Data Breach Investigations Report (DBIR), which has been published annually since 2008. These reports analyze tens of thousands of cybersecurity incidents and breaches and provide valuable information regarding the overall cybersecurity environment in which local governments find themselves. While local governments are not within the Verizon reports' primary foci, the DBIRs do analyze cybersecurity incidents in the public sector. Most striking, the 2021 DBIR notes that of the 3236 incidents analyzed in the public sector, just over a quarter (885 or 27 percent) involved confirmed data disclosure (Verizon, 2021). External threat actors made up 83 percent of breaches (17 percent of which originated internally) in the sector. Organized crime made up roughly 80 percent of threat actors involved in data breaches against public organizations. In nearly all of these incidents the actor's motivation was financial. Worse, 92 percent of breaches in the public sector were caused by social engineering, miscellaneous errors, and other incidents involving theft of user credentials (80 percent). These findings are not surprising because the financial opportunities of attacking local government information systems are enormous due to the sensitivity of information stored there.

Finally, the professional services organization Ernst & Young Global Limited (known as EY) conducts an annual survey of more than 1000 senior cybersecurity leaders on Global Information Security and the role of CISO (Lovejoy, 2021). Eighty-one percent of respondents indicated that during the pandemic their organization had bypassed established cybersecurity processes for speed and efficiency and did not consult with cybersecurity teams while planning (see Chapter 11 for more on the impact of the pandemic on local government cybersecurity). Three-quarters (76 percent) of respondents from government organizations identified an increase in the number of disruptive attacks over the previous 12 months. Government CISOs lacked confidence of their cybersecurity team being able to understand and anticipate new strategies used by threat actors (only 45 percent confident), ensure supply chain can defend and recover against threat actors (38 percent), and ensure that third parties disclose breaches (33 percent). Cybersecurity threats stemming from third parties and the software supply chain are a consistent theme of recent research.

Almost half of government respondents (43 percent) in the EY report indicated that they anticipated their organizations would make significant investments in data and technology in the next 12 months. Specifically, the largest anticipated budget increases for government entities related to overall risk reduction (35 percent), crisis response (15 percent), and enabling, in EY's language "new business," although for governments possibly meaning new services (11 percent). Cybersecurity can foster risk reduction in government, is a significant component to crises, may even undergo its own crises, and is also essential to enabling new government services. Considering that funding is the largest barrier to local government cybersecurity, local government officials might find these budget justifications helpful when advocating for increases or maintaining their existing budget.

4.3.2 Public Sector

In 2020 IBM and The Harris Poll conducted a survey of state and local government employees regarding cybersecurity threats (IBM Security & The Harris Poll, 2020). Over half (58 percent) of respondents were from local governments. Seventy-three percent of state and local government employees were concerned about ransomware attacks to cities in the US and 64 percent were somewhat/very concerned about cyberattacks, more so than natural disasters (61 percent) or terrorist attacks (54 percent). However, these respondents were also somewhat optimistic about their governments' ability to overcome such attacks (65 percent confident) and 74 percent were confident of their own ability to recognize and prevent a ransomware attack. This is surprising given that only 66 percent of these respondents were somewhat/very familiar with ransomware, 26 percent had not received any basic cybersecurity training, and only 54 percent believed they had received adequate training on responding to a cyberattack. Last, 80 percent of these respondents did not believe it was likely that their governments would make a ransomware payment. However, 56 percent believed the impact of a ransomware attack on public safety should be a very important consideration in making the decision to pay or not.

Under a research fellowship from the International City/County Management Association (ICMA), in 2020 Norris conducted a survey of local government CISOs (Norris, 2021). Because the findings of this survey are discussed in some detail in Chapters 5 and 6, this review will only briefly summarize its most important findings. First, local governments do not adequately fund cybersecurity, as they are well below what the public sector spends on this function. Not surprisingly, then, the CISOs in the survey said that funding (followed by staffing) were the two biggest barriers to effective cybersecurity that they faced. Half of the governments in the survey had suffered data breaches in the previous year, suggesting that these governments are not doing as good a job protecting their information assets as they should. Last, and consistent with other findings in this literature, the CISOs reported that most parties in their governments were not sufficiently aware of the need for high levels of cybersecurity as would be ideal.

In 2019, the IBM Center for the Business of Government published an implementation model for how to manage cybersecurity risk in government known as the PRISM model

(Goel et al., 2018).[1] The authors structured this model on the theory that the lack of prioritization of cybersecurity is the root cause of gaps in government risk management programs. The authors presented the PRISM model after introducing the NIST Cybersecurity Framework and discussing how cybersecurity risk was managed in the federal government. The PRISM model was developed after the authors analyzed key terms in 32 documents (e.g., white papers, academic research, the NIST Framework, and other risk management documents) to craft a thematic association with and between the core functions of the NIST Cybersecurity Framework.

These themes can help local government decision-makers decide what to do in order to improve their cybersecurity risk management. *Prioritize* means to categorize cybersecurity risks in levels from high to low priority. *Resource* involves assessing the amount of funding required to accomplish cybersecurity goals. *Implement* means undertaking the proper practices and procedures to manage cybersecurity risks effectively. *Standardize* involves "creat[ing] standard knowledge and solutions to share across agencies to prevent risks" (p. 29). *Monitoring* means continual systematic observation and review of what is going on in the information systems.

Local governments can utilize the PRISM model as a continuous decision framework from a macro-level perspective by focusing on what to prioritize within the NIST Cybersecurity Framework's categories, as reporting under the Federal Information Security Management Act (FISMA) does not address gaps in an organization's cybersecurity program. PRISM is essentially the *how* (the process of improving cybersecurity) and the NIST Framework provides the *what* (outcomes to improve).

Local government officials should first identify what in the NIST Cybersecurity Framework needs to be addressed. For example: awareness and training within the Protect category. Given the unique cybersecurity environment and exposure faced by a local government, the officials should then **prioritize** what types of awareness and training are the most appropriate. Then, the **resources** and funding necessary for the awareness and training must be secured in order to **implement** the programs. This information can then be **standardized** and shared with similar organizations. And ultimately, the awareness an training programs should be continuously **monitored** in order to ensure effectiveness. The PRISM model may help some local governments initiate a review of the Cybersecurity Framework in order to determine what to focus on and implement. Because local governments face many competing interests, a priority model may help identify which best practices are most needed. But ultimately, it is up to local government officials and cybersecurity staff to develop explanations and justifications for *why* these measures are important and must be taken, something this book can help them accomplish.

4.3.3 Ransomware

Although local governments must be prepared for many types of cyberattacks, as of this writing, ransomware attacks are perhaps the single worst threat they face. As noted elsewhere in this book, ransomware attacks are also increasing in number and severity. As such, ransomware is discussed throughout this book (see especially Chapters 3, 11, and 12), and the works discussed in this section specifically focus on the threats of ransomware attacks.

The cybersecurity firm Black Fog tracks ransomware attacks by industry, country, and month (Black Fog, 2021). Between January 2021 and this writing, the government sector had received the highest number of attacks (40), followed by education (29), services (27), healthcare (23), technology (21), manufacturing (18), retail (12), utilities (8), finance (4), and other (14), totaling 196 successful attacks. Of these, 97 took place in the US. This report and its monthly updates describing each attack can be valuable to local governments to help them remain aware of the evolving level of this threat, the types of attacks to anticipate, and the kinds of flaws that attackers are exploiting in peer organizations.

The anti-malware company Emsisoft also tracks ransomware attacks in the United States. In 2020, Emsisoft identified 113 ransomware attacks against federal, state and municipal governments and agencies, 560 against healthcare facilities, and 1681 against schools, colleges, and universities (Emsisoft Malware Lab, 2021). However, during the same period, ransomware attacks doubled across organizations in the US (Nakashima, 2021).

The Emsisoft report also highlighted significant attacks experienced in each sector. Additionally, the report made predictions and recommendations to help close the intelligence gap caused by the of lack of available information on ransomware incidents and better predict when attacks are likely to occur. Reports from firms like Emsisoft provide helpful, if not essential information for local governments, and these governments should learn as much as possible from them in order to incorporate lessons learned and improve their own cybersecurity posture.

4.3.4 Costs

It is important to be able to measure the impact of cybercrime on the global economy and individual organizations, and there are many organizations that endeavor to do just that. IBM is one as are Accenture, Cybersecurity Ventures, McAfee, among others. IBM began publishing its annual Cost of a Data Breach Report in 2004 (IBM Security, 2021). In its 2021 report, IBM analyzed 537 breaches in 17 countries and regions and in 17 industries. Overall, IBM found a 10 percent increase in the average cost of a breach from $3.9 million to $4.2 million between 2020 and 2021. Also, it took an average of 287 days to identify and contain a data breach, with breaches taking more than 200 days to identify and contain costing more ($4.9 million) versus $3.6 million for those that were identified in 200 days or less. While breaches in the public sector were the lowest average cost of any sector ($1.93 million), the sector also experienced the highest cost increase over the past year (79 percent). The cost of cybercrime continues to increase, and this is especially true for the public sector, which has experienced more growth than any other sector.

There are both direct and indirect or hidden costs associated with successful cybersecurity attacks. Direct costs include the costs of remediating the breach by repairing and replacing devices, applications, software and systems, and other expenses like notifying those whose data has been breached, public relations and litigation expenses, the loss of any funds that may have been stolen, and more. In 2020, McAfee published the fourth of its biennial reports highlighting the hidden costs of cybercrime in 2020 (Smith and

Lostri, 2020). The report identified hidden costs incurred as the result of a successful cybersecurity attack, including opportunity costs (e.g., "reduced research and development spending, risk-adverse behavior and increased spending on cyber defenses"). Although increased spending on cybersecurity can also be considered a direct cost, the authors of the report indicated that increased spending is a common reaction to suffering a breach and that these funds otherwise might be better spent due to the "risk premium" in the cybersecurity market because of the massive amount of ongoing criminal activity. Other hidden costs discussed in the report include system downtime, reduced efficiency, brand damage and loss of trust, intellectual property (IP) theft, incident response costs, outside assistance (e.g., consultants and legal assistance), cyber risk insurance, and damage to employee morale. The highest cost attacks in the government sector involved ransomware, phishing, and a greater likelihood of malicious insider attacks.

4.4 Conclusion

From the perspective of cybersecurity scholars, local government cybersecurity is considerably under-researched. That there are only 14 academic and peer-reviewed research articles from the social sciences and computer science and related journals on local government cybersecurity between 2000 and 2021 (a period when the internet became a necessary infrastructure for government, business, and society to function) strongly supports this conclusion. By contrast, there is a large and growing number of high quality publications on cybersecurity in general and a smaller but growing number on local government cybersecurity in the professional realm. Taken together, these publications provide strong evidence-based findings about cybersecurity along with helpful recommendations about how to improve cybersecurity programs that can be highly beneficial to local governments. This body of knowledge is constantly growing and evolving, and therefore also offers keen insights into cybersecurity threats and challenges facing all organizations, including local governments.

Some of the major themes from this review of that combined literature are not surprising. Lack of adequate cybersecurity funding hampers nearly all organizations. Many top officials and managers in organizations are not fully aware of the need for cybersecurity and do not support it adequately. Ransomware and other cyberattacks continue to plague organizations. Threats continue to evolve, becoming increasingly sophisticated. The cost of cybercrime continues to increase. Most organizations do not practice or manage cybersecurity well. And more.

The available scholarly and professional literature clearly confirm that there are ongoing problems with implementing cybersecurity in organizations of all types and sizes, but especially in local governments. Accordingly, local government officials should be aware of and use this wealth of information and analysis to better understand the cybersecurity environment and learn about what actions they can take to ensure a robust and effective cybersecurity posture for their communities.

Note

1 PRISM is an acronym for the five steps for governments to take to help ensure effective risk management: Prioritize, Resource, Implement, Standardize, and Monitor.

References

Ali, O., Shrestha, A., Chatfield, A., and Murray, P. (2020). Assessing information security risks in the cloud: A case study of Australian local government authorities. *Government Information Quarterly*, 30 (1), 101419. https://doi.org/10.1016/j.giq.2019.101419

Black Fog (2021, August 02). *The State of Ransomware in 2021*. https://www.blackfog.com/the-state-of-ransomware-in-2021

Caruson, K., MacManus, S.A., and McPhee, B.D. (2012). Cybersecurity policy-making at the local government level: An analysis of threats, preparedness, and bureaucratic roadblocks to success. *Homeland Security & Emergency Management*, 9(2), 1–22. https://doi.org/10.1515/jhsem-2012-0003

Deloitte-NASCIO (2020). *2020 Deloitte-NASCIO Cybersecurity Study: States at risk: The cybersecurity imperative in uncertain times*. https://www.nascio.org/wp-content/uploads/2020/10/2020-Deloitte-NASCIO-Cybersecurity-Study-1.pdf

Emsisoft Malware Lab (2021, January 18).*The state of ransomware in the US: Report and statistics 2020*. https://blog.emsisoft.com/en/37314/the-state-of-ransomware-in-the-us-report-and-statistics-2020

Falco, G., Noriega, A., and Susskind, L. (2019). Cyber negotiation: A cyber risk management approach to defend urban critical infrastructure from cyberattacks. *Journal of Cyber Policy*, 4(1), https://doi.org/10.1080/23738871.2019.1586969

Goel, R., Haddow, J., and Kumar, A. (2018). *Managing cybersecurity risk in government: An implementation model*. IBM Center for the Business of Government. http://www.businessofgovernment.org/sites/default/files/Managing%20Cybersecurity%20Risk%20in%20Government.pdf

Habibzadeh, H., Nussbaum, B.H., Anjomshoa, F., Kantarci, B., and Soyata, T. (2019). A survey on cybersecurity, data privacy, and policy issues in cyber-physical system deployments in smart cities. *Sustainable Cities and Society*, 50, 101660. https://doi.org/10.1016/j.scs.2019.101660

Hatcher, W., Meares, W.L., and Heslen, J. (2020). The cybersecurity of municipalities in the United States: An exploratory survey of policies and practices. *Journal of Cyber Policy*, 5(2), https://doi.org/10.1080/23738871.2020.1792956

Heid, A. (2020, October 15). *State of the states*. SecurityScorecard. https://securityscorecard.pathfactory.com/state-of-the-states/state-to-states-map-

Ibrahim, A., Valli, C., McAteer, I., and Chaudhry, J. (2018). A security review of local government using NIST CSF: A case study. *The Journal of Supercomputing*, 74(10), 5171–5186. https://doi.org/10.1007/s11227-018-2479-2

IBM Security (2021). *Cost of a Data Breach Report 2021*. https://www.ibm.com/downloads/cas/OJDVQGRY

IBM Security and The Harris Poll (2020). *Public sector security research IBM-Harris Poll Survey 2020*. https://www.ibm.com/downloads/cas/74JKYWZQ

Kesan, J. P. and Zhang, L. (2019). An empirical investigation of the relationship between local government budgets, IT expenditures, and cyber losses. *IEEE Transactions on Emerging Topics in Computing*, 9(2), Advance online publication. Doi:. https://doi.org/10.1109/TETC.2019.2915098

Li, Z. and Liao, Q. (2018). Economic solutions to improve cybersecurity of governments and smart cities via vulnerability markets. *Government Information Quarterly*, 35(1), 151–160. https://doi.org/10.1016/j.giq.2017.10.006

Lovejoy, K. (2021). *Global information security survey 2021*. EY. https://www.ey.com/en_us/cybersecurity/cybersecurity-how-do-you-rise-above-the-waves-of-a-perfect-storm

MacManus, S.A., Caruson, K., and McPhee, B.D. (2012). Cybersecurity at the local government level: Balancing demands for transparency and privacy rights. *Journal of Urban Affairs*, 35(4), 451–470. https://doi.org/10.1111/j.1467-9906.2012.00640.x

Multi-State Information Sharing & Analysis Center [MS-ISAC] (2019). *2019 Nationwide cybersecurity review*. https://www.cisecurity.org/wp-content/uploads/2021/06/2019-NCSR-Summary-Report.pdf

Multi-State Information Sharing & Analysis Center [MS-ISAC] (n.d.). *Nationwide cybersecurity review (NCSR)*. https://www.cisecurity.org/ms-isac/services/ncsr

Nakashima, E. (2021, September 18). *U.S. aims to thwart ransomware attacks by cracking down on crypto payments*. Washington Post. http://thewashingtonpost.pressreader.com/epaper/viewer.aspx?noredirect=true&bookmarkid=9C6VEMQN3SD6

Norris, D.F. (2021, July 14). *A new look at local government cybersecurity: Recommendations for staying vigilant against persistent cyber threats*. Local Government Review/Public Management. Washington, DC: International City/County Management Association.

Norris, D.F., Mateczun, L., Joshi, A., and Finin, T. (2018). Cyber-Security at the Grassroots: American Local Governments and the Challenges of Internet Security. *Journal of Homeland Security and Emergency Management*, 15(3), 1–14.

Norris, D.F., Mateczun, L., Joshi, A., and Finin, T. (2019). Cyberattacks at the grassroots: American local governments and the need for high levels of cybersecurity. *Public Administration Review*, 79(6), 895–904. https://doi.org/10.1111/puar.13028

Norris, D.F., Mateczun, L., Joshi, A., and Finin, T. (2020). Managing cybersecurity at the grassroots: Evidence from the first nationwide survey of local government cybersecurity. *Journal of Urban Affairs*. Published online 17 April 2020. https://doi.org/10.1111/puar.13028

Phin, P.A., Abbas, H., and Kamaruddin, N. (2020). Physical security problems in local governments: A survey. *Journal of Environmental Treatment Techniques*, 8(2), 679–686. http://www.jett.dormaj.com/docs/Volume8/Issue%202/html/Physical%20Security%20Problems%20in%20Local%20Governments%20A%20Survey.html

Pries, B., and Susskind, L. (2020). Municipal cybersecurity: More work needs to be done. *Urban Affairs Review*. https://doi.org/10.1177/1078087420973760

Public Technology Institute and the Computing Technology Industry Association [PTI/CompTIA] (2020). *PTI/CompTIA 2020 National Survey of Local Government Cybersecurity Programs*. https://comptiacdn.azureedge.net/webcontent/docs/default-source/advocacy-documents/2020-pti-cybersecurity-national-survey.pdf?sfvrsn=b0488502_2

Public Technology Institute and the Computing Technology Industry Association [PTI/CompTIA] (2021). *2021 Public Technology Institute (PTI) State of City and County IT National Survey*. https://comptiacdn.azureedge.net/webcontent/docs/default-source/research-reports/2021-pti-state-of-city-and-county-it-national-survey.pdf?sfvrsn=bf5e8d49_0

Smith, Z.M. and Lostri, E. (2020, December 7). *The hidden costs of cybercrime*. McAfee. https://www.mcafee.com/enterprise/en-us/assets/reports/rp-hidden-costs-of-cybercrime.pdf

Sorrel, S. (2016). Worldwide smart cities: Energy, transport and lighting 2016–2021. In *Technical Report*. Juniper Research.

Verizon (2021). *Verizon 2021 Data Breach Investigations Report*. https://enterprise.verizon.com/resources/reports/2021-data-breach-investigations-report.pdf

Vitunskaite, M., He, Y., Brandstetter, T., and Janicke, H. (2019). Smart cities and cyber security: Are we there yet? A comparative study on the role of standards, third party risk management and security ownership. *Computers & Security*, 83, 313–331. https://doi.org/10.1111/puar.13028

5

Cyberattacks: Targeting Local Government[1]

5.1 Introduction

This chapter discusses the nature of cyberattacks that local governments contend with on an almost daily basis. It uses data from several sources, including from the first-ever nationwide survey of cybersecurity among American's grassroots or local governments to address cyberattacks against these governments (Norris et al., 2019). Included also are data from a more recent survey conducted by Hatcher et al. in 2018, a survey of a small group of CISOs of mainly large cities by one of the authors in 2020 (Norris, 2021), and findings from the professional literature where relevant.

Governments of all types and sizes, and increasingly local governments, are under constant or nearly constant attack (e.g., Norris et al., 2018, 2019). This should not be surprising because, among other things, more than half of the cyberattacks against organizations in the United States are against small- and medium-size businesses. Additionally, like such businesses, local governments often lack the funds and skills to combat such attacks.

This chapter begins by briefly discussing the methodology employed to conduct the 2016 survey from which the data in the chapter are derived. Then it examines the data from that survey concerning attacks and attackers against local government information assets, local government cybersecurity preparedness, and the barriers to achieving high levels of cybersecurity in them. The chapter then concludes by providing some recommendations to local governments for improving their levels of cybersecurity and makes suggestions for future research into local government cybersecurity. Appendix 5.1, which discusses in detail the methodology behind the 2020 survey, follows.

To conduct the 2016 survey, the authors partnered with the International City/County Management Association (ICMA), and in the summer of 2016 ICMA mailed the survey to all municipal governments with populations of 25,000 and greater and to all county governments of the same size (a total of 3423 local governments). The survey produced a response rate of 11.9 percent (n = 406 local governments). The survey results are reasonably representative of the overall population of the local governments that we surveyed, although larger local governments are proportionately overrepresented, smaller local governments are numerically overrepresented.

Cybersecurity and Local Government, First Edition. Donald F. Norris, Laura K. Mateczun and Richard F. Forno.
© 2022 John Wiley & Sons Ltd. Published 2022 by John Wiley & Sons Ltd.

For the 2020 survey, which was conducted under a research fellowship from ICMA, the author revised the 2016 survey instrument and administered it by email as part of a combined convenience and expert sample to member CISOs of the Coalition of City CISOs (https://cityciso.org) and a few non-member local governments. The survey received a response rate of 50 percent. (For a more detailed discussion of the research methodology behind both surveys, see Appendix 5.1.)

5.2   Cyberattacks on Local Governments

This section begins by examining the exposure of American local governments to cyberattacks. To do so, it was necessary to ensure that all respondents (in both the 2016 and 2020 surveys) had a common understanding of three important terms used in the survey – attack, incident, and breach. Therefore, the survey instruments provided definitions of those terms. **Attack** was defined as: *any attempt by any party to gain unauthorized access to any component of your local government's information technology system for the purpose of causing mischief or doing harm.* Then, the survey instrument provided definitions of incident and breach found in the industry-accepted annual Verizon Data Breach Investigations Report (2015). The definition of **incident** provided was: *"Any event that compromises the confidentiality, integrity or availability of an information asset"*; and of **breach** was: *"An incident that resulted in confirmed disclosure (not just exposure) to an unauthorized party."*

5.2.1   Attacks, Incidents, and Breaches

With these definitions in mind, the survey asked if local governments catalogued or counted attacks, incidents, and breaches. Fewer than half (47 percent) said that they catalogued or counted attacks; followed by 58 percent that catalogued or counted incidents; and 60 percent that did so for breaches (Table 5.1). In terms of the method of cataloguing or counting, only 33 percent of local governments employed a formal system, while 41 percent used an informal system and 38 percent used no system at all (Table 5.2).

Next, the survey inquired about the frequency of attacks, incidents, and breaches (Table 5.3). Attacks occurred the most frequently: hourly or more – 28 percent; at least daily – 19 percent; less than daily – 24 percent. However, 29 percent said that they *did not know* how frequently their system was attacked. Earlier research found that local

Table 5.1   Does your local government catalogue and count attacks, incidents, and breaches?

	Yes		No		Total
	N	%	N	%	
Attacks	173	46.5	199	53.5	372
Incidents	217	58.3	155	41.7	372
Breaches	221	60.1	147	40.0	368

Table 5.2 Does your local government employ a formal or informal method of cybersecurity management?

	N	%
Formal	80	33.1
Informal	161	66.9
Total	241	100.0

Table 5.3 How frequently is your local government's information system subject to attacks, incidents, and breaches (in %s)?

	Attacks	Incidents	Breaches
Hourly or more	27.7	4.8	4.3
At least once a day	19.4	7.7	3.4
Less than daily	23.8	53.1	29.9
Don't know	29.1	34.4	62.4
Total	100.0	100.0	100.0

governments are under constant or near constant attack (Norris et al., 2018). It is possible, even likely that the 24 percent who responded that attacks occurred less than daily were not well informed of the frequency of attacks against their systems.

Findings from the 2020 survey suggest that attacks have become more frequent. More than half of the local governments reported that attacks were constant: 29 percent said hourly, and 14 percent said daily. None responded that they did not know how frequently they were being attacked.

As expected, the local governments in the 2016 survey reported that incidents occurred less frequently than attacks, and breaches occurred less frequently than incidents. Just over one-third of responding local governments *did not know* how frequently incidents occurred, and nearly two-thirds *did not know* how often their systems were breached. These data suggest that in 2016, at least, sizeable numbers of local government were guilty of cybersecurity malpractice. Not knowing if a government's IT system has experienced an incident or breach is fundamental to proper cybersecurity.

All but one of the governments in the 2020 survey reported that they had experienced incidents. Only 7 percent said no incidents; 21 percent had experienced one incident; 14 percent – two incidents; 29 percent – four; and 21 percent more than five. Regarding breaches, half reported no breaches; 29 percent reported one breach; 7 percent reported having been breached twice; and 7 percent said more than three times.

The data, especially the "did not knows," in the 2016 survey strongly suggest that at least some local governments were not practicing cybersecurity well. The situation improved in the 2020 survey, although the number of governments in that survey reporting multiple breaches in the past year is troublesome. The 2016 data also suggest that, despite providing a definition of the term breach in the instrument, some respondents

Table 5.4 In the past 12 months, has your local government's information system experienced more, less, or about the same number of attacks, incidents, and breaches?

	Attacks		Incidents		Breaches	
	N	%	N	%	N	%
Fewer	27	7.4	47	13.1	47	13.1
Same	125	34.4	149	41.4	164	45.8
More	118	32.5	65	18.1	20	5.6
Don't know	93	25.6	99	27.5	127	35.5
Total	363	100.0	360	100.0	358	100.0

apparently did not understand what constituted breach because nearly 8 percent said that their governments were breached at least daily.

When asked whether the frequency of attacks, incidents, and breaches had changed over the 12 months prior to the survey (Table 5.4), one-third of local governments reported that attacks remained about the same, four in ten said the same about incidents as did nearly half about breaches. Much smaller percentages said they had experienced fewer attacks – 7 percent; incidents – 13 percent; and breaches – 13 percent. One-third of respondents said that attacks had increased; fewer than one in five (18 percent) said incidents had increased; and very few (6 percent) said breaches had increased. Again, however, the number of local governments that *did not know* was not trivial: 25 percent for attacks; 27 percent for incidents; and 35 percent for breaches.

The responses in 2020, however, were clear that the frequency of attacks had increased in the past year with almost 93 percent saying so. Only 7 percent of local governments said that the frequency of attacks had remained about the same.

Next, the survey asked if respondents could determine the types of attackers during the previous year and the attackers' motives. A clear majority said that they *could not determine* the types of attackers (Table 5.5). Of those who were able to determine the types of attackers, 50 percent said attackers included external actors-organizations, 43 percent said they included external actors-individuals, 21 percent said state actors, and 9 percent said malicious insiders (Table 5.6). By contrast, nearly two-thirds of respondents to the 2020 survey said that they could identify their attackers. When asked, respondents to the 2016 survey said that the top reasons for the attacks were: ransom, mischief, sensitive information, hacktivism, and theft of money (Table 5.7) These findings are consistent with the 2020 survey in which ransom, theft of money, and theft of PII were the top three attack purposes, and with a report by PNC released in 2018 (Kozlik, 2018).

5.2.2 Preparedness

To better understand how well local governments can defend their IT assets, the 2016 survey asked how prepared these governments felt they were to detect, prevent, and recover from several potential events that could adversely affect their systems, including incident and attack detection and recovery (Table 5.8). Only small percentages of local

Table 5.5 Is your local government able to determine the types of attackers that attack your system?

	N	%
Yes, can determine	151	41.6
No, cannot	212	58.4
Total	363	100.0

Table 5.6 Types of attackers.

	Yes		No		
	N	%	N	%	Total
External Actors/ Organizations	76	50.3	31	20.5	107
External actors/ individuals	65	43.0	42	27.8	107
State actors	31	20.5	76	50.3	107
Malicious insiders	14	9.3	94	62.3	108

Table 5.7 Purpose of attacks.

	Yes		No		
	N	%	N	%	Total
Ransom	60	39.7	41	27.2	101
Mischief	38	25.2	63	41.7	101
PII	28	18.5	73	48.3	101
Hacktivism	26	17.2	75	49.7	101
Theft of money	21	13.9	80	53.0	101
Employee records	15	9.9	86	57.0	101
Confidential records	14	9.3	87	57.6	101
Customer/ citizen records	12	7.9	89	58.9	101
Espionage	5	3.3	96	63.6	101
Revenge	2	1.3	99	65.6	101
Terror	2	1.3	99	65.6	101

governments reported having a very good or excellent ability to do so, ranging from 48 percent with a very good or excellent ability to recover from ransomware attacks to 21 percent with a similar ability to detect exfiltration. As seen in Table 5.8, responses to the remainder of this question do not inspire confidence in these governments' ability to

Table 5.8 Preparedness of local governments to.

	Detect Attacks		Detect Incidents		Prevent Breaches		Recover from Breaches	
	N	%	N	%	N	%	N	%
Poor/fair	97	28.0	98	28.3	98	28.5	90	26.5
Good	88	25.4	98	28.3	103	29.9	79	23.2
Very good/ excellent	145	41.9	132	38.2	125	36.3	125	36.8
Don't know	16	4.6	18	5.2	18	5.2	46	13.5
Total	346	100.0	346	100.0	344	100.0	340	100.0
	Detect Exfiltration		Prevent Exfiltration		Recover from Exfiltration		Recover from Ransomware	
	N	%	N	%	N	%	N	%
Poor/fair	168	49.3	146	42.9	107	31.7	64	18.7
Good	54	15.8	64	18.8	68	20.1	77	22.5
Very good/ excellent	70	20.5	85	25.0	94	27.8	165	48.3
Don't know	49	14.4	45	13.2	69	20.4	36	10.5
Total	341	100.0	340	100.0	338	100.0	342	100.0

Table 5.9 Confidence in your local government's ability to prevent all breaches.

	N	%
Not at all/slightly confident	100	30.3
Somewhat confident	103	31.2
Confident/highly confident	115	34.9
Don't know	12	3.6
Total	330	100.0

withstand attacks, incidents, and breaches or to recover from them. Consistent with findings thus far in this chapter, once again it appears that local governments were not practicing high levels of cybersecurity.

This finding is also consistent with the results of a 2018 survey of over 1000 respondents from companies in the UK and the US. Among other things, it found that nearly half of participants had "no understanding of how to protect their companies against cyber attacks [*sic*]" (Keeper Security, Inc and Ponemon Institute, 2018).

Next, the 2016 survey inquired about the level of confidence that these governments had in their ability to prevent all breaches (Table 5.9). Three in ten reported being not at all or only slightly confident, 31 percent said somewhat confident, and 34 percent replied confident or highly confident of being able to prevent all breaches. Viewed differently, nearly two-thirds of respondents were less than confident in the ability of their local government to prevent all breaches. This finding will doubtless come as no surprise because, as cybersecurity professionals know, it is not a matter of whether, but when an organization will be breached (see also Ponemon Institute, 2015).

5.2.3 Barriers to Cybersecurity

Clearly, a number of factors may contribute to American local governments' failure to practice higher levels of cybersecurity. With this in mind, the survey included a number of questions about barriers to the effective practice of cybersecurity (Table 5.10). The specific barriers considered were based on the barriers identified in the prior literatures on IT and government and e-government. The five most important barriers reported in the 2016 survey were: 1) the inability to pay competitive salaries to cybersecurity employees; 2) insufficient number of cybersecurity staff; 3) lack of funds; 4) lack of adequately

Table 5.10 Barriers to achieving highest possible level of cybersecurity.

	Not/Small Barrier		Modest Barrier		Somewhat/ Severe Barrier		Don't Know		Total	
	N	%	N	%	N	%	N	%	N	%
Inability to pay competitive salaries	67	19.8	42	12.4	198	58.6	31	9.2	338	100.0
Insufficient number of staff	68	20.2	71	21.1	179	53.1	19	5.6	337	100.0
Lack of funds	57	16.6	95	27.7	181	52.8	10	2.9	343	100.0
Lack of adequately trained personnel	86	25.5	76	22.6	158	46.9	17	5.0	337	100.0
Lack of end user accountability	121	35.8	78	23.1	127	37.6	12	3.6	338	100.0
Lack of trained personnel to hire	120	35.3	73	21.5	108	31.8	39	11.5	340	100.0
Lack of adequate cybersecurity Awareness	118	35.1	104	31.0	104	31.0	10	3.0	336	100.0
No end user training at all	172	51.3	64	19.1	86	25.7	13	3.9	335	100.0
Some, but insufficient end user training	158	48.2	88	26.8	65	19.8	17	5.0	328	100.0
Federated nature of local government	183	55.8	41	12.5	58	17.7	46	14.0	328	100.0
Too many IT networks/ systems	222	66.1	43	12.8	55	16.4	16	4.8	336	100.0
Lack of support from department managers	209	61.5	70	20.6	47	13.8	14	4.1	340	100.0

trained personnel; and 5) lack of end user accountability. All other potential barriers were selected by less than one-third of respondents.

Perhaps most importantly, four of the top five barriers identified in the 2016 survey centered around *inadequate funding for cybersecurity* (Table 5.11). If local governments cannot pay competitive salaries, it is because of their financial limitations (i.e., lack of funds). If local governments lack sufficient numbers of cybersecurity staff, it is also due to financial limitations. This said, it is also true that local governments find it difficult to compete for IT and cyber personnel because private-sector salaries are typically much higher than the public sector is able to pay. Last, lack of adequately trained personnel is also related to funding because training is not free. Indeed, training is often cut when local governments face budgetary difficulties, like those experienced during the "Great Recession" of 2009 and the "Pandemic Recession" of 2020.

These findings are consistent with several years of research into IT and government and e-government (e.g., Holden et al., 2003; Norris and Kraemer, 1996; Norris and

Table 5.11 Top three things needed to ensure the highest level of cybersecurity.

	1		2		3		Total	
	N	%	N	%	N	%	N	%
Greater funding for cybersecurity	76	54.7	37	26.6	26	18.7	139	100.0
Better cyber policies	46	38.3	36	30.0	38	31.7	120	100.0
Greater CS awareness	42	35.3	29	24.4	48	40.3	119	100.0
More end user training	22	25.3	32	36.8	33	37.9	87	100.0
More cyber personnel	26	30.2	37	43.0	23	26.7	86	100.0
Improved cyber hardware	35	42.2	26	31.3	22	26.5	83	100.0
More training for cyber personnel	21	28.8	24	32.9	28	38.4	73	100.0
Pay competitive salaries for cyber personnel	15	23.1	30	46.2	20	30.8	65	100.0
More end user accountability	13	20.0	18	27.7	34	52.3	65	100.0
Better enforcement of cyber policies	11	20.4	26	48.1	17	31.5	54	100.0
Greater support – top electeds	9	29.0	9	29.0	13	41.9	31	100.0
Greater support dept managers	5	16.7	13	43.3	12	40.0	30	100.0
Greater support top appointeds	7	35.0	3	15.0	10	50.0	20	100.0
Consolidation of networks/systems	3	23.1	3	23.1	7	53.8	13	100.0

Reddick, 2013) as well as evidence produced by the literature review for this book (Caruson et al., 2012; Deloitte-NASCIO, 2010 through 2020; Ponemon Institute, 2015). These findings are also consistent also with the 2020 survey in which the top two barriers were lack of funding and lack of sufficient and adequately trained staff, and with a recent survey of state governments that found the top two barriers were lack of funding and lack of cyber staff (Deloitte-NASCIO, 2020).

5.3   Conclusions and Recommendations

Evidence available from a variety of sources including but not limited to the 2016 survey of local government cybersecurity shows that organizations including local governments are under frequent, if not constant attack and that they often practice cybersecurity poorly. This is almost certainly a function of the several barriers to cybersecurity identified in the survey and other sources – of which *lack of funding was the most serious.* Indeed, when asked about the top three things needed to ensure the highest level of cybersecurity, respondents to the 2016 survey first named a need for greater funding, followed by better cybersecurity policies, and greater cybersecurity awareness among local government employees (Table 5.11). Thus, a first recommendation is that, within budgetary limitations, local governments must provide adequate finding for cybersecurity.

What might American local governments consider to improve their practice of cybersecurity? First, as noted above, they must fund cybersecurity adequately, an issue that is addressed in greater detail in Chapter 6. Second, top local elected and appointed officials must be fully committed to cybersecurity. One of the most frequent complaints heard from IT and cybersecurity staff is that their organizations' top executives do not understand and are not sufficiently supportive of cybersecurity and that cybersecurity does not get their attention until a serious adverse event occurs, which, of course, is too late. If top local government officials do not fully understand or support cybersecurity, those who work for them will, understandably, ask, "Why should I?" And lack of support from the top will make it difficult to ensure, establish, and maintain cybersecurity at high levels.

One way these officials can make cybersecurity a priority is to address existing barriers to cybersecurity. This is a third recommendation. Within their fiscal and administrative limitations, local governments must address known barriers to cybersecurity, especially funding, staffing, and accountability. Although lack of funding ranked at the top of the list of reported barriers to cybersecurity, local governments can take action in a number of areas where cost is not as great a factor, such as adopting and implementing cybersecurity policies and providing end user training, which are addressed in greater detail in Chapter 6.

Fourth, top officials must insist that their governments be aware of and follow the latest cybersecurity best practices, such as those published by relevant federal government agencies. At the minimum, these currently include the NIST Cybersecurity Framework and the DHS cybersecurity strategy document and resources (DHS, 2018a, 2018b; NIST, 2014, 2018a, 2018b).

The 2016 survey found numerous cases in which local governments did not know that they were under cyberattack and had experienced incidents or breaches (mercifully, this was not the case in the 2020 survey). No top local government official, whether elected or appointed, and certainly no IT or cybersecurity official should ever have to answer "I do not know" to questions about the cybersecurity of their organizations. Knowing the security status of their information system is fundamentally important to a local government's ability to address vulnerabilities and improve cyber-outcomes. For local officials and staff not to know about important aspects of their government's cybersecurity is akin to malpractice. So, a fifth recommendation is to eliminate the "don't knows."

Last, local governments must create and maintain a culture of cybersecurity within their organizations. The concept of a culture of cybersecurity began to gain traction among practitioners only within the past decade or so (e.g., Deloitte-NASCIO, 2010). Among other things, a culture of cybersecurity means that the elected officials and top managers fully embrace and support cybersecurity, play important roles in it, insist that others in their governments do so as well, and hold all accountable when they do not. Chapter 6 provides greater detail on the meaning of a culture of cybersecurity.

Local governments are currently attractive targets for cyberattackers, and they are likely to remain so well into the future. This is partly because of the failure of so many of these governments to provide high levels of cybersecurity. The effects of cyberattacks at the local level can have devastating consequences for governmental operations and service delivery, local business activities, citizen engagement, local trust, and more. Therefore, local government leaders must understand and actively support cybersecurity operations that are proactive, effective, and capable of making it more difficult for adversaries to cause significant harm to local government information assets. While total security is a noble goal – but, sadly, one that is never fully achievable – there is much that can be done by local governments to make it more difficult for attacks and incidents to be successful.

Having discussed cyberattacks against local governments in these pages, Chapter 6 will explore the assorted management issues related to implementing, managing, and sustaining an effective local government cybersecurity program.

Appendix 5.1   Research Method and Data

2016 Survey

To produce the data for the 2016 study, the survey's authors partnered with the International City/County Management Association (ICMA) for a nationwide survey of local government cybersecurity. ICMA is the premier membership organization of local government professionals in the United States and is widely recognized for its research into many aspects of local governance, including information technology. ICMA also has a survey capability that is unsurpassed in reaching local governments across America.

In cooperation with staff at the ICMA, the authors prepared a draft survey instrument based on the limited available information about local government cybersecurity from previous research on this subject (e.g., Caruson et al., 2012; Norris et al., 2018), and on the professional literature that is discussed in the literature review in Chapter 4. The draft survey instrument was then submitted for review and comment to a volunteer advisory group created to assist in this project. The group consisted of the IT directors, Chief Technology Officers (CTO), CISOs or equivalent officials in ten cities and counties in the authors' home state of Maryland as well as the CIO and CISO of their university. After receiving comments and suggestions from these advisors, the survey instrument was appropriately revised. ICMA then pre-tested the instrument, and final adjustments were made to it. The process used to develop the instrument creates face validity for the instrument, and provides confidence that, on the whole, the questions in it produce reliable data.

The instrument examined a wide range of local government cybersecurity issues. For the purposes of this chapter, we have focused on those related to cyberattacks. Chapter 6 focuses on issues relating to cybersecurity management.

The survey received a final response rate of 11.9 percent (n = 406 local governments), which is considered low. However, there were several reasons for it. Chief among them is, first, the substantial decline in response rates to surveys in recent years (e.g., Anseel et al., 2010), including those conducted by ICMA. A second reason is that IT and cybersecurity officials across the nation are reluctant to respond to such surveys because they are afraid that their responses might reveal sensitive information about their governments' cybersecurity problems and practices.

There is some degree of satisfaction that a response of 406 to a random sample of 3400 local governments would have produced a margin of error of 5 percent at a confidence level of 95 percent. Clearly, however, this was not a random sample but rather a population survey. As a result, there are other reasons that these results should be taken seriously. Consider, for example, two factors. First, as seen in Table 5.A.1, the survey results are reasonably representative of the overall population of the local governments that were surveyed. While larger local governments are proportionately overrepresented, smaller local governments are numerically overrepresented. This is not surprising because it reflects the relative distribution of local governments in the US. There is also some regional variation, with local governments in the Northeast and North Central regions being underrepresented and those in the South and West being overrepresented. This is also not surprising and is probably because the occurrence of the council manager form of government is greater in the latter two regions and, as Table 5.A.1 shows, council manager governments were overrepresented.

Second, the survey's authors are confident of these results because the great majority of respondents (83.9 percent) were experienced, local government IT and cyber professionals, mostly CIOs, ITDs, and CISOs (Table 5.A.2). Thus, the men and women who responded to this survey were knowledgeable, expert local government practitioners who "knew their stuff."

The 2020 Survey

The 2020 survey was conducted to provide data for an exploratory study that employed a combination of convenience and expert sampling. A convenience sample is a method of sampling that includes participants because they were easily reached by the researchers (Battaglia, 2014). By contrast, an expert sample involves the selection if participants who are knowledgeable experts in the field of the survey, in this case local government

Table 5.A.1 Local government demographics.

	Number Surveyed	Number Responding	Response Rate (%)
Total	3423	406	11.9
population size			
500,000+	140	31	22.1
250,000–499,999	168	26	15.5
100,000–249,999	532	63	11.8
50,000–99,999	939	107	11.4
25,000–49,999	1644	179	10.9
Geographic division			
Northeast	574	42	7.3
North Central	1048	120	11.5
South	1148	139	12.1
West	653	105	16.1
City/county			
Municipalities	1893	262	13.8
Counties	1530	144	9.4
Form of government 1			
Elected (Mayor-Council, County Council-Elected Executive, County Commission)	1541	117	7.6
Appointed (City Council-Manager, County Administrator/Manager)	1588	276	17.4
Form of government 2			
Mayor-Council	570	46	8.1
County Commission	685	33	4.8
County Council-Elected Executive	286	38	13.3
City Council-Manager	1035	204	19.7
County CA/CM	553	72	13.0

cybersecurity (Patton, 2018). To gather data for this study, the author surveyed top IT and cybersecurity officials in 11 cities and three counties in the US (Table 5.A.3). Respondents to this survey included 11 CISOs, one CIO, and two ITDs. These officials, or key informants, all had considerable expertise, experience in and knowledge of the cybersecurity of their local governments, including their governments' cybersecurity management, practices, risks, strengths, limitations, and problems. The use of knowledgeable key informants who are trained, experienced practitioner experts working as the top cybersecurity or IT officials for their local governments should mean that the data from the survey is both valid and reliable.

The principal strengths and limitations of this method are that it is simpler, easier, and less expensive than probability sampling, and therefore useful for studies like this. It also

Table 5.A.2 Respondent profession and experience.

Profession	N	%
IT professionals	193	83.9
Other government	28	14.5
Other	3	1.6
Total	193	100.0
IT Experience		
0–5 Years	25	24.8
6–10 Years	30	29.7
11–19 Years	30	29.7
20+ Years	16	15.8
Total	101	100.0

Table 5.A.3 What is your official title?

	Number	%
CISO	11	78.6
CIO	1	7.1
ITD	2	14.3
Other		
Total	14	100.0

produces information from knowledgeable key informants, so the data should be both valid and reliable. The principal limitations of this type of research include that the results are not representative of a broader population and, therefore, cannot be generalized to that population. It is also prone to contain bias and sampling error. For exploratory studies, the strengths appear to outweigh the limitations of this research method.

The survey was conducted between mid-April and late August 2020. The initial plan was to conduct a combination of face-to-face and telephone interviews. However, because of the COVID-19 pandemic, conducting face-to-face interviews was unsafe. It was also clear that telephone interviews would not be feasible because of the difficulty finding the telephone numbers of IT and cybersecurity officials on many local government websites, the time pressure under which cybersecurity and IT officials across the nation were working during the pandemic, and a reluctance among such officials to respond to surveys (Norris et al., 2019). Hence, we used email only (see Norris et al., 2019).

Initially, emails were directed only to the then approximately 17 members of the *Coalition of City CISOs* (https://cityciso.org) that was established in the spring of 2019, and we are especially grateful for the coalition's support for this survey. Indeed, most of the local governments that participated (at least nine) are members of the coalition. Two

Table 5.A.4 Participating local governments and their population.

Boston, MA	692,600
Chicago, IL	2,693,976
Dallas, TX	1,343,573
Detroit, MI	670,031
Fairfax County, VA	1,457,532
Los Angeles, CA	3,979,576
Memphis, TN	651,073
Nashville, TN	670,820
San Francisco, CA	881,549
Seattle, WA	753,675

Population data from the 2019 Census estimates for counties and for cities and towns. Please note that the authors received explicit permission from the ten listed local governments to identify them by name.

anonymous colleagues who were familiar with this research, one in a city government and one in a local government membership organization, volunteered to solicit responses from other local governments, and we thank them for their assistance as well. These efforts produced only five additional responses for a total of 14 responses, of which nine were from coalition members. See Table 5.A.4 for participating jurisdictions.

Perhaps the most prominent reason for low response rates in this type of research is the concern among CISOs and other officials that revealing anything about their cybersecurity might put the local government at risk. Revealing too much might also be embarrassing. In this and previous research, more than one official has essentially replied: "Our policy is not to respond to such surveys."

The refusal of local government cybersecurity and IT officials to participate in surveys and other types of research into their cybersecurity is unfortunate for at least three reasons. First, it deprives local governments across the nation of reliable information about the state of cybersecurity management and practice among their peers, which knowledge can benefit all local governments. Second, it deprives these governments with evidence-based recommendations to improve their management and practice of cybersecurity. And the third reason involves cybersecurity researchers, whose job it is to gather and make sense of the data that can influence local government cybersecurity management and practice. If researchers cannot gather the data, they cannot analyze it and provide results to local governments to help in their cybersecurity planning or to other scholars conducting similar research.

Beyond gathering and analyzing data and providing results to local governments, these scholars can also begin theorizing about aspects of local government cybersecurity management and practice, such as what are the factors or conditions that produce certain cybersecurity outcomes among local governments and why? However, without data from studies of various kinds about local government cybersecurity, such theorizing is not likely to occur.

Respondents were promised anonymity and confidentiality for their participation in the survey because they are essential elements for the conduct of research into sensitive topics. However, it is clear from this and other cybersecurity surveys, that this promise was not sufficient to produce higher response rates. For example, the 2016 survey achieved only an 11.9 percent response rate after several mailings and personal contact by telephone (Norris et al., 2019). In their 2018 nationwide survey of municipal government cybersecurity (based in part on Norris et al., 2019), Hatcher et al. achieved only a 7 percent response rate (2020).

Note

1 This chapter is a revised and expanded version of Donald F. Norris, Laura Mateczun, Anupam Joshi, and Tim Finin. 2020. Cyberattacks at the grassroots: American local governments and the need for high levels of cybersecurity. *Public Administration Review.* 79(6): 895–904. It is included with the permission from the publisher, John Wiley and Sons, Inc.

References

Anseel, F., Lievens, F., Schollaert, E., and Choragwicka, B. (2010). Response rates in organizational sciences, 1995–2008: A meta-analytic review and guidelines for survey researchers. *Journal of Business Psychology*, 25(3), 335–349. https://link.springer.com/article/10.1007/s10869-010-9157-6

Battaglia, M.P. (2014). Nonprobability sampling. In P.J. Lavrakas (Ed.), *Encyclopedia of Survey Research Methods* (pp. 524–527). Sage Publications.

Caruson, K., MacManus, S.A., and McPhee, B.D. (2012). Cybersecurity policy-making at the local government level: An analysis of threats, preparedness, and bureaucratic roadblocks to success. *Homeland Security & Emergency Management*, 9(2), 1–22. https://www.degruyter.com/document/doi/10.1515/jhsem-2012-0003/html

Deloitte and National Association of State Chief Information Officers (2010). *State governments at risk: A call to secure citizen data and inspire public Trust*. Lexington, KY. https://www.nascio.org/Portals/0/Publications/Documents/Deloitte-NASCIOCybersecurityStudy2010.PDF

Deloitte and National Association of State Chief Information Officers (2012). *2012 Deloitte-NASCIO cybersecurity sStudy–state governments at risk: A call for collaboration and compliance*. https://www.nascio.org/Portals/0/Publications/Documents/Deloitte-NASCIOCybersecurityStudy2012.pdf

Deloitte and National Association of State Chief Information Officers (2014). *2014 Deloitte-NASCIO cybersecurity study–state governments at risk: Time to move forward*. https://www.

nascio.org/Portals/0/Publications/Documents/Deloitte-NASCIOCybersecurityStudy_2014.pdf

Deloitte and National Association of State Chief Information Officers (2016). *2016 Deloitte-NASCIO cybersecurity study–state governments at risk: Turning strategy and awareness into progress.* https://www.nascio.org/Portals/0/Publications/Documents/2016/2016-Deloitte-NASCIO-Cybersecurity-Study.pdf

Deloitte and National Association of State Chief Information Officers (2018). *2018 Deloitte-NASCIO cybersecurity study–states at risk: bold plays for change.* https://www.nascio.org/wp-content/uploads/2019/11/2018DeloitteNASCIOCybersecurityStudyfinal.pdf

Deloitte and National Association of State Chief Information Officers (2020). *2020 Deloitte-NASCIO cybersecurity study.* https://www.nascio.org/wp-content/uploads/2020/10/2020-Deloitte-NASCIO-Cybersecurity-Study-1.pdf

Hatcher, W., Meares, W.L., and Heslen, J. (2020). The cybersecurity of municipalities in the United States: An exploratory survey of policies and practices. *Journal of Cyber Policy*, 5(2), https://doi.org/10.1080/23738871.2020.1792956

Holden, S.H., Norris, D.F., and Fletcher, P.D. (2003). Electronic government at the local level: Progress to date and future issues. *Public Productivity and Management Review*, 26(3), 1–20. https://www.tandfonline.com/doi/abs/10.1177/1530957603252580

Keeper Security, Inc., and Ponemon Institute (2018, November). *2018 State of cybersecurity in small and medium size businesses.* https://www.keepersecurity.com/assets/pdf/Keeper-2018-Ponemon-Report.pdf

Kozlik, T. (2018, April 23). *Cyberattacks: A real threat to state and local governments, infrastructure.* PNC. https://www.pnc.com/content/dam/pnc-com/pdf/corporateandinstitutional/MunicipalBond/Cyberattacks-a-real-threat.pdf

Norris, D.F. (2021). *A new look at local government cybersecurity in 2020 Recommendations for staying vigilant against persistent cyber threats.* Local Government Review. A publication of the International City/County Management Association. https://icma.org/sites/default/files/2021-07/PM%20%2B%20LGR%20July%202021%20LOW-RES.pdf

Norris, D.F. and Kraemer, K.L. (1996). Mainframe and PC computing in American cities: Myths and realities. *Public Administration Review*, 56(6), 568–576. doi: 10.2307/977255

Norris, D.F., Mateczun, L., Joshi, A., and Finin, T. (2018). Cybersecurity at the grassroots: American local governments and the challenges of internet security. *Journal of Homeland Security and Emergency Management*, 15(3), 1–14. https://www.degruyter.com/document/doi/10.1515/jhsem-2017-0048/html

Norris, D.F., Mateczun, L., Joshi, A., and Finin, T. (2019). Cyberattacks at the grassroots: American local governments and the need for high levels of cybersecurity. *Public Administration Review*, 76(6), 895–904. https://onlinelibrary.wiley.com/doi/abs/10.1111/puar.13028

Norris, D.F., and Reddick, C.G. (2013). Local E-government in the United States: Transformation or incremental change? *Public Administration Review*, 73(1), 165–175. https://doi.org/10.1111/j.1540-6210.2012.02647.x

Patton, M.Q. (2018). Expert sampling. In B.B. Frey (Ed.), *The SAGE Encyclopedia of Educational Research, Measurement, and Evaluation.* SAGE Publications.

Ponemon Institute (2015). *State of cybersecurity in local state & federal government.* https://ssl.www8.hp.com/ww/en/secure/pdf/4aa6-2563enw.pdf

U.S. Department of Homeland Security (2018a). *Cybersecurity strategy.* https://www.dhs. gov/sites/default/files/publications/DHS-Cybersecurity-Strategy_1.pdf

U.S. Department of Homeland Security (2018b). *Cybersecurity resources.* https://www.dhs. gov/topic/cybersecurity (This resource continuously updated by DHS.)

U.S. National Institute of Standards and Technology (2014). *NIST roadmap for improving critical infrastructure cybersecurity.* National Institute of Standards and Technology. https:// www.nist.gov/sites/default/files/documents/cyberframework/roadmap-021214.pdf

U.S. National Institute of Standards and Technology. (2018a). *Framework for improving critical infrastructure cybersecurity, version 1.1.* National Institute of Standards and Technology. https://nvlpubs.nist.gov/nistpubs/CSWP/NIST.CSWP.04162018.pdf

U.S. National Institute of Standards and Technology (2018b). *Cybersecurity framework state, local, tribal and territorial perspectives.* https://www.nist.gov/cyberframework/ perspectives/state-local-tribal-and-territorial-perspectives

Verizon (2015). *2015 data breach investigations report.* http://www.verizon.com/about/ news/2015-data-breach-report-info

6

Managing Local Government Cybersecurity[1]

6.1 Introduction

Since the early 2000s, cybersecurity has become an essential function within organizations because entities of nearly all types and sizes are under constant or nearly constant cyberattack and routinely experience incidents and breaches (e.g., Verizon, 2019 Data Breach Investigations Report). This chapter examines data from the 2016 nationwide survey of cybersecurity among local governments in the US to examine these governments' management of cybersecurity (Norris et al., 2020). Those data are supplemented with data from a 2018 survey (Hatcher et al., 2020) and a survey that one of this books' authors conducted in 2020 (Norris, 2021).

As a result of an extensive literature review, it is clear that there are very few publications of any kind, especially scholarly works, on *local government* cybersecurity and exactly fewer still on *local government* cybersecurity management. This said, since at least the 1980s, if not earlier, scholars from various academic disciplines have shown that "management matters" in the world of information technology (IT) in local government (e.g., King and Kraemer, 1985; Kraemer and Dedrick, 1997; Kraemer et al., 1989)

More recently, scholars and professionals in the fields of computer science, information technology, and cybersecurity have concluded that management matters for cybersecurity as well. Indeed, it is now common for cybersecurity experts and practitioners, for example, to strongly recommend that the CEOs, corporate board members, and top managers of private sector organizations understand the need for and fully support cybersecurity in their organizations (e.g., Buszta, 2003; Gibson, 2015; Merko and Breithaupt, 2014; Whitman and Mattord, 2010; Wood, 2010). These experts also argue that top officials must play key roles in creating and maintaining what is also commonly known as a "culture of cybersecurity" throughout their organizations (e.g., Norris et al., 2018, 2019).

While such recommendations have been directed mainly at top officials in private sector organizations, they apply equally to the chief elected officials, elected legislators, and top appointed managers of America's local governments. This is because without these officials' full support, the management of cybersecurity and, therefore, cybersecurity outcomes, will likely be less than optimal.

Cybersecurity and Local Government, First Edition. Donald F. Norris, Laura K. Mateczun and Richard F. Forno.
© 2022 John Wiley & Sons Ltd. Published 2022 by John Wiley & Sons Ltd.

Therefore, it is important to understand how local governments manage cybersecurity and how effective (or not) they are at it. Understanding cybersecurity management among local governments will help frame recommendations that local governments can act upon to achieve high levels of cybersecurity.

6.2 Scholarly Studies of Local Government Cybersecurity Management

As noted in Chapters 1 and 4, in preparation for this book, an extensive search was conducted for works about local government cybersecurity in *journals in the social sciences and computer science* since 2000 (see Chapter 4). This review identified only 14 articles from those disciplines that address local government cybersecurity. However, few of them addressed local government cybersecurity management.

The scarcity of scholarly literature on local government cybersecurity management led to examination of scholarly works from related areas, in particular research that began in the 1980s on IT and government that has since both continued that focus and expanded into research on electronic or e–government and most recently cybersecurity among local governments. In a then ground-breaking study of management of computing in organizations, King and Kraemer (1985) tested the then widely accepted belief that "computing is manageable in a rational manner" (p. 12). They examined "a much larger set of variables…in keeping with the view of computing as a 'package' consisting of many interrelated parts, rather than simply a tool consisting of hardware and software techniques" (p. 14). In particular, they "investigated the relationships between the characteristics of organizations, the policies used to manage computing, and the benefits and problems of computing in those organizations" (p. 14). They found that the management of computing itself was one of the most important, variables affecting computing in local governments, if not the most important one.

In a later study, Kraemer et al. (1989) noted that prior research had held that technological advancement was the prime driver of computing in organizations and that the literature gave little consideration to the role of managers and management. What they discovered, however, was that external forces played little role in computing outcomes. Instead, management played an overarching role. Thus, they concluded that management action was the *single* most important factor for computing in organizations.

Additional works by Kraemer and his associates between the early 1980s and the 2000s routinely found evidence of the importance of management in computing. For example, in a 1997 review of the public administration literature between 1981 and 1995, Kraemer and Dedrick again observed the importance of management to computing in local governments. To give but one example, the application of IT in local and state governments can be significantly affected by actions of management. This was true even though many of their works also showed how complex and difficult managing computing in organizations could be (e.g., King and Kraemer, 1985).

Thus, by the late 1980s, the message, at least among social science scholars, was that management is critical to computing development and success. Indeed, as recently as 2019, King and Kraemer advocated for a greater role for the information systems community in the creation of policy to help ensure desired management outcomes (King and Kraemer,

2019). This message also resonated with many scholars who followed in the footsteps of Kraemer and associates to examine the adoption of PCs by local governments and these governments' adoption of e-government (e.g., Norris, 2010; Norris and Kraemer, 1996; Norris and Jae Moon, 2005; Norris and Reddick, 2013 among others). One of the principal findings of the latter studies is that professionally managed local governments (versus those with elected chief executives) generally are more advanced in their adoption and use of PCs and e-government and have arguably better PC and e-government use outcomes.

It is also common among scholars and practitioners in the information systems field to argue that management matters. For example, managers need to understand and participate in IT decisions because those systems affect the entire enterprise and also to ensure that these decisions have the support, funding, and other resources necessary to succeed (e.g., Laudon and Laudon, 2014; Pearlson and Saunders, 2006). Likewise, the importance of management to the achievement of high levels of cybersecurity in organizations is widely accepted and highly recommended by authors in this field (e.g., Whitman and Mattord, 2010).

In the foreword to Whitman and Mattord's text, long-time information security consultant Charles Cresson Wood wrote that his experience conducting risk assessments of more than 125 different organizations around the world led him to conclude that, regardless of type, size, sector, or other characteristics of organizations, management is not sufficiently well informed about or committed to cybersecurity. This is partly because cybersecurity is a new field that competes with (and often loses to) other organizational needs. Nevertheless, Wood has argued that top executives and managers should understand and fully support cybersecurity and should not allow information security to be the domain of technologists alone (see also: Wood, 2005, 2016).

Many cybersecurity practitioners and researchers echo Wood's observations. Buszta (2003) argued that the chief executive and the company board of directors (analogous to the chief elected officials, elected legislators, and top appointed manager of local governments) must be committed to information security. If they are not, then this can result in the likely failure of information security. According to Merko and Breithaupt (2014), effective cybersecurity requires sponsorship from the top of the organization in order to be successful. Last, Gibson (2015) has argued that top managers must be committed to cybersecurity because in the absence of their commitment others in the organization will realize that it is not valued and may act accordingly.

This body of research makes clear that management is exceptionally important to positive IT and e-government outcomes. More recent works by scholars and practitioners in the fields of IT and cybersecurity make the same argument for the management of cybersecurity in organizations. By extension, it might be expected that the same will be true of local government cybersecurity. That is, management matters to cybersecurity among those organizations as well.

6.3 Managing Local Government Cybersecurity

Since implementing effective cybersecurity is more than just addressing a technical challenge, the rest of this chapter discusses a number of items related to cybersecurity management, such as cybersecurity governance, policies, and investing in cybersecurity protections. After all, in the absence of an adequate if not exemplary management process, it is likely that efforts to improve or enhance local government cybersecurity will suffer.

6.3.1   The Structure of Cybersecurity Management

This section discusses some important structural characteristics of cybersecurity management. The first of which is the location of responsibility for cybersecurity management in these governments; that is, which local government office was in charge of cybersecurity (Table 6.1). The 2016 survey found that cybersecurity was the responsibility of information technology departments (ITDs) for nine in ten local governments (Norris et al., 2020). In 3 percent of governments, responsibility for cybersecurity resided in the top appointed manager's office; in 2 percent, in the chief elected official's office; in 1 percent in a stand-alone cybersecurity office; and, last, in 5 percent in some "other" office.

In the 2018 survey, cybersecurity resided in the ITD in 80 percent of responding governments and in the chief administrator's office in 15 percent (Hatcher et al., 2020). Respondents to the 2020 survey were mostly CISOs (86 percent) versus 14 percent that were CIOs (Norris, 2021). Most of these officials (86 percent) reported to the CIO or chief technology officer (CTO) or equivalent in their organizations while 14 percent reported to the chief administrator. That survey also found all local government employees fell under the jurisdiction of the CISO in more than three-quarters of these local governments. There were three outliers with CISO responsibility, respectively, for 25, 60, and 75 percent of their governments' employees (Norris, 2021).

That cybersecurity management is housed mostly in local government ITDs is not surprising because in most local governments the ITD has responsibility for the government's IT system. Logically, therefore, the ITD should also have responsibility for protecting that system and all associated assets from cyberthreats.

6.3.2   Outsourcing

The 2016 survey inquired about whether the local governments outsourced any of their cybersecurity functions. The main reasons that local governments may decide to outsource

Table 6.1   Location of responsibility for cybersecurity management within local government.

	n	%
IT department	353	89.4
Appointed manager	11	2.8
Chief executive's office	8	2.0
Stand-alone department	3	0.8
Other	20	5.1
Total	395	100.0

cybersecurity include: 1) their inability to hire and retain qualified cybersecurity staff due to insufficient budgetary resources; 2) to benefit from the cybersecurity expertise of organizations that specialize in this area; 3) to reduce both cost and risk; and 4) to increase the organization's focus on its core functions; and perhaps others (CivicPlus, 2018).

Although there is little data about cybersecurity outsourcing by local governments, it is increasingly common for organizations in general to outsource at least some responsibility for cybersecurity (e.g., EY.com, 2017; Landi, 2017). For example, 85 percent of participants in a Deloitte survey said that they had "some level of reliance on vendors and managed service providers to provide cybersecurity operations, with 66 percent of those outsourcing between 21 and 50 percent of cybersecurity operations" (Deloitte, 2019).

Nearly four in ten respondents to the 2016 survey reported that their local governments either fully (8 percent) or partially (31 percent) outsourced this function (Table 6.2). This rate of outsourcing is consistent with that found by Deloitte and NASCIO (2018) in their survey of state government cybersecurity and among other types of organizations (e.g., Earnst and Young, 2016; EY.com, 2017; Medical Group Management Association, 2017). It is also a much higher outsourcing rate than reported in the Multi-State Information Sharing and Analysis Center (MS-ISAC) 2016 Nationwide Cyber Security Review, which found that only 7 percent of local governments outsourced at least some cybersecurity functions (Center for Internet Security, 2017). Hatcher et al. found that 51 percent of local governments outsourced, of which 36 percent said that they outsourced all of their cybersecurity needs (2020).

6.3.3 Cybersecurity Contractor Reporting

Next, the 2016 survey inquired into the office to which local governments required their cybersecurity contractor to report (Table 6.3). It is not surprising that most local governments (79 percent) required their outsourcing contractor to report to one of their top technology offices. This is almost certainly because those offices, among all offices in local governments, are likely to be the most well prepared to manage this function. In most cases, cybersecurity contractors were properly required to report to the ITD or CIO/IT director.

6.3.4 Cybersecurity Insurance

In addition to outsourcing cybersecurity, local governments appear to be increasingly purchasing cybersecurity insurance to help manage this function. (For more about

Table 6.2 Does your local government outsource its cybersecurity responsibility?

	n	%
Fully outsource	31	8.2
Partially outsource	119	31.3
Do not outsource	230	60.5
Total	380	100.0

Table 6.3 Local government office to whom outsourced contractor reports.

	n	%
IT department	49	33.1
CIO or IT director	39	26.4
Top appointed manager's office	17	11.5
CISO	13	8.8
Elected chief executive's office	7	4.7
CTO	4	2.7
Other	19	12.8
Total	148	100.0

cybersecurity insurance see Chapter 3.) According to the Cybersecurity and Infrastructure Security Agency (CISA) of the US Department of Homeland Security (DHS) cybersecurity insurance "is designed to mitigate losses from a variety of cyber incidents, including data breaches, business interruption, and network damage" (CISA, n.d.). Local governments may also consider cybersecurity insurance because doing so can result in these governments adopting technologies, policies, procedures, and practices that can improve their levels of cybersecurity and also enable them to purchase better insurance coverage at lower cost. As part of the application process for cybersecurity insurance, local governments may be required to engage in cybersecurity risk management exercises. These exercises can help local governments identify cybersecurity weaknesses that they then can address, even if they do not ultimately purchase the insurance (e.g., Norris et al., 2018).

With this in mind, the 2016 survey asked whether the local governments had purchased cybersecurity insurance (Table 6.4). Slightly under half of the responding governments (45 percent) had purchased cybersecurity insurance, while just over half (55 percent) had not. Although there is little or no data about previous rates of local government adoption of cybersecurity insurance, adoption by nearly half of local governments appears impressive and likely represents a substantial increase over the past few years (Public Technology Institute, 2019). This is also at least partly so because cybersecurity insurance is a relatively new insurance product (Marvin, 2018).

When local governments purchase cybersecurity insurance, they can be fully or partially covered. Hence, the 2016 survey asked those local governments that had purchased cybersecurity insurance about the extent of their coverage (Table 6.5). One in five (21 percent) said very little or limited coverage, one in three (36 percent) said moderate coverage, and one in four (27 percent) said most or full coverage. Just under one in six respondents (15 percent) said that they did not know the extent of their cybersecurity insurance coverage.

Half of the respondents to the 2020 survey outsourced cybersecurity partially and half did not outsource at all. The principal functions that they reported were outsourced

Table 6.4 Cybersecurity insurance adoption rates.

	n	%
Yes	150	44.6
No	186	55.4
Total	336	100.0

Table 6.5 Extent of cybersecurity insurance coverage.

Extent of coverage	n	%
Very/limited coverage	32	21.1
Moderate coverage	53	36.1
Most/full coverage	41	27.0
Don't know	22	15.0
Total	147	100.0

included: PCI scanning and penetration testing; monitoring vendor tools on the network; 24/7 monitoring of the IPS; IT Security Operation Center (SOC) monitoring; and monitoring and vulnerability scanning. These functions are described in Appendix 6.1.

Due to the limited space available in the 2016 survey, it was unable to examine the coverages that these governments had secured, the elements of cybersecurity insurance they had forgone, and the cost of their policies. These should be areas for further research.

6.3.5 Cybersecurity Tools and Actions

The 2016 survey also asked which of eight tools (see Appendix 6.2 for descriptions of these tools) local governments employed in their cybersecurity efforts (Table 6.6). In order of frequency of adoption these included: anti-virus software (84 percent had adopted); web and email gateways (72 percent); virtual private networks or VPNs (71 percent); intrusion detection and prevention systems (65 percent); next-generation firewalls (63 percent); automated malware protection systems (53 percent); network traffic analysis or network virtualization (47 percent); and multi-factor or biometric authentication (23 percent). There should be an element of reassurance about these governments' awareness of the importance of cybersecurity since four types of tools were adopted by about two-thirds or more of local governments, and nearly half reported adopting two additional tools. Yet, it might also be argued that anything short of nearly total adoption of highly recommended cybersecurity tools by local governments places the laggard governments at unnecessary risk.

In addition to tools, the 2016 survey asked which of a set of commonly recommended actions had local governments taken to improve their cybersecurity practice. The actions are in two categories: 1) actions involving testing of some sort (Table 6.7); and 2) actions involving training (Table 6.8). The survey instrument also asked how frequently these

Table 6.6 Cybersecurity tools utilized.

	n	%
Antivirus software	339	83.5
Web and email gateways	292	71.9
Virtual private networks (VPNs)	289	71.2
Intrusion detection and prevention systems	265	65.3
Next-generation firewalls	255	62.8
Automated malware protection systems	214	52.7
Network traffic analysis or network visualization	189	46.6
Multi-factor/biometric authentication	92	22.7
Other	18	4.4
Total	406	100.0

Table 6.7 Actions to improve cybersecurity (testing).

	Monthly/ Quarterly		1–2 years		Never		Don't Know		Total	
	n	%	n	%	n	%	n	%	n	%
Scanning and testing	199	57.5	103	29.8	26	7.5	18	5.2	346	100.0
Risk assessment	78	22.5	198	57.1	47	13.5	24	6.9	347	100.0
Technical security review	88	25.4	190	54.9	41	11.9	27	7.8	346	100.0
Audit of our cybersecurity practices	28	8.2	191	56.0	92	27.0	30	8.8	341	100.0
Cybersecurity exercises	35	10.2	127	37.0	141	41.1	40	11.7	343	100.0
Forensic services after incidents or breaches	34	16.0	44	20.7	92	43.2	43	20.2	213	100.0

governments had taken any of these actions (at least monthly, at least quarterly, at least annually, at least every two years, never, or don't know). For ease of analysis, the results were combined into four groups: monthly/quarterly, every one to two years, never, and don't know.

Certainly, not all actions should be taken at the same frequency. For example, organizations should conduct scanning and testing regularly to learn, at the minimum, their systems' vulnerabilities and whether they are under cyberattack. Some sources recommend that organizations scan at least monthly while others suggest continually (Browning, 2017; SecureWorks, 2019). Organizations should undertake other actions more or less frequently depending on such things as the risks that they face, legal requirements, contractual

Table 6.8 Actions to improve cybersecurity (training).

	Monthly/ Quarterly		1–2 years		Never		Don't Know		Total	
	n	%	n	%	n	%	n	%	n	%
Cybersecurity staff training	66	19.2	178	51.7	72	20.9	28	8.1	344	100.0
End user training	51	15.0	156	45.8	101	29.6	33	9.7	341	100.0
Cybersecurity awareness training for local government IT personnel	71	20.8	164	48.0	81	23.7	26	7.6	342	100.0
Cybersecurity awareness training for local government cybersecurity personnel	82	24.6	137	41.0	84	25.2	31	9.3	334	100.0
Cybersecurity awareness training for local government employees	45	13.2	159	46.8	109	32.1	27	8.0	340	100.0
Cybersecurity awareness training for local government elected officials	19	5.6	104	30.4	171	50.0	48	14.0	342	100.0
Cybersecurity awareness training for contractors	15	4.5	45	13.4	208	61.9	68	20.2	336	100.0
Cybersecurity awareness training for citizens	5	1.5	20	6.0	239	71.6	70	21.0	334	100.0
Other	1	2.3	4	9.1	12	27.3	27	61.4	44	100.0

obligations, and whether they have adopted cybersecurity best practices. Last, forensic services should be employed not on any schedule but, rather, after any known incident that compromises the integrity of an information system.

Over half of respondents (58 percent) reported having conducted scanning and testing on a monthly or quarterly basis. However, 30 percent said one-to-two years, 8 percent said never, and 5 percent did not know (totaling 43 percent).

Next, came the frequency with which local governments undertake risk assessments. Here, nearly eight in ten reported conducting risk assessments at least every one to two years, which is probably a reasonable frequency. However, 14 percent said never, and 7 percent did not know (for a total of 21 percent). Next came technical security review where slightly more than half said at least every one to two years. One quarter said monthly/quarterly, which seems rather unusual because of the nature of such reviews. Almost one in eight said never and 8 percent did not know (totaling 20 percent).

This was followed by the frequency of audits of cybersecurity practices, where 8 percent said monthly/quarterly and just under two-thirds said at least one to two years. However, slightly more than one in four said never and 9 percent did not know (for a total of 36 percent). Cybersecurity exercises came next, where nearly half reported that they conducted these exercises at least every one to two years. However, 41 percent said never, and 12 percent did not know (for a total of 53 percent).

6.3.6 Forensic Services

The 2016 survey next inquired about local government use of forensic services after cybersecurity incidents or breaches. Extrapolating from the survey responses, about one in six governments said they were used monthly/quarterly and just over one in five said one to two years (for a total of 37 percent). A plurality of governments (43 percent), however, said they never used forensic services, and 20 percent did not know (totaling 63 percent).

6.3.7 Training

The 2016 and 2020 surveys both addressed training provided by local governments for several groups in or associated with those governments. Here again frequencies will vary, although this time by audience, where those more closely associated with cybersecurity practice should receive training more frequently, but all should receive at least some training (PCI Security Standards Council, 2014). For example, it is essential that local governments ensure that cybersecurity staff undertake periodic training so that they can stay abreast of developments in the rapidly changing field. However, it is probably reasonable to provide training less frequently to others, e.g., annual training to end users and contractors and cybersecurity awareness training every one to two years for all categories of personnel (e.g., CivicPlus, 2018; ICMA, 2018).

Respondents to the 2016 survey reported that slightly over half (52 percent) of local governments provided training to cybersecurity staff every one to two years, while 19 percent said monthly/quarterly (totaling 70 percent). However, one in five said never and 8 percent did not know (totaling 29 percent).

Next, the survey addressed end user training, which as suggested above should occur at least annually. Here, 15 percent of local governments reported providing end user training saying monthly/quarterly and close to half (46 percent) said every one to two years (totaling 60.8 percent). Nearly one in three, however, said never, and 10 percent did not know (totaling 40 percent). The 2018 survey found that nearly six in ten local governments provided cybersecurity training regularly to their employees (Hatcher et al., 2020). The 2018 survey did not ask which employees or inquire about the frequency of training, although its overall finding is not terribly dissimilar from the 2016 survey.

Now to the frequency with which local governments provided cybersecurity *awareness* training to various constituencies from the 2016 survey. Nearly seven in ten respondents reported they provided awareness training on a regular basis, with the vast majority doing so at least annually. This frequency of awareness training seems quite reasonable.

However, it is troubling that nearly one-third of local governments either did not offer such training or did not know if they did.

This was followed by cybersecurity awareness training for cybersecurity personnel where 25 percent of local governments said monthly/quarterly, and 41 percent said one or two years (totaling 66 percent). This frequency of awareness training also seems quite reasonable. However, it is bothersome that so many governments either did not offer such training (25 percent) or did not know (9 percent – totaling 34 percent). Cybersecurity awareness training for local government employees came next with 13 percent responding monthly/quarterly and 47 percent responding one or two years (totaling 60 percent). Still, nearly one-third said never, and 8 percent did not know (totaling 40 percent, another disturbing figure).

The 2020 survey asked whether local governments provided *mandatory* cybersecurity training (and how frequently) to their various stakeholders ranging from elected officials to executives, managers, and end users (Table 6.9). Note that the 2016 and 2018 surveys did not inquire if training was mandatory.

Nearly eight in ten governments responded that they required annual cybersecurity training for all users. Seven in ten said that they provided annual cybersecurity training to the city/county manager/administrator. Seven percent each said some other period for all of those parties or did not know.

The data from the 2016 survey suggest that majorities of local governments appear to be doing a decent job of providing cybersecurity training for certain categories of employees, at least as measured by the frequency of training offered. However, substantial minorities of them are not. As can be seen in the remainder of Table 6.8, however, this is not the case for cybersecurity awareness training for local elected officials, contractors, and local residents. As noted above, the data from the 2020 survey represent a considerable improvement from the 2016 survey, offering some degree of cautious optimism that awareness of the need for high levels of cybersecurity within local governments may be improving.

Table 6.9 Cybersecurity policies adopted.

	Yes		No		Total	
	n	%	n	%	n	%
Password creation rules	188	70.7	78	29.3	266	100.0
Periodic password change requirement	187	70.0	80	30.0	267	100.0
Personally-owned device use policy for officials and employees	155	54.2	131	45.8	286	100.0
Cybersecurity policy, standards, strategy, or plan	120	40.1	179	59.9	299	100.0
Cybersecurity risk management plan	83	26.7	228	73.3	311	100.0
Cybersecurity standards for contracts with vendors for cloud-based services	82	27.6	215	72.4	297	100.0
Plan for recovery from breaches	85	27.6	223	72.4	308	100.0

6.3.8 Cybersecurity Policies

Cybersecurity policies are important for several reasons. They establish roles and responsibilities for all involved parties in an organization and describe proper and responsible cybersecurity practice. They also describe actions that are neither proper nor responsible. And they set the rules of behavior around several consequential cybersecurity matters including but not limited to password management, software patching, cyber risk management, incidence response planning, use of external (including personal) devices on an organization's IT system, policies for vendors, and contractor use of an organization's IT system.

The 2016 survey asked about the extent to which local governments had adopted policies that are important to effective cybersecurity management (Table 6.9). It also asked adopting governments to rate the effectiveness of these policies (Table 6.10). Responses are discussed in the order of most to least frequently adopted policy. Only three policies had been adopted by majorities of local governments: password creation rules (71 percent); periodic password change requirements (70 percent); and policies regarding the use of personally owned devices (54 percent). All remaining policies had been adopted by less than half of respondents: cybersecurity policy, standards, strategy or plan (40 percent); plan for recovery from breaches (28 percent); cybersecurity standards for contracts with vendors for cloud-based services (28 percent); and cybersecurity risk management plan (28 percent). These data suggest that far too many local governments had not adopted policies that are essential to the effective management of cybersecurity.

Majorities of respondents rated only two policies highly/very highly effective – periodic password creation requirement (58 percent) and password creation rules (56 percent). These were also the two most frequently adopted. However, the National Institute of Standards and Technology (NIST) has recommended removing periodic password

Table 6.10 Effectiveness of cybersecurity policies.

	Very Low/ Low		Average		High/Very High		Total	
	n	%	n	%	n	%	n	%
Periodic password change requirement	19	11.3	51	30.4	98	58.3	168	100.0
Password creation rules	20	12.0	53	31.7	94	56.3	167	100.0
Personally-owned device use policy for officials and employees	25	18.8	52	39.1	56	42.1	133	100.0
Cybersecurity standards for contracts with vendors for cloud-based services	20	27.0	27	36.5	27	36.5	74	100.0
Plan for recovery from breaches	24	31.6	36	47.4	16	21.1	76	100.0
Cybersecurity policy, standards, strategy, or plan	32	29.9	54	50.5	21	19.6	107	100.0
Cybersecurity risk management plan	23	31.5	36	49.3	14	19.2	73	100.0

change requirements because some studies have indicated they may be counterproductive to ensuring security (NIST Special Publication 800-63B, 2017).

The remaining policies were rated highly effective by fewer (some by far fewer) governments: policies governing personally owned devices – 42 percent; policies governing vendors – 37 percent; and the rest by one-fifth or fewer governments.

The 2020 survey examined adoption of seven cybersecurity policies, as well as their perceived effectiveness (Tables 6.11 and 6.12). Seventy-nine percent had fully adopted formal cybersecurity policies, which is 30 percent above the 2016 survey, and 21 percent had partially adopted such policies. Similarly, 79 percent had fully adopted password management policies, compared to 70 percent in 2016. Twenty-one percent had partially adopted, and 21 percent had not adopted. Seventy-one percent had fully adopted policies regarding software patches, while 21 percent had partially adopted, and seven percent had not adopted this policy.

Just over half of the governments (57 percent) had fully adopted cyber risk management plans, while 21 percent had partially adopted them, and 21 percent had not adopted them. Another slightly over half of governments (57 percent) had fully adopted incident response plans/disaster recovery/business continuity plans (in 2016 the adoption rate was 28 percent), while just over one-third had partially adopted them, and 7 percent had not adopted. Forty-three percent had adopted policies on the use of external devices

Table 6.11 Has your local government adopted any of the cybersecurity policies listed below (2020 survey).

	Adopted Fully No. %	Adopted Partially No. %	Not Adopted No. %	Don't Know No. %	Total No. %	% adopted in 2016 Survey
Formal cybersecurity policy	11 78.6	3 21.4			14 100	40.1
Password management policy	11 78.6	3 21.4			14 100	70.7
Policy regarding applying software patches	10 71.4	3 21.4	1 7.1		14 100	Not asked
Cyber risk management plan	8 57.1	3 21.4	3 21.4		14 100	26.7
Incident response/ disaster recovery/ business continuity plan	8 57.1	5 35.7	1 7.1		14 100	27.6
Policy on use of external devices (e.g., cell phones/flash drives)	6 42.9	4 28.6	4 28.6		14 100	54.2
Policy for vendors, contractors, cloud services	6 42.9	6 42.9	1 7.1	1 7.1	14 100	27.6

[1]The question in the 2016 survey was binary, yes or no, and did not ask fully or partially, so the percentages reported there may include governments that had only partially adopted policies

Table 6.12 How effective, if at all, are these policies (2020 survey)?

	Highly No. %	Somewhat No. %	Not Very No. %	Not at All No. %	Don't Know No. %	Total No. %	% High/ Very High 2016
Formal cybersecurity policy	4 28.6	9 64.3	1 7.1			14 100	19.6
Password management policy	6 42.9	6 42.9	2 14.3			14 100.1	56.3
Policy regarding applying software patches	4 28.6	8 57.1	1 7.1	1 7.1		14 100	Not asked
Cyber risk management plan	2 14.3	6 42.9	4 28.6	2 14.3		14 100.1	19.2
Incident response/disaster recovery/ business continuity plan	3 21.4	9 64.3	1 7.1	1 7.1		14 100	21.1
Policy on use of external devices (e.g., cell phones/ flash drives)	2 14.3	8 57.1	1 7.1	2 14.3	17.1	14 100	42.1
Policy for vendors, contractors, cloud services	2 14.3	7 50.0	2 14.3	1 7.1	2 14.3	14 100	36.5

(compared to 54 percent in 2016), while 29 percent had partially adopted them, and 29 percent had not adopted. Last, 43 percent had adopted policies for vendors and cloud contractors (this figure was 28 percent in 2016), 43 percent had partially adopted, 7 percent had not adopted, and 7 percent did not know.

Overall, these data show that larger percentages of the governments in the 2020 survey had adopted cybersecurity policies than in the 2016 survey. This said, once again too few local governments had adopted policies or had adopted them only partially. The latter is not terribly surprising since only 44 percent of firms worldwide had adopted cybersecurity policies (PWC, 2018).

Aside from the full adoption of two important policies, these data reveal a surprising lack of full adoption of cybersecurity policies among the responding governments in the 2020 survey, especially since these governments are, for the most part, large as measured by population with presumably adequate budgetary resources and trained professionals managing their cybersecurity. The lack of full adoption, in turn, likely means that these governments are not able to derive the full benefits of these policies, their implementation, and enforcement. These data do not provide clarity regarding how much "partial" adoption meant to the respondents, which could be important in understanding the policies' perceived effectiveness.

Next, the 2020 survey asked about the perceived effectiveness of the adopted policies (Table 6.12). Forty-three percent of respondents said that their password management policies were highly effective (compared to 56 percent in 2016), 21 percent said somewhat, and 7 percent said not very. Just over one-quarter said their formal cybersecurity policies were highly effective (versus 19 percent in 2016), and seven percent said not very. Another 29 percent said that their software patching policies were highly effective, just over half said somewhat, and one each (7 percent) said not very and not at all.

Twenty-one percent said that their incident response plans were highly effective (compared to the same percentage in 2016), two-thirds said somewhat, and one each (7 percent) said not very, and not at all. Fourteen percent said their cyber risk management plans were highly effective (versus 19 percent in 2016), more than four in ten respondents (43 percent) said highly effective, 29 percent said somewhat, and 14 percent said not at all. Fourteen percent also said their policies on the use of external devices were highly effective (compared to 42 percent in 2016), 57 percent said somewhat, 7 percent said not very, 14 percent said not at all, and 7 percent did not know. Finally, 14 percent said their policies for vendors, etc., were highly effective (versus 37 percent in 2016), half said somewhat, 14 percent said not very, 7 percent said not at all, and 14 percent did not know.

For the most part, responses to the questions of policy effectiveness in both surveys do not inspire confidence that the policies are working as needed to achieve their objectives. Somewhat and not very effective responses suggest that the policies (and/or their enforcement) contain gaps that are likely to allow problems, perhaps serious ones, of cybersecurity practice and management to occur. Consider, for example, the policy on applying software patches in the 2020 survey where only 28 percent of respondents said that this policy was highly effective. If software patches are not applied in a timely manner, and especially if not at all, seriously consequential cybersecurity outcomes can be expected. Indeed, failure to apply software patches as soon as possible after they are released by vendors is a major reason that cybercriminals are able to breach local government IT systems.

What the data cannot reveal, however, is why the respondents rated the effectiveness of these policies so low. Could it be that the policies themselves were not well written, and, as a result, they would be unlikely to be effective or that the policies had not been properly implemented or were not being enforced? The data also cannot reveal what the term "somewhat effective" meant to the respondents. Were the policies good but not perfect, which generally could suggest a positive outcome. Or were they weak but yet with some positive qualities, or something in between?

6.3.9 Cybersecurity Technology, Practices, Policies, and Ability

Next, the survey explored whether respondents believed that their local governments had kept their cybersecurity technologies (hardware and software), practices (methods used, etc.) and policies (written or unwritten "rules" or procedures) up-to-date and whether they had the ability to address various cybersecurity events. These are important to know because local governments that lag behind the current state of the practice likely place themselves at greater cybersecurity risk than those at least at the state of the practice. Likewise, those that are not able to respond to adverse events are more likely to experience breaches, data exfiltration, ransomware attacks, etc.

The 2016 survey asked whether local governments considered their cybersecurity technology, practices, and policies to be state of the art, current best practice, one generation behind current best practice, more than one generation behind, or don't know (Table 6.13). Because only 5 percent of governments rated their technology as state of the art and 1 percent each did so for practices and policies, the ratings of state of the art and current best practice were collapsed to simply "best practice." Just over half rated their cybersecurity technologies as best practice, nearly three in ten said one generation behind, almost one in ten said more than one generation behind, and only a small fraction did not know. This reinforces what local government cybersecurity practitioners have previously reported – that they have the technology part of the cybersecurity equation reasonably well in hand (Norris et al., 2019).

The same cannot be said of local government cybersecurity practices and policies. Slightly more than four in ten said that their cybersecurity practices were best practice. One-third said one generation behind, nearly one in five said more than one generation behind, and 7 percent did not know. Just under one-third said that their policies were best practice, while almost six in ten said either one generation, or one quarter said more than one generation behind, and one in ten did not know. The previously noted lack of effectiveness of cybersecurity policies among local governments in the 2016 survey may well be due to the fact many of those governments policies do not reflect today's best practices.

The 2016 survey also asked respondents to rate their local governments' ability to address eight potential cybersecurity events (Table 6.14). A rating of anything other than very good/excellent strongly suggests that a policy is not sufficiently effective, leaving these governments unnecessarily vulnerable to adverse cybersecurity events. The results are decidedly poor. Less than half of local governments rated their ability to respond to the listed events as very good/excellent: Recover from ransomware attack – 48 percent; detect attacks – 42 percent; detect incidents – 38 percent; and the rest about one-third or

Table 6.13 Rate technologies, practices, and policies.

	Best Practice		One Generation Behind		More Than One Generation Behind		Don't Know		Total	
	n	%	n	%	n	%	n	%	n	%
Technology	189	55.8	99	29.2	30	8.9	21	6.2	339	100.0
Practices	146	43.1	109	32.2	62	18.3	22	6.5	339	100.0
Policies	106	31.3	109	32.2	89	26.3	35	10.3	339	100.0

Table 6.14 Ability of your local government to do the following.

	Poor/Fair		Good		Very Good/ Excellent		Don't Know		Total	
	n	%	n	%	n	%	n	%	n	%
Recover from ransomware attack	64	18.7	77	22.5	165	48.3	36	10.5	342	100
Detect attacks	97	28	88	25.4	145	41.9	16	4.6	346	100
Detect incidents	98	28.3	98	28.3	132	38.2	18	5.2	346	100
Detect breaches	98	28.5	103	29.9	125	36.3	18	5.2	344	100
Recover from breaches	90	26.5	79	23.2	125	36.8	46	13.5	340	100
Recover from exfiltration of data/info	107	31.7	68	20.1	94	27.8	69	20.4	338	100
Prevent exfiltration of data/info	146	42.9	64	18.8	85	25.0	45	13.2	340	100
Detect exfiltration of data/info	168	49.3	54	15.8	70	20.5	49	14.4	341	100

fewer. These data suggest that local governments' ability to respond to adverse cybersecurity events is severely lacking.

6.3.10 Cybersecurity Awareness, Support, Responsibility, and Funding

Three additional factors may help to explain the weaknesses in cybersecurity management among US local governments. The first two are awareness of and support for cybersecurity among elected officials and top managers. The third is the extent to which those officials embrace an important role in responsibility for cybersecurity.

Awareness of and support for cybersecurity within an organization can operate as facilitators of, or barriers to, how it practices cybersecurity. For example, if top local government officials (for present purposes this means top elected officials and top appointed managers) are aware of the need for cybersecurity and provide high levels of support for it, then their governments will be more likely to be able to establish and maintain high levels of cybersecurity. Here, the focus is only on whether officials provided high levels of awareness and support (moderately/exceptionally aware in Table 6.15) because anything else, we argue, suggests the opposite (i.e., inadequate levels of support).

Respondents to the 2016 survey reported that top appointed managers possessed the greatest cybersecurity awareness in their organizations – 62 percent moderately/exceptionally aware (Table 6.15). However, respondents also reported that one-third were not aware, slightly aware, or only somewhat aware of cybersecurity. Next in order were department managers at 42 percent moderately/exceptionally aware. This was followed by the average end user, 33 percent, and all others falling below one-third.

Table 6.15 How would you rate the cybersecurity awareness of each of the following in your local government?

	Not/ Slightly Aware		Somewhat Aware		Moderately/ Exceptionally Aware		Don't Know		Total	
	n	%	n	%	n	%	n	%	n	%
Top appointed managers	47	14.0	64	19.0	208	61.7	18	5.3	337	100.0
Department managers	76	21.3	117	32.8	151	42.3	13	3.6	357	100.0
Elected executives	85	27.5	82	26.5	99	32.0	43	13.9	309	100.0

Table 6.16 How would you rate the amount of support cybersecurity receives in your local government from each of the following?

	No/ Limited Support		Moderate Support		Strong/Full Support		Don't Know		Total	
	n	%	n	%	n	%	n	%	n	%
Top appointed manager	51	15.7	76	23.5	175	54.0	22	6.8	324	100.0
Elected executive	71	25.4	72	25.7	99	35.4	38	13.6	280	100.0
Department managers	94	26.9	122	35.0	115	33.0	18	5.0	349	100.0

A similar pattern emerged regarding support for cybersecurity from each group (Table 6.16). Here, a bare majority of respondents felt that only one official, the top appointed manager, provided either strong or full support for cybersecurity, and about one-third reported strong or full support from the elected executive and department managers.

The 2020 current survey also asked about the awareness of (Table 6.17) and support for (Table 6.19) cybersecurity among these local governments' 1) mayor/elected county executive, 2) city/county council members, 3) city/county manager/administrator, 4) department heads, and 5) average end users. The results are not encouraging. Respondents did not believe that these parties were highly aware of the need for cybersecurity. In only one case (mayor/elected county executive) did a slight majority of respondents believe that incumbents in this office were highly or mostly aware of the need for cybersecurity. And one-third of respondents said these office holders were only somewhat/a little aware, and 7 percent said not at all aware.

Perceptions of the cybersecurity awareness of the remaining officials and staff were bleak. Half of respondents said that the city/county manager/administrator was highly/mostly aware. Slightly under three in ten said somewhat/a little, one said not at all, and two didn't know. Half responded that department heads were highly/mostly aware, while 43 percent said somewhat/a little, and one said not at all. Four in ten said that city/county council members were highly/mostly aware; half said somewhat/a little and one

Table 6.17 In your opinion, how aware are the following of the need for high levels of cybersecurity (2020 survey)?

	Highly/ Mostly	Somewhat/ A Little	Not At All	Don't Know	Total
	No %	No. %	No. %	No. %	No. %
Mayor/elected county executive	8 57.1	5 35.7	1 7.1		14 100.0
City/county council members	6 42.9	7 50.0	1 7.1		14 100.0
City/county manager/ administrator	7 50.0	4 28.6	1 7.1	2 14.3	14 100.0
Department heads	7 50.0	6 42.9	1 7.1		14 100.0
Average end user	6 42.9	7 50.0	1 7.1		14 100.0

Table 6.18 In your opinion, how supportive of the need to maintain high levels of cybersecurity are the following (2020 survey)?

	Highly/ Mostly	Somewhat/A Little	Not At All	Don't Know	Total
	No. %	No. %	No. %	No. %	No. %
Mayor/elected county executive	11 78.6	2 14.3	1 7.1		14 100.0
City/county council members	7 50.0	6 42.9	1 7.1		14 100.0
City/county manager/ administrator	8 57.1	3 21.4	1 7.1	2 14.3	14 100.0
Department heads	10 71.4	3 21.4	1 7.1		14 100.0
Average end user	8 57.1	5 35.7	1 7.1		14 100.0

said not at all. Finally, four in ten responded that end users were highly/mostly aware; half said somewhat/a little; and one said not at all.

In theory, awareness of the need for cybersecurity among local government officials and staff should lead them to provide support for it. The results of the 2016 survey do not support this notion. In that survey, a bare majority of respondents felt that only one official and that official alone, the top appointed manager, provided either strong or full support for cybersecurity, and about one-third each reported the same for elected executive and department managers.

Unlike the 2016 survey, respondents to the 2020 survey felt that most of the parties in their governments provided a good deal of support for cybersecurity (Table 6.18). Nearly

Table 6.19 Responsibility of top elected and appointed officials versus technologists for cybersecurity.

	Mainly with Technologists		Both		Important Role for Officials		Don't Know		Total	
	n	%	n	%	n	%	n	%	n	%
Top elected officials	224	67.3	34	10.2	31	9.3	44	13.2	333	100.0
Top appointed officials	189	57.3	45	13.6	56	17.0	40	12.1	330	100.0

eight in ten said that the mayor/elected county executive was highly/mostly supportive of cybersecurity. Close behind seven in ten said that department heads were highly/ mostly supportive. This was followed by city/county manager administrator (57 percent); average end users (57 percent); and city/county council members (50 percent).

A common proposition in the cybersecurity field, especially in private sector organizations, is that top executives and board members must be fully engaged in and supportive of cybersecurity and should not leave cybersecurity solely to technologists. Thus, the 2016 survey asked whether top elected and appointed officials in American local governments believed that responsibility for cybersecurity lies mainly with technologists or if these officials felt that there was an important role for them to play in cybersecurity (Table 6.19). Not surprisingly, respondents said that, for the most part, top elected and appointed officials believed that cybersecurity belonged mainly with technologists: top elected officials (67 percent) and top appointed officials (57 percent). Respondents also reported that only 9 percent of top elected officials and 17 percent of top appointed officials felt that there was an important role in cybersecurity for them.

The data from the 2016 survey, reporting limited awareness of and support for cybersecurity and the lack of acceptance of cybersecurity roles and responsibility by top elected and appointed officials may help to explain why local governments in that survey, on average, practiced cybersecurity so poorly. The results of the 2020 survey provide some measure of optimism that at least support for cybersecurity among various parties in local governments is improving, if not awareness as well.

Another reason for poor cybersecurity management may also be lack of funding. It is important to know whether local governments' annual cybersecurity investment has fluctuated in recent years. According to the executive director of the US Cyberspace Solarium Commission (CSC), Mark Montgomery, most organizations' cybersecurity budgets have been flat "but the cyberattacks are growing exponentially" (Morgan, 2019). Thus, the 2016 survey asked if local government cybersecurity budgets had changed over the past five years regarding technology, additional staffing, staff compensation, staff training, and policies and procedures (Table 6.20).

Only in one category, technology, did most local governments report that their spending over the previous five years had increased slightly or greatly. For all others, majorities

Table 6.20 Cybersecurity investment changes over the last five years.

	Decreased Greatly/ Slightly		About the Same		Increased Slightly/ Greatly		Don't Know		Total	
	n	%	n	%	n	%	n	%	n	%
Technology	22	6.4	107	31.3	201	58.8	12	3.5	342	100.0
Additional staff	39	11.5	187	55.0	100	29.4	14	4.0	340	100.0
Higher staff compensation	38	11.2	213	62.8	100	29.4	14	4.0	339	100.0
Training for staff	43	12.7	167	49.0	113	33.2	17	5.0	340	100.0
Policies and procedures	25	7.4	163	47.9	132	38.8	20	5.9	340	100.0

or near majorities said that spending had remained about the same: higher staff compensation – 63 percent; additional staff – 55 percent; training for staff – 49 percent; and policies and procedures – 48 percent. Few governments reported that spending in these areas actually decreased.

These findings should be understood in the context of local government budgeting and finance. First, there is rarely if ever enough money in a local government's budget to meet all needs, real and perceived. Second, local government budgets are especially sensitive to economic downturns, such as the "Great Recession," when many are obliged to reduce funding to some functions and/or initiate service cutbacks. Third, arguably important things like higher salary and additional hiring, and "frills," such as travel and staff training, are often cut to preserve core functions. Last, even in good times, funding of such things as travel, training, policies, and procedures has historically been low across many if not most local governments. So, these data, especially when combined with knowledge that local governments consider lack of adequate funding to be among the top barriers to cybersecurity, suggest anything but a robust pattern of recent investment for cybersecurity at the grassroots (Norris et al., 2019).

6.4 Conclusion and Recommendations

The findings in Chapter 5 showed that most of local governments do not *practice* cybersecurity very well. The evidence presented in this chapter strongly suggests that an important reason for poor cybersecurity practice is that local governments do not *manage* cybersecurity well. In other words, while there are some local governments, especially those that are larger, better financed, and more well-staffed, that are doing exceptional jobs of managing and practicing cybersecurity, there many are others that are not. One area of future analysis might be to identify a number of local governments that practice excellent cybersecurity management and conduct in-depth case studies of them to learn how they are able to achieve such results.

Perhaps this can be explained by the fact that the top elected and appointed officials in local governments are insufficiently aware of the need for cybersecurity, do not support cybersecurity strongly enough, and/or believe that cybersecurity only is the responsibility of technologists and not themselves. If this is true, and there is ample evidence that it is, then unless this situation changes and top elected and appointed officials become more knowledgeable about, and supportive of, cybersecurity and accept responsibility to play active roles in cybersecurity, the problems related to local government cybersecurity management discussed in this chapter likely will persist.

The findings from the surveys discussed in this chapter offer what can only be considered an indictment of the current state of local government cybersecurity management. This said, local governments certainly are not alone in this regard. Few organizations of any kind in the public or private sectors manage and practice cybersecurity well. On a more positive note, despite these findings (indeed, perhaps because of them), substantial opportunities exist for local governments to improve their cybersecurity management.

Tables: All tables in this Appendix present data from the 2016 survey, except those explicitly noted as from the 2020 survey.

Appendix 6.1 Outsourced Cybersecurity Functions from 2020 Survey

Function	Description
Payment card industry data security standards (PCI DSS) scanning	Quarterly scan of internal and external networks and applications processing and storing credit card data required to be PCI DSS compliant. (See Chapter 10 for more on PCI DSS).
Penetration testing	Also known as "pen tests," penetration testing is an authorized simulated attack/breach on the local government's systems to test the security measures in place.
Monitoring vendor tools on network	Vendor monitoring software allows local governments to monitor third party controls and maintain awareness of the vendor relationship. The software can alert local governments of rising risks of vendors they are using.
24/7 Intrusion prevention system (IPS) monitoring	IPS monitoring allows local governments to know of any abnormal network traffic to help prevent vulnerability exploits. In addition to alarming the system administrator of anomalous activity, IPS can autonomously drop bad packets and block traffic.
IT security operation center (SOC) monitoring	A SOC team monitors, prevents, and responds to cyber threats facing the local government. SOCs can be outsourced as can the monitoring of those services and logs.
Vulnerability scanning	Vulnerability scans test networks and computers for known weaknesses to identify any security flaws and predict the effectiveness of countermeasures.

Appendix 6.2. Cybersecurity Tools

Tool	Description
Anti-virus software	Antivirus software is a class of program designed to prevent, detect, and remove malware infections on individual computing devices, networks, and IT systems.
Web and email gateways	An email security gateway is a product or service that is designed to prevent the transmission of emails that break company policy, send malware or transfer information with malicious intent.
Virtual private networks of VPNs	A virtual private network (VPN) is programming that creates a safe and encrypted connection over a less secure network, such as the public internet. A VPN works by using the shared public infrastructure while maintaining privacy through security procedures and tunneling protocols. In effect, the protocols, by encrypting data at the sending end and decrypting it at the receiving end, send the data through a "tunnel" that cannot be "entered" by data that is not properly encrypted. An additional level of security involves encrypting not only the data, but also the originating and receiving network addresses.
Intrusion detection and prevention systems	An intrusion detection system (IDS) is a system that monitors network traffic for suspicious activity and issues alerts when such activity is discovered. While anomaly detection and reporting is the primary function, some intrusion detection systems are capable of taking actions when malicious activity or anomalous traffic is detected, including blocking traffic sent from suspicious IP addresses.
Next-generation firewalls	A next-generation firewall (NGFW) is a part of the third generation of firewall technology that is implemented in either hardware or software and is capable of detecting and blocking sophisticated attacks by enforcing security policies at the application, port, and protocol levels.
Automated malware protection systems	Antimalware (anti-malware) is a type of software program designed to prevent, detect, and remove malicious software (malware) on IT systems, as well as individual computing devices. Antimalware software protects against infections caused by many types of malware, including all types of viruses, as well as rootkits, ransomware, and spyware. Antimalware software can be installed on an individual computing device, gateway server, or dedicated network appliance. It can also be purchased as a cloud service – such as McAfee's CloudAV product – or be embedded in a computing device's firmware.
Network traffic analysis or network virtualization	Network virtualization is a method of combining the available resources in a network by splitting up the available bandwidth into channels, each of which is independent from the others, and each of which can be assigned (or reassigned) to a particular server or device in real time. Each channel is independently secured. Every subscriber has shared access to all the resources on the network from a single computer.

(Continued)

Tool	Description
Multi-factor or biometric authentication	Two-factor authentication (2FA), sometimes referred to as two-step verification or dual factor authentication, is a security process in which the user provides two different authentication factors to verify themselves to better protect both the user's credentials and the resources the user can access. Two-factor authentication provides a higher level of assurance than authentication methods that depend on single-factor authentication (SFA), in which the user provides only one factor – typically a password or passcode. Two-factor authentication methods rely on users providing a password as well as a second factor, usually either a security token or a biometric factor like a fingerprint or facial scan.
	Biometric authentication is a security process that relies on the unique biological characteristics of an individual to verify that he is who is says he is. Biometric authentication systems compare a biometric data capture to stored, confirmed authentic data in a database. If both samples of the biometric data match, authentication is confirmed. Typically, biometric authentication is used to manage access to physical and digital resources such as buildings, rooms, and computing devices.

[1]These definitions have been taken verbatim from https://searchsecurity.techtarget.com.

Note

1 This chapter is a revised and expanded version of Donald F. Norris, Laura Mateczun, Anupam Joshi, and Tim Finin. 2021. Managing cybersecurity at the grassroots: Evidence from the first nationwide survey of local government cybersecurity. *Journal of Urban Affairs* 43(8), 1173–1195. Published online April 2020. Included by permission of the publisher, Taylor & Francis.

References

Browning, E. (2017). *Scanning for vulnerabilities: When, why and how often – prevent threat actors from exploiting vulnerabilities in your network by eliminating the risks*. SecureWorks, Inc. https://www.secureworks.com/blog/scanning-for-vulnerabilities-when-why-and-how-often

Buszta, K. (2003). Security management. In H.F. Tipton and M. Krause (Eds.), *Information Security Management Handbook* (4th ed., pp. 263–274). Auerbach Publications.

Center for Internet Security (2017). *National cyber security review: Summary report*. https://www.cisecurity.org/wp-content/uploads/2018/10/NCSR-2017-Final.pdf

CivicPlus (2018). *The reality of the local government cybersecurity skill gap*. Governing. http://www.governing.com/topics/mgmt/Cybersecurity-Month-Addressing-the-Biggest-Cybersecurity-Challenges-Facing-Local-Governments.html

Cybersecurity and Infrastructure Security Agency (CISA), US Department of Homeland Security (n.d.). *Cybersecurity insurance*. https://www.cisa.gov/cybersecurity-insurance

Cybersecurity and Infrastructure Security Agency (CISA), US Department of Homeland Security (2019). *Cybersecurity insurance.* https://www.dhs.gov/cybersecurity-insurance

Deloitte (2019). *The future of cyber survey 2019: Cyber everywhere. Succeed anywhere.* https://www2.deloitte.com/us/en/pages/advisory/articles/future-of-cyber-survey.html

Deloitte and National Association of State Chief Information Officers (2018). *2018 Deloitte-NASCIO Cybersecurity study – States at risk: Bold plays for change.* https://www2.deloitte.com/insights/us/en/industry/public-sector/nascio-survey-government-cybersecurity-strategies.html

Earnst and Young (2016). *Path to cyber resilience: Sense, resist, react. EY 19th Global information security survey 2016.* https://www.ey.com/Publication/vwLUAssets/Global_Information_Security_Survey_2016/$FILE/REPORT%20-%20EY's%2019th%20Global%20Information%20Security%20Survey.pdf

EY.com (2017). *Cybersecurity regained: Preparing to face cyber attacks. 20th Global information security survey 2017-2018.* https://assets.ey.com/content/dam/ey-sites/ey-com/en_gl/topics/digital/ey-cybersecurity-regained-preparing-to-face-cyber-attacks.pdf

Gibson, D. (2015). *Managing Risk in Information Systems* (2d ed.). Jones and Bartlett Learning.

Hatcher, W., Meares, W.L., and Heslen, J. (2020). The cybersecurity of municipalities in the United States: An exploratory survey of policies and practices. *Journal of Cyber Policy,* 5(2). https://doi.org/10.1080/23738871.2020.1792956

International City/County Management Association (ICMA) (2018, February 2). *Expert interview: Cybersecurity awareness training for local government employees.* https://icma.org/blog-posts/expert-interview-cybersecurity-awareness-training-local-government-employees

King, J.L., and Kraemer, K.L. (1985). *The Dynamics of Computing.* Columbia University Press.

King, J.L., and Kraemer, K.L. (2019). Policy: An information systems frontier. *Journal of the Association for Information Systems,* 20(6), 842–847, DOI: 10.17705/1.jais.00553

Kraemer, K.L., and Dedrick, J. (1997). Computing and public organizations. *Journal of Public Administration Research and Theory,* 7(1), 89–112, https://doi.org/10.1093/oxfordjournals.jpart.a024344

Kraemer, K.L., King, J.L., Dunkle, D.E., and Lane, J.P. (1989). *Managing Information Systems: Change and Control in Organizational Computing.* Jossey-Bass.

Landi, H. (2017, July 24). *Survey: 47 Percent of healthcare orgs outsourcing some of their cybersecurity needs.* Healthcare Informatics. https://www.hcinnovationgroup.com/cybersecurity/news/13028942/survey-47-percent-of-healthcare-orgs-outsourcing-some-of-their-cybersecurity-needs

Laudon, K.C., and Laudon, J.P. (2014). *Management Information Systems: Managing the Digital Firm* (13th ed.). Pearson.

Marvin, R. (2018, January 24). *What is cyber insurance and should you get it?* PC Magazine. https://www.pcmag.com/feature/358453/what-is-cyber-insurance-and-should-you-get-it

Medical Group Management Association (2017, July 18). *Practice leaders manage cybersecurity with in-house and outsourced resources.* https://www.mgma.com/data/data-stories/practice-leaders-manage-cybersecurity-with-in-hous

Merko, M.S. and Breithaupt, J. (2014). *Information Security: Principles and Practices* (2d ed.). Pearson.

Morgan, S. (2019). *2019 Official annual cybercrime report: Cybercriminal activity is one of the biggest challenges humanity will face in the next two decades.* Cybersecurity Ventures and Herjavec Group. https://www.herjavecgroup.com/wp-content/uploads/2018/12/CV-HG-2019-Official-Annual-Cybercrime-Report.pdf

Norris, D.F. (1984). Small local governments and information technology: Uses and users. *Public Administration Review*, 44(1), 70–78, https://doi.org/10.2307/975666

Norris, D.F. (2010). E-government 2020: Plus ca change, plus c'est la meme chose. *Public Administration Review*, 70 (Special Issue), S180, https://doi.org/10.1111/j.1540-6210.2010.02269.x

Norris, D.F. (2021). *A new look at local government cybersecurity in 2020: Recommendations for staying vigilant against persistent cyber threats.* Local Government Review. A publication of the International City/County Management Association. https://icma.org/sites/default/files/2021-07/PM%20%2B%20LGR%20July%202021%20LOW-RES.pdf

Norris, D.F., and Kraemer, K.L. (1996). Mainframe and PC computing in American cities: Myths and realities. *Public Administration Review*, 56(6), 568–576, https://doi.org/10.2307/977255

Norris, D F., Mateczun, L., Joshi, A., and Finin, T. (2018). Cybersecurity at the grassroots: American local governments and the challenges of Internet security. *Journal of Homeland Security and Emergency Management*, 15(3), 1–14, https://doi.org/10.1515/jhsem-2017-0048

Norris, D.F., Mateczun, L., Joshi, A., and Finin, T. (2019). Cyberattacks at the grassroots: American local governments and the need for high levels of cybersecurity. *Public Administration Review*, 79(6), 895–904. https://doi.org/10.1111/puar.13028

Norris, D.F., Mateczun, L., Joshi, A., and Finin, T. (2020). Managing cybersecurity at the grassroots: Evidence from the first nationwide survey of local government cybersecurity. *Journal of Urban Affairs*, 43(8), 1173–1195. Published online 17 April 2020. https://doi.org/10.1080/07352166.2020.1727295

Norris, D.F., and Jae Moon, M. (2005). Advancing e-government at the grass roots: Tortoise or hare? *Public Administration Review*, 65(1), 64–75. https://doi.org/10.1111/j.1540-6210.2005.00431.x

Norris, D.F., and Reddick, C.G. (2013). Local E-government in the United States: Transformation or incremental change? *Public Administration Review*, 73(1), 165–175. https://doi.org/10.1111/j.1540-6210.2012.02647.x

PCI Security Standards Council (2014). *Information Supplement: Best Practices for Implementing a Security Awareness Program.* https://www.pcisecuritystandards.org/documents/PCI_DSS_V1.0_Best_Practices_for_Implementing_Security_Awareness_Program.pdf

Pearlson, K.E., and Saunders, C.S. (2006). *Managing and Using Information Systems: A Strategic Approach.* John Wiley and Sons.

Public Technology Institute (2019). *Local government survey research.* http://www.pti.org/civicax/inc/blobfetch.aspx?BlobID=23038

PWC (2018). *Strengthening digital society against cyber shocks: Key findings from the 2018 global state of information security survey.* https://www.pwc.com.br/pt/global-state-of-information-security-survey-2018/pwc-2018-gsiss-strengthening-digital-society-against-cyber-shocks.pdf

SecureWorks (2019, May 30). *Achieving PCI compliance.* https://www.secureworks.com/blog/achieving-pci-compliance

US National Institute of Standards and Technology (NIST) (2020, March 3). *Special Publication 800-63B, Digital Identity Guidelines – Authentication and Lifecycle Management.* https://pages.nist.gov/800-63-3/sp800-63b.html

Verizon (2015). *2015 Data breach investigations report.* http://www.verizon.com/about/news/2015-data-breach-report-info

Verizon (2019). *2019 Data breach investigations report.* https://enterprise.verizon.com/resources/reports/dbir

Whitman, M.E., and Mattord, H.J. (2010). *Management of Information Security* (4th ed.). Cengage Learning.

Wood, C.C. (2005). All aboard! *Information Security*, 8(7), 52–55.

Wood, C.C. (2010). Preface. In M.E. Whitman and H.J. Mattord (Eds.), *Management of Information Security* (4th ed.). Cengage Learning.

Wood, C.C. (2016). Solving the information security and privacy crisis by expanding the scope of top management personal liability. *Journal of Legislation*, 43(1), 65–121. https://scholarship.law.nd.edu/jleg/vol43/iss1/5

7

Cybersecurity Policies for Local Government

7.1 Introduction

This chapter discusses the various cybersecurity policies needed to establish an effective framework for local government cybersecurity programs. First, it discusses the policy design and development process to ensure that cybersecurity policies are developed effectively and include key stakeholders from across local government. Then, the chapter presents a series of cybersecurity policy recommendations in general order of importance to local governments. The goal is to provide readers with an understanding of the necessary components of cybersecurity policy and also how to best implement them.

7.2 Policy Design and Development

Although developing and implementing cybersecurity policies in local governments typically is a staff function, it is important to involve relevant stakeholders, including elected officials, in this process. Local governments are perfect examples of this situation because they often have subordinate departments, divisions, or agencies that might have their own unique cybersecurity requirements. In large local governments, cybersecurity staff might use a centralized policy planning process to craft a high-level strategic framework that establishes a robust cybersecurity vision, goals, standards, and responsibilities that would be respected by subordinate entities in drafting their own respective policies and procedures. By contrast, in smaller local governments, developing jurisdiction-wide cybersecurity policies might be the responsibility of a small group of staff, if not even a single official. Regardless of the size of the local government, the cybersecurity policy development process should not only identify the involved stakeholders but also, more importantly, allow the stakeholders' specific concerns and needs to be heard and appropriately addressed in the process.

At a minimum, developing local government cybersecurity policy should include representatives from the following departments: IT, human resources, legal, facilities and infrastructure management, law enforcement, fire and emergency services, public affairs, and each administrative and operating department. Additionally, representatives

Cybersecurity and Local Government, First Edition. Donald F. Norris, Laura K . Mateczun and Richard F. Forno.
© 2022 John Wiley & Sons Ltd. Published 2022 by John Wiley & Sons Ltd.

of elected officials (chief elected executive and members of the local government legislative body), who ultimately bear public responsibility for what happens in their jurisdiction, should be kept informed throughout this process to help maintain their much needed support for cybersecurity within their governments. At the conclusion of the process, the elected officials should be briefed regarding its outcomes, especially because at some point they may be called upon to approve any policy recommendations that result.

Once key stakeholders are identified, the next step is to conduct and review all existing policies, procedures, practices, and documentation related to the local government's cybersecurity to determine how cybersecurity is currently governed, practiced, and managed. Here, emphasis should be placed on identifying gaps between existing policy, procedure, and practice and identified cybersecurity needs in the local government. Some of the questions that might be asked and the information gathered during this review might include:

- What facilities, servers, and networks are used to conduct government business by employees and with citizens? Which systems or workflows are considered "critical" services, such as 911 centers, online tax collection websites, voter registration, or other digital self-service systems?
- What third-party vendors are relied upon to provide internet connectivity or critical services like official email or cloud services, and do these vendors practice good cybersecurity themselves? Are minimum standards of cybersecurity included when evaluating new products and vendors? If not, no matter how robust the local government cybersecurity posture might be, such platforms and services, many of which have direct and trusted access into local government networks, represent potential serious cybersecurity risks (Velazco and Lerman, 2021).
- Do local IT and cybersecurity officials actually know what their network looks like? What software, services, platforms, or external linkages are used within the local government network environment? Prior research (Norris et al., 2019) suggests that if officials don't know if they're under attack, it's probably safe to presume they don't have a complete picture of their information environment. Failing to know the details and/or any changes to information resources can lead to cyber incidents or attacks that seemingly "come out of nowhere" or allow an attacker to remain hidden for longer periods of time within the official network environment. But even if IT staff have that knowledge, is that knowledge kept current?
- Are there any federal, state, or local requirements that local government must comply with, and is it doing so?
- Are there any existing policies, procedures, or processes, formal or informal, that can help inform developing new or updated cybersecurity policies and procedures? For example, is there a contact list of individuals in key leadership and technical positions, along with subject matter experts, that can be reached in an emergency?

For larger governments with many subordinate departments, the information-gathering process can be time-consuming and require the active participation and discussion of many staff, offices, and officials. This said, the cybersecurity policy development process is likely to vary according to local government size, staffing, budgets, and potentially other considerations. It is also likely that small local governments may not have the staff or financial resources to adopt all of the policy recommendations presented in this chapter. Regardless, it is important that local governments use this process to adopt policies that will enhance cybersecurity readiness.

Once cybersecurity policies have been developed, they should undergo legal review to ensure both legal sufficiency and compliance with applicable local, state, or federal laws (see also Chapter 10). In the case of all cybersecurity policies, those who develop them should write in clear and concise language that fosters maximum understanding and minimizes confusion or misinterpretation.

Having discussed the process of developing cybersecurity policies in local governments, this chapter now turns to presenting some of the most important policies that local governments must adopt in order to establish high levels of cybersecurity within their organizations.

7.3 About Cybersecurity Policy

For the purposes of this chapter, *policies* are considered the strategic documents establishing broad enterprise-wide expectations, requirements, and standards that govern IT activities. *Procedures* are derived from policies and describe how organizations and the people in them will carry out the policies in practice. For example, while an incident-handling policy might provide high-level guidance for managing cybersecurity emergencies, incident response *procedures* derived from that policy provide operational task-oriented guidance on responding to certain types of incidents like phishing attacks or data breaches. Under this management model, policies tend not to be changed very often but operational processes and procedures will as situations on the ground change, such as the emergence of new cyberattack modes and techniques.

Well-crafted cybersecurity policies typically reflect a traditional defense in depth cybersecurity posture (US National Security Agency, 2010). This approach to security is based on the medieval castle model that establishes strong perimeter defenses and then layers additional security controls upon the facilities and the people within. This is a time-tested approach to cybersecurity. The defense in depth model is being enhanced by the concept of "zero trust" security which considers every device and every person connected to the local government's IT system to be potentially untrustworthy (see also Chapter 11). While many cybersecurity controls are technical in nature (such as firewalls, encryption, network monitoring, and more), the adoption and implementation of the policies governing their use are critical to the success of any formal cybersecurity program.

Whether local government cybersecurity policy is a single document or is divided among smaller, more specific policies (as this chapter does), the important thing is to develop and adopt them. One good example of a local government cybersecurity policy comes from San Francisco, California (thank you CISO Mike Makstman!). It is a little over six pages long and covers such issues as the purpose and scope of the policy, cybersecurity requirements that all departments must follow, and the cybersecurity roles and responsibilities of various officials and departments in the city. It is attached as Appendix 7.1. Additionally, and although it is not a local government, the

Commonwealth of Massachusetts has adopted an eight-page cybersecurity policy establishing the basic foundations of the commonwealth's cybersecurity program, and several of its policy provisions reflect many of the policies discussed below (Commonwealth of Massachusetts, 2018). It is found as Appendix 7.2. Examples like these can be invaluable in helping local governments, especially those with limited cybersecurity staff or resources, as they work to establish a minimum cybersecurity policy framework.

Next, this chapter presents essential cybersecurity policies for local governments and then considers policies that may not be essential but nevertheless are desirable. These policy recommendations are based on industry recommended best cybersecurity practices and reflect the guidance provided in government publications like the NIST Cybersecurity Framework (National Institute for Standards and Technology [NIST], 2018) and Risk Management Framework (NIST, n.d.). In many cases, there is no need for local governments to spend their scarce resources to hire policy development specialists or consultants. There are easily identifiable no-cost cybersecurity policies or policy templates that they can use to develop their own policies, such as from the SANS Institute. Asking other local governments to share their cybersecurity policies can also produce beneficial results and may as well help to establish mutually beneficial working relationships on cybersecurity matters. Local governments should also consider contacting various representative and professional organizations for cybersecurity advice and assistance (e.g., National League of Cities (NLC), National Association of Counties (NACo), International City/County Management Association (ICMA), National Association of State CISOs (NASCIO), US Conference of Mayors (USCM) and others).

Essential cybersecurity policies are those absolutely necessary to establish a cybersecurity program. Desirable policies, on the other hand will support, enhance, and expand upon those essential foundations. Of course, operational priorities and resourcing will determine which policies in either category local governments will adopt. This said, the more comprehensive and more effective local government cybersecurity programs will include all of the policy items mentioned below as well as potentially others.

7.4 Essential Cybersecurity Policies

Perhaps the most fundamental of the essential policies, which is the document that establishes baseline cybersecurity requirements, is the **Acceptable Use Policy** (AUP) or **Policy for Responsible Computing**. This may also be known as the site's **Terms of Service** (TOS) policy (Baltimore County, MD, n.d.). Regardless of its name (and in this book we stick with AUP), this policy describes what activities are and are not permitted by employees, contractors, visitors, and other users of a local government's computer systems and networks, and what expectations of privacy, if any, users should expect while working on those systems. AUPs generally require official systems to be used for official business, used within the authorized scope of a user's privileges, and/or prohibit intentional misuse (such as introducing malware, visiting pornography sites, uploading copyrighted materials, or attempting to break into a site's web form). AUPs may also include prohibitions against using employee-owned devices on the local government network or when conducting official business unless authorized to do so.

A key benefit of the AUP is to confirm that users and site visitors understand how they are expected to behave when using official information resources and also the extent of privacy they can expect when using such systems. Most AUPs inform users that there is no expectation of privacy and that anything they do on the system or site potentially can be used as evidence against them in a criminal or civil court action. Such policy declarations help protect system operators and cybersecurity staff from legal liability and accusations of wiretapping when monitoring official systems or user actions for suspicious activity or system support purposes.

Increasingly, AUPs governing the use of official computer resources tend to allow incidental personal use of those resources as long as such use does not interfere with employee productivity or system availability and security. Examples of incremental uses include such things as conducting online banking from a work computer, shopping Amazon during breaks, printing a college application or paper from the workplace printer, sending personal, non-work-related emails to friends and family members and more. However, users should understand that there typically is no expectation of privacy when conducting personal activities on local government computer systems.

AUPs frequently are presented to and signed by new employees during their initial orientations and onboarding processes when starting employment. Additionally, users often are reminded of the AUPs terms each time they log in to the system. Here, they're greeted by a login banner that summarizes the key provisions of the AUP and are again reminded they should have no expectation of privacy while using the system. Users are required to agree to the terms before continuing to log in.

From a legal or compliance perspective, an employee's signed AUP and/or clicking through the login banner has been interpreted for decades as evidence of employees providing informed awareness of and agreement to the terms of the AUP. Depending on the situation, violations of the AUP may lead to employee sanctions up to and including termination of employment and/or criminal prosecution, especially if the employee's actions constitute abuse or misuse of a local government's information resources.

While creating an AUP is fairly straightforward in most situations, readers should note that crafting an AUP for public K-12 schools requires more extensive planning and legal review. Specifically, AUPs in this context must reflect and comply with relevant laws regarding educational privacy while balancing the needs of school cybersecurity and respecting student freedom of expression when using a school-provided information resource. In some situations, schools might need to develop specific carve-outs in their AUP to accommodate educational activities like computer science education or cybersecurity competition teams. Such activities often require specific software, tools, and network access and can generate seemingly-suspicious activity during legitimate activities such as classes, club meetings, or scholastic competitions (Forno, 2015).

An **Information Security Policy** describes how the information that is created, exchanged, and stored on a local government information system is protected and handled, including the requirement that data at rest be encrypted at all times. In the federal government, often this is expressed as a security classification such as confidential, secret, and top secret. For local governments, an information security policy might prescribe enhanced protections for sensitive information about municipal operations, citizen tax records, business license transactions, and/or citizen complaints about law enforcement. By extension, local health authorities will need to develop an information security policy to comply with not only local government cybersecurity requirements but also federal mandates such as the Health Insurance Portability and Accountability Act (HIPPA) and any state mandates. Likewise, local law enforcement agencies should establish their own policy governing how they handle, process, and store information related to investigations, evidence and how they will handle sensitive information received from the federal government or industry (see Chapter 10 for more).

In some cases, the Information Security Policy will develop a method of categorizing information by sensitivity to help staff understand the nature of that information and the persons and organizations with whom staff are authorized to share it. The Traffic Light Protocol is one such method, using a color to signify the level of sensitivity as a determinant of who is authorized to access it (FIRST, n.d.). See Figure 7.1.

Using the TLP in a local government setting might entail applying TLP:RED to information related to a cybersecurity incident such as specific technical details about how the attack occurred, relevant network information (such as internal IP addresses or server names), and the initial assessment of financial costs arising from the incident.

Color	When should it be used?	How may it be shared?
TLP:RED Not for disclosure, restricted to participants only.	Sources may use TLP:RED when information cannot be effectively acted upon by additional parties, and could lead to impacts on a party's privacy, reputation, or operations if misused.	Recipients may not share TLP:RED information with any parties outside of the specific exchange, meeting, or conversation in which it was originally disclosed. In the context of a meeting, for example, TLP:RED information is limited to those present at the meeting. In most circumstances, TLP:RED should be exchanged verbally or in person.
TLP:AMBER Limited disclosure, restricted to participants' organizations.	Sources may use TLP:AMBER when information requires support to be effectively acted upon, yet carries risks to privacy, reputation, or operations if shared outside of the organizations involved.	Recipients may only share TLP:AMBER information with members of their own organization, and with clients or customers who need to know the information to protect themselves or prevent further harm. **Sources are at liberty to specify additional intended limits of the sharing: these must be adhered to.**
TLP:GREEN Limited disclosure, restricted to the community.	Sources may use TLP:GREEN when information is useful for the awareness of all participating organizations as well as with peers within the broader community or sector.	Recipients may share TLP:GREEN information with peers and partner organizations within their sector or community, but not via publicly accessible channels. Information in this category can be circulated widely within a particular community. TLP:GREEN information may not be released outside of the community.
TLP:WHITE Disclosure is not limited.	Sources may use TLP:WHITE when information carries minimal or no foreseeable risk of misuse, in accordance with applicable rules and procedures for public release.	Subject to standard copyright rules, TLP:WHITE information may be distributed without restriction.

Figure 7.1 Traffic light protocol. The traffic light protocol is a color-coded method of easily assigning levels of sensitivity to cybersecurity information to help determine if/when/how it can be shared and to whom.
Source: FIRST (n.d.).

Law-enforcement investigative or attorney/client privileged information might also be given the TLP:RED designation. However, material considered TLP:WHITE, such as the generalized nature and scope of the incident, incident chronology, current status of the response, and estimated times to recover, likely would be acceptable for media or public statements since they would not disclose information that is sensitive or potentially aid in subsequent attacks. But it is important to remember that the TLP framework is a guideline and every incident, situation, and/or context is different. As such, local governments may need to bend the boundaries of this protocol, such as sharing TLP:RED-derived information with elected officials despite them not being directly involved with the response activity. Similarly, TLP:AMBER and TLP:GREEN information often gets distributed to external cybersecurity experts, academics, and researchers on a regular basis since they have a greater need for early warnings about a given cybersecurity risk than the average user or citizen. For example, the FBI and other agencies may release a TLP:GREEN Flash Alert providing proactive general details regarding a new type of ransomware attack that can inform operational practices by local governments or support research and analysis into this emerging threat by academics and other experts.

An information security policy should also describe how to properly sanitize surplus computer hardware, software, and data before disposal to ensure that devices and their contents are properly deleted or destroyed. This is especially important since used hard drives and other storage media containing sensitive information show up on eBay or at government auctions and often result in unauthorized public data disclosures (Leyden, 2016).

Elements of an Information Security Policy may also be used to establish the local government's **Privacy Policy** (Montgomery County, MD, n.d.). Often appearing on public-facing websites alongside the AUP, a privacy policy describes the types of information that is collected by the website, how that information is used, stored, and shared by local governments and the security procedures employed to protect that information. This document might also offer guidance to users on how they can control their privacy preferences on that site or service, such as prohibiting sharing with third parties or disabling web browser cookies.

In essence, an Information Security Policy (and/or Privacy Policy) helps local governments categorize data and information assets within their organizations, and specifies how certain types of data is stored, handled, and processed. They also establish formal guidance and set public expectations for how information submitted from local governments to others is protected.

Once local governments have categorized the various sensitivities of its data and has determined who is authorized to access it, an **Identity and Access Management** (IAM) policy will govern *how* users are able to access it (NIST, 2017). Among other things, local government IAM policies should establish the process for creating and removing user accounts, categories of users, and the various roles and permissions that may be assigned to users based on their function within the organization. Care must be taken to grant the minimum amount of access necessary for each user to perform their work under the notion of the "least privilege" principle. For example, there likely is no reason for a human resources specialist to have access to local tax records, a clerical assistant in the procurement office to have privileged (or elevated) system administrator access to the city's main website, or for a local police department to have access into the local health department's electronic records unless a specific need is identified, and the proper authority authorizes the access.

In addition to the technical requirements of the Information Security Policy discussed above, the IAM policy describes how privileged administrative, remote, or shared access to information resources is administered by IT staff for cybersecurity purposes. For example, to protect against rogue IT staff and/or other insider threats, an IAM policy may establish a two-person rule for accessing sensitive systems such as a firewall system or the system that creates new user accounts. A two-person rule is a security control requiring two authorized users to approve or be aware of every attempt to conduct a certain type of transaction. This is similar to rules governing the launch of nuclear missiles by the US military, which requires two authorized officers to turn four keys while sitting on opposite ends of the control room – something impossible for one person to accomplish alone.

Perhaps most important, a local government IAM policy describes how user accounts and privileges are created, deleted, administered, and validated. Among many other reasons, this is important to ensure that former employees or visitors no longer have access to government systems and information resources. Relatedly, the IAM policy may describe characteristics of user passwords such as password length and complexity, password aging, validation for password changes, and/or how the organization employs biometrics or hardware tokens to authorize privileged access.

Local governments might use their IAM policies to link computer and network access to streamline user and facility administration, similar to what the Department of Defense (DoD) does with its Common Access Card (Department of Defense, n.d.) by assigning users one physical smartcard that can be used to access both buildings and computer resources. In such cases, it is helpful to establish working relationships with other departments or offices (such as human resources, facilities management, or procurement officials) to verify user accounts and employee rosters regularly to be prepared for situations where a user must be removed from system or facility access quickly.

Another essential local government cybersecurity policy is the **Incident Handling Policy (IHP).** This policy describes how local governments will respond in the event of a cyberattack, incident, and breach and is especially important when the critical governmental functions and services are disrupted or disabled. At minimum, a local government incident handling policy needs to describe who is in charge of the response, identify what expertise and support are available from within and outside of the government to help respond, and what sort of operational workarounds are authorized to facilitate some level of continued governmental operations.

An Incident Handling Policy and the operational processes derived from it may also address how local governments respond to specific types of cybersecurity incidents such as ransomware attacks, denial of service attacks, data breaches, malware attacks insider threats, and other adverse cyber events. The selection of particular threats and events addressed should be based on what the government's cybersecurity staff understand to be the most probable attacks and adverse cyber events that they might encounter. Presumably, this understanding will be based upon the findings of the infor-mation-gathering process mentioned earlier and a careful consideration of the key ser-vices, facilities, and workflows necessary for the continuing performance of local government business.

> The Carnegie Mellon University Software Engineering Institute's Computer Emergency Response Team continues to be the gold standard for guidance, documentation, and training for local governments on incident handling. Similarly, the US-CERT at the Cybersecurity and Infrastructure Protection Agency (CISA) offer excellent guidance on developing incident handling capabilities for local governments.
> CERT/CC: https://www.sei.cmu.edu/about/divisions/cert; US-CERT: https://us-cert. cisa.gov/resources/sltt.

Local governments also need to adopt **Disaster Recovery/Business Continuity Policies (DR/BCP)** that describe the organization's priorities and response to major emergencies that disrupt governmental operations, including cyberattacks as well as natural disasters, terrorist attacks, and other events that disrupt or destroy the local gov-ernment's ability to function. Frequently, incident handling and DR/BCP overlap or intersect in various ways since both require the same knowledge generated earlier in the policy development process. Thus, it might be helpful for local governments to develop these policies concurrently and to include the relevant stakeholders in the process. In some cases, an IT-related DR/BCP may be part of a broader set of policies and procedures related to how local government will continue to function during emergencies that dis-rupt the community.

A DR/BCP seeks to minimize the impact of emergencies that might prevent some, if not all, local government functions from operating. For instance, it might define alter-nate email or mobile capabilities that can allow government to communicate if their primary services are offline. Or, from an information infrastructure perspective, the DR/BCP might ensure that any backup capabilities, such as diesel generators or the water to feed data center cooling systems, can be replenished during a crisis. The need for a DR/BCP policy again underscores the importance of identifying the key assets, facilities, and necessary workflows required to sustain critical government operations.

During the 2019 Baltimore ransomware incident, city employees created so many free Gmail accounts so quickly that Google deemed it suspicious and blocked them until learning these were city employees trying to get online to do business while their official city systems were paralyzed (Duncan and Zhang, 2019). Also during this incident, due to poor IT planning, the city was unable to deploy software patches quickly across its enter-prise and frequently had to visit each computer in-person to conduct manual technical activities, further slowing down its recovery efforts. These are some of the consequences of failing to establish incident response and DR/BCP plans, procedures, and capabilities.

Local governments should understand that incident response and DR/BCP plans rarely work perfectly. Such policies and procedures must be firm enough to provide effective guidance in the spirit of a successful resolution to a given situation but flexible enough to adapt as necessary. It is important not to become dogmatically locked into a particular course of action simply because "it's policy." Doing so could potentially make the situation worse, especially if the policy suddenly becomes incompatible with a changing circumstance.

7.5 Desirable Cybersecurity Policies

In addition to the essential, if not required, cybersecurity policies mentioned above, there are several others that are desirable to include when establishing a local government cybersecurity program. In many cases, they draw upon the likely provisions of the policies discussed above.

Closely related to, if not potentially part of, the Identity and Access Management Policy (IAM) is how users connect to local government computing services remotely. This can also be known as a **Remote Access Policy**. At a minimum, this policy describes how remote access is granted or revoked, to which systems, and what types of additional security requirements are needed to do so. Since users operating remotely are part of the local government IT system, in addition to complying with the Remote Access Policy, they remain governed by the Acceptable Use Policy (AUP).

A remote access policy takes into account the security of the computers and other devices used to conduct remote work. In most cases, such policies prohibit employees from using their personal computers and other devices for remote access to sensitive systems and information since there is no assurance that those devices are trustworthy or secure. Instead, the policy may require remote users to be issued government-configured computers and/or other devices with proper security configurations established and controlled by the IT department. However, in cases where it's financially or otherwise not possible to issue such devices to remote workers or when a rapid pivot to remote work is necessary, this policy might define the security and configuration requirements needed to use employee-owned devices (i.e., the **Bring-Your-Own-Device Policy**) when accessing government information systems.

Remote Access Policies will become more important for local governments because, as the COVID-19 pandemic demonstrated, many office workers can effectively perform their duties remotely. Accordingly, as the pandemic winds down, they may request the ability to continue doing so, and local governments may be inclined to grant such requests in the interest of employee recruiting, retention, or well-being. However, local officials must realize that the benefits of remote work could be offset by the increased likelihood of a successful cyberattack against these potentially less-protected systems as a way of infiltrating the larger government network (Miller, 2020). Thus, expanded remote access requires additional cybersecurity protections and monitoring. Such operational and cybersecurity trade-offs must be considered and adequately addressed by local officials to avoid creating new cybersecurity problems.

Local governments should also consider establishing separate **Email Use Policies** governing the use of official email. As the name implies, this policy establishes what may and may not be transmitted by official email. Further, as a compliment to an Information Security Policy, it may also prescribe special procedures such as mandatory encryption or specific accounts when using email to exchange sensitive or personal information. In some cases, this policy may outline any email retention requirements since email sent by official accounts might be considered official government documents. Additionally, email use policies typically reiterate provisions of the Acceptable Use Policy (AUP) such as setting privacy expectations for use of the local government's email and prohibiting the use of third-party accounts, such as Gmail, for conducting official business unless otherwise authorized.

During cybersecurity emergencies, it is essential that local governments maintain coherent messaging both internally and externally. Thus, it is important that local governments adopt **Media and Communications Policies**. The purpose of this policy is to establish *who* is empowered to speak to the media, the public, employees, and other audiences on matters related to cybersecurity. Admittedly, media relations capabilities differ among local governments. Some, especially larger local governments, have dedicated media or public relations staff, but smaller ones may not have such a capability. Regardless, local governments of all sizes need to identify the appropriately trained and knowledgeable staff members or officials to handle public messaging and media relations during cybersecurity emergencies.

A Media and Communications policy should establish clear lines of communication and outreach to these audiences and describe what can or cannot be disclosed during a crisis based on the nature of the incident. For example, during an adverse cybersecurity event, it is appropriate to announce that a cyberattack shut down a tax collection website. However, it would not be appropriate to discuss specific technical details about how the attack took place, the names of people involved, or anything related to law enforcement investigation of that attack. In many cases, Media and Communications Policies prohibit all but expressly authorized persons from speaking to the public about a cybersecurity event. Thus, from department heads down the hierarchy to rank-and-file employees and contractors, staff are prohibited from speaking publicly about such events.

To help with public messaging, the Media and Communications Policy may require that authorized staff or officials develop prepared statements to issue during cyber events. It may also recommend that elected leadership and senior executives be given appropriate talking points to use in response to press inquiries, so they don't make the situation worse by issuing poorly-crafted statements or engaging in uninformed speculation.

A **Change (or Configuration) Management Policy** (CMP) establishes a formal method for making changes to the local government's information system. Although CMPs are often overseen by the IT department, cybersecurity officials should be intimately involved in developing and implementing them. This is because changes to an information system, even slight ones, may inject new vulnerabilities that can be exploited by adversaries or manifested through user error. A CMP centers around four key questions:

1) What changes are being proposed?
2) What systems, services, and/or processes are involved or impacted?
3) Who is responsible for this change?
4) Who and what will be affected by this action?

Answering these questions allow IT and cybersecurity staff to understand how local government information resources may be affected, and they then can provide appropriate advice on any cybersecurity issues that may arise as a result of the changes. By contrast, failing to be aware of changes to systems may lead to self-inflicted cybersecurity incidents or operational failures such as update patches that change existing and approved software configurations (Bigelow, 2013; Lawler, 2021).

Increasingly, systems and devices unrelated to traditional notions of the IT infrastructure connect to or rely on the local government's network. Therefore, the CMP should be applied to systems such as access control, security cameras, HVAC, elevators, parking control systems, and others to ensure these systems do not inadvertently introduce cybersecurity risks to local government information systems (Turton, 2021). In some cases, the questions raised by the CMP are simple to answer while for others it may be prudent to test proposed technical changes in a simulated environment first if possible before going live with it. Indeed, the CMP should specify when and under what circumstances such testing should occur.

Local governments should also adopt **Vulnerability and Patch Management Policies** to address how cybersecurity weaknesses and vulnerabilities discovered in technology products are handled. This can be included in the CMP or governed by a separate policy. For example, some technology products might require immediate updates to fix emerging security problems while others might be able to wait to be updated on a less urgent schedule. Extending the provisions of the CMP, this policy should describe how and when various types of product updates are received and deployed to ensure that updates do not disrupt functionality or cause new security or operational concerns by modifying previously approved configurations (Lawler, 2021). This policy also may describe approved assorted workarounds to address situations where a cybersecurity problem is known publicly but a product fix is not yet available. Known as zero-day vulnerabilities, these are often the most serious cybersecurity threats facing organizations, including local governments, and must be patched immediately when a fix is announced (FireEye, n.d.). For example, it was a zero-day vulnerability that allowed hackers to break into the Microsoft Exchange Server in January 2021, which subsequently infected at least 30,000 organizations in the US alone (KrebsOnSecurity, 2021).

Last, local governments should adopt an appropriate **Back-up Policy** that will be administered by the IT staff. As the name implies, this policy establishes data back-up expectations and recovery procedures. At a minimum, this policy addresses how user or server data is backed up, how and where they are backed up, how often, where the back-ups will be located (preferably off-site) and how long back-ups will be retained (preferably months or longer). Such policies also must identify any particular categories of information requiring special security protection in accordance with the existing information security policy and what those additional protections might be. For example, the policy should require that back-ups of tax information, personally identifiable information, medical data, voter registration databases, etc. be encrypted to prevent unauthorized information disclosures.

Solid back-up procedures are essential defenses against cyberattacks of all types, technology failures, and common user errors. For local governments in particular, having an effective back-up policy is a critical countermeasure to the ongoing threat of ransomware attacks and can make recovering from such incidents easier.

7.6   Striving for Continuous Improvement and Quality

Once local governments have adopted and published their cybersecurity policies, such policies should not simply go onto a webpage or into a binder never to be seen again. Policies must be implemented and must be reviewed regularly and updated to ensure they remain relevant and effective in the ever-changing cybersecurity landscape. Additionally, over time, emerging concerns or gaps in local government cybersecurity policies may be identified and addressed as technologies, user expectations, and the official workflows evolve. In other words, the cybersecurity policy process is iterative and ongoing, not just a one-time project.

Therefore, it is important that each local government establishes a cybersecurity philosophy of **Continuous Improvement** to assess and evaluate its IT and cybersecurity policies, procedures, practices, and controls for effectiveness over time. While it doesn't necessarily need to be a separate policy per se (although it could be), a commitment to continuous improvement helps keep IT and cybersecurity policies and procedures current. In management parlance, this iterative process evaluates the as-is current state of IT and cybersecurity to inform planning for its to-be desired future state.

Continuous improvement mandates that several activities take place after every adverse cybersecurity event. These include at least the following: periodic policy and procedure reviews, regularly scheduled audits, tabletop what-if war-game exercises, periodic vulnerability assessments, scheduled penetration tests by outside experts, cybersecurity awareness campaigns, and lessons-learned meetings.

Activities like these not only help foster a cybersecurity culture, but also develop and share institutional knowledge that can keep cybersecurity policies and procedures current and relevant.

While it is important to regularly assess all policies and procedures, local government incident response and DR/BCP plans, and especially emergency contact lists should be reviewed regularly to keep them current. Participation in cybersecurity exercises coordinated by external organizations like the Army Cyber Institute's (ACI) Jack Voltaic Project are additional ways of both testing local response procedures and networking with other local, state, and federal officials to enhance cybersecurity preparedness while learning new things and building relationships that can be invaluable when a crisis occurs (FTI, 2020).

7.7   Conclusion

This chapter has described the key cybersecurity policies that establish a necessary foundation for any local government cybersecurity program. Over time, and as the cybersecurity landscape changes, local governments will need to consider adoption of additional cybersecurity policies. Although many cybersecurity concerns are shared by organizations of all sizes and types, the capabilities, culture, context, and expectations of organizations can differ. As such, there is no single, correct approach to developing cybersecurity policies other than aligning them with accepted industry best practices such as the NIST Cybersecurity Framework whenever practicable. What is fundamentally important is that local governments *formally address cybersecurity in whatever ways are appropriate for their jurisdictions given their available resourcing and other constraints.*

Establishing the policies described in this chapter will not prevent every cybersecurity incident, attack or breach. However, such measures, properly developed, implemented, and sustained over time can make them less likely to occur, easier to respond to, and potentially much less costly to recover from afterwards.

Appendix 7.1 City and County of San Francisco, CA, Cybersecurity Policy

https://sf.gov/resource/2021/citywide-cybersecurity-policy

The City and County of San Francisco (City) is dedicated to building a strong cybersecurity program to support, maintain, and secure critical infrastructure and data systems. The following policy is intended to maintain and enhance key elements of a citywide cybersecurity program.

PURPOSE AND SCOPE

The COIT Cybersecurity Policy lays the foundation for the City's Cybersecurity Program as a whole and articulates executive level support for the effort. Cybersecurity operations across the City are in different stages of deployment. The Cybersecurity Policy supports the City's Cybersecurity Program established to:

- protect our connected critical infrastructure
- protect the sensitive information placed in our trust
- manage risk
- continuously improve our ability to detect cybersecurity events
- contain and eradicate compromises, restoring information resources to a secure and operational status
- ensure risk treatment is sufficient and in alignment with the criticality of the information resource
- facilitate awareness of risk to our operations within the context of cybersecurity

The requirements identified in this policy apply to all information resources operated by or for the City, and County of San Francisco and its departments, and commissions. Elected officials, employees, consultants, and vendors working on behalf of the City and County of San Francisco are required to comply with this policy.

POLICY STATEMENT

The COIT Cybersecurity Policy requires all departments to:

1. Appoint a Departmental Information Security Officer (DISO) to coordinate cybersecurity efforts. Larger Departments may appoint a Chief Information Security Officer (CISO) to recognize the increased scope of responsibility.

2. Adopt a cybersecurity framework as a basis to build their cybersecurity program. The City recommends adopting the National Institute of Standards and Technology (NIST) Cybersecurity Framework as a methodology to secure information resources.
3. Support cyber incident response as needed in accordance with Emergency Support Function 18 (ESF-18) Unified Cyber Command.
4. Conduct and update, at least annually, a department cybersecurity risk assessment. Departments with dedicated Risk Management staff may elect to integrate cybersecurity risk management into the department's Risk Management program.
5. Develop and update, at least annually, department cybersecurity requirements to mitigate risk and comply with legal and regulatory cybersecurity requirements. Department will develop and adopt cybersecurity requirements that should be equivalent to or greater than the citywide security requirements.
6. Participate in citywide cybersecurity forum meetings.

CYBERSECURITY FRAMEWORK

The Cybersecurity Policy requires all departments to adopt a cybersecurity framework to guide their operations.

In order to adequately protect information resources, systems and data must be properly categorized based on information sensitivity and criticality to operations. A risk-based methodology standardizes security architecture, creates a common understanding of shared or transferred risk when systems and infrastructure are connected, and makes securing systems and data more straightforward.

The NIST framework provides five elements to a cybersecurity program:

Function	Description
Identify	Develop the organizational understanding to manage cybersecurity risk to systems, assets, data, and capabilities.
Protect	Develop and implement appropriate safeguards to ensure delivery of infrastructure services.
Detect	Develop and implement appropriate activities to identify the occurrence of a cybersecurity event.
Respond	Develop and implement appropriate activities to respond to a cybersecurity event.
Recover	Develop and implement appropriate activities to maintain plans for resilience and to restore any capabilities or services impaired by a cybersecurity event.

Departments, in consultation with the City Chief Information Security Officer (CCISO), may choose alternatives to the NIST Cybersecurity Framework. However, all departments shall implement or consume central standards and services from their respective framework, such as access control and management, risk assessment and management, awareness and training, and data classification.

Cybersecurity Risk Assessment

As defined in NIST Special Publication 800-30, "Guide for Conducting Risk Assessments," risk assessment is the process of identifying, estimating, and prioritizing information security risks.[1] Assessing risk requires the careful analysis of threat and vulnerability information to determine the extent to which circumstances or events could adversely impact an organization [i.e. City departments] and the likelihood that such circumstances or events will occur.

The purpose of risk assessment is to inform decision makers and support risk responses by identifying:

  i. relevant threats to [departments]
  ii. vulnerabilities both internal and external to [departments]
  iii. impact (i.e., harm) to [departments] that may occur given the potential for threats exploiting vulnerabilities
  iv. likelihood that harm will occur

The end result is a determination of risk (i.e., typically a function of the degree of harm and likelihood of harm occurring).

To ensure their cybersecurity programs comply with an approved cybersecurity framework, including NIST CSF, ISO 2700x, and CIS Top 20, and a risk-based approach, the City Services Auditor conducts readiness assessments to measure implementation.

Readiness assessments align with an approved cybersecurity framework and enable departments to determine their current cybersecurity capabilities, set individual goals for a target state, and establish a plan for improving and maintaining cyber security programs. Readiness assessments also assist the Department of Technology and the Controller in the efficient and effective planning of cybersecurity activities.

CYBERSECURITY REQUIREMENTS

Departments are required to develop and update cybersecurity requirements to mitigate risk profiles and comply with legal and regulatory cybersecurity requirements. The City Chief Information Security Officer will develop baseline cybersecurity requirements to address the citywide risk profile. All proposed requirements will be reviewed and approved by the Architecture Policy and Review Board (APRB). Upon adoption by the APRB, Departments should subsequently develop cybersecurity requirements that should be equivalent to or greater than the citywide security requirements to address department risks. APRB should establish meaningful timelines for adoption based on the complexity of the proposed requirements.

City-wide cyber-security requirements shall not supersede State or Federal requirements that may apply to certain specific city departments.

---

[1] ISO 31000 "Risk Management — Guidelines" is another framework for risk assessment.

Roles and Responsibilities

1. Department Heads shall:

a. Promote a culture of cybersecurity awareness and compliance with the City's cybersecurity policy. Department heads must remind their employees and contractors about the City's Cybersecurity policies, standards, procedures, guidelines, and best practices.
b. To the extent resources allow, budget and staff the cybersecurity function for systems procured, operated, or contracted by their departments to ensure that all systems and the data contained by them are protected in accordance with the category / classification of the data and systems.
c. Designate a Departmental Information Security Officer (DISO) or a Chief Information Security Officer

2. City Chief Information Security Officer (CCISO) shall:

a. Establish and maintain a security team and function with the ability to identify, protect, detect, respond, and recover from attacks against City information resources.
b. Develop and maintain a centralized incident response program capable of addressing major compromises of City information resources.
c. Review Emergency Support Function 18 Unified Cyber Command annex annually and ensure it is updated as needed.
d. Support departments' cyber emergency exercises and conduct periodic City-wide cybersecurity emergency exercise with City leaders.
e. Ensure that Department, Commission, and the Centralized Information Technology Cybersecurity Programs employ a risk-based assessment and treatment program, and regularly report the status of the City's residual risk profile to City leadership.
f. Develop cybersecurity risk assessment methodology and provide training to DISOs on conducting cybersecurity risk assessments.
g. Provide guidance on building the security organization at the department level.
h. Ensure that Departments' cybersecurity risk assessment results are protected adequately and access is restricted to limited City cybersecurity personnel.
i. At least annually, develop and update citywide cybersecurity requirements to mitigate the City's residual risk profile, and comply with legal and regulatory cybersecurity requirements. All cybersecurity requirements will be approved by the Architecture Policy & Review Board (APRB) before going into effect.
j. Support departments' implementation of citywide cybersecurity requirements.
k. Support department DISOs in their cybersecurity responsibilities, including through the centralized incident response program, cybersecurity defense capabilities, and a citywide cybersecurity toolset.
l. Organize citywide cybersecurity forum meetings.

3. **Departmental Information Security Officers (DISOs) shall:**

   a. Ensure information resources are properly protected through risk treatment strategies that meet the acceptable risk threshold for the category / classification of the information resource.
   b. Develop the necessary security organizations based on the available resources and budget.
   c. Inform the City Chief Information Security Officer when there is an event which compromises the control, confidentiality, integrity, or availability of a system or data involving Personally Identifiable Information, Regulatory Protected Information (such as HIPAA or Social Security Numbers), and/or data that is not considered public as soon as practical.
   d. Participate in the citywide cybersecurity round table meetings.
   e. Conduct and update, at least annually, department cybersecurity risk assessments, and confidentially share results with the City Chief Information Security Officer.
   f. Meet annually with department Disaster Preparedness Coordinator to review results of cyber risk assessment and update department COOP cyber appendix as needed. Departments with dedicated Emergency Management Functions shall review the results of their department's cyber-security risk assessments and update their incident response procedures as appropriate
   g. Conduct, at least annually, department cybersecurity emergency exercise with department leadership, City partners, and critical third parties. Departments with dedicated Emergency Management Functions may elect to incorporate cybersecurity as part of their department emergency exercises.
   h. Develop and update, at least annually, department cybersecurity requirements to mitigate department risk profile and comply with legal and regulatory cybersecurity requirements, and confidentially share requirements with the City Chief Information Security Officer. Department requirements that should be equivalent to or greater than the citywide security requirements.
   i. When appropriate, consult with the City Chief Information Security Officer when gathering the requirements for new information systems to ensure the security design is vetted before selection and deployment.

4. **Department of Emergency Management**

   a. Activate the city emergency operations center to coordinate response to emergency level cyber event as outlined in Emergency Support Function 18 Unified Cyber Command.
   b. Support Citywide cybersecurity emergency exercise for City leaders in coordination with the City Chief Information Security Officer.

5. **Department Disaster Preparedness Coordinators (DPC)**

   a. Train department leadership and cybersecurity incident response staff with Department and Emergency Operation Center roles and responsibilities
   b. Work with the DISO to adopt the reporting processes for Emergency Support Function 18 Unified Cyber Command.

   c. Participate, at least annually, in the department cybersecurity emergency exercise.

6. **COIT and Mayor's Budget Office shall:**

   a. To the extent possible, adequately support and fund City and Department cybersecurity operations in alignment with the risk assessment.

7. **Chief Data Officer shall:**

   a. Work with the City Chief Information Security Officer to develop and maintain an information classification system and support departments in their data classification efforts.

8. **City Services Auditor shall:**

   a. Evaluate City cybersecurity efforts with regular readiness assessments and assist in the evaluation of cybersecurity audit controls.

   b. Review, at least annually, department implementation plans for adoption of citywide and department-specific cybersecurity requirements.

   c. Perform security testing for departments in alignment with the citywide cybersecurity requirements to validate that departments effectively implement the requirements.

   d. Share results of this testing with the Department Head, and when requested, facilitate the discussion of potential risk reduction strategies between the department and the City CISO.

9. **City Employees, contractors, and vendors shall:**

   a. Comply with cybersecurity practices, requirements, and acceptable use agreement, and promptly report any incidents to the appropriate officials.

COMPLIANCE

To the extent resources allow:

1. Department heads are accountable for ensuring that systems procured, operated, or contracted by their respective department or commission meet the appropriate security protections required by the system's risk category /classification, in addition to any regulatory requirements.

2. Employees, consultants, and vendors shall ensure that information resources are appropriately and securely utilized, administered, and operated while authorized access is granted, according to the Acceptable Use Policy.

3. City Services Auditor shall evaluate City cybersecurity efforts and validate departments' implementation of the applicable security requirements.

EXCEPTIONS

No exceptions to this policy will be approved.

Authorization

SEC. 22A.3. Of the City's Administrative Code states, "COIT shall review and approve the recommendations of the City CIO for ICT standards, policies and procedures to enable successful development, operation, maintenance, and support of the City's ICT."

References

- NIST Cybersecurity Framework Website - http://www.nist.gov/cyberframework/
- Cyber Safe SF which contains documentation for the CCSF cybersecurity requirements and ESF-18 Unified Cyber Command - https://sfgov1.sharepoint.com/sites/TIS-NationalCybersecurity-Awareness

Definitions

For a list of definitions please refer to: httplinvlpubs.nist.govinistpubs/ir/2013/NIST.IR.7298r2.pdf

Appendix 7.2   Commonwealth of Massachusetts Cybersecurity Policy

https://www.mass.gov/doc/is000-enterprise-information-security-policy/download

Enterprise Information Security Policy

Document Name: Enterprise Information Security	Effective Date. October 15th, 2018
Document ID: IS.000	Last Revised Date: July 15th, 2020

1. PURPOSE

1.1 The Commonwealth of Massachusetts. ("the Commonwealth") collects, manages, and stores information on a regular basis in order to support business operations. The Commonwealth is committed to preserving the confidentiality, integrity, and availability of its information assets*.

The Commonwealth must protect its information assets, provide for the integrity of business processes and records, and comply with applicable laws and regulations.

This document, the Enterprise Information Security Policy (hereafter, the "Policy"), reinforces Leadership's commitment, establishes high-level functions of an information security program, and outlines information security requirements to safeguard information assets and assist the Commonwealth to achieve its strategic objectives.

2. AUTHORITY

2.1 M.G.L. Ch. 7d provides that "Notwithstanding any general or special law, rule, regulation, executive order, policy or procedure to the contrary, all executive department agencies shall, and other state agencies may, adhere to the policies, procedures and objectives established by the Executive Office of Technology Services and Security (EOTSS) with respect to activities concerning information technology."

3. SCOPE

3.1 This document applies to the use of information, information systems, electronic and computing devices, applications, and network resources used to conduct business on behalf of the Commonwealth. The document applies to all state agencies in the Executive Department including all executive offices, boards, commissions, agencies, departments, divisions, councils, bureaus, and offices within an executive office. Other Commonwealth entities that voluntarily use or participate in services provided by the Executive Office of Technology Services and Security, such as mass.gov, must agree to comply with this document, with respect to those services, as a condition of use.

4. RESPONSIBILITY

4.1 The Enterprise Security Office is responsible for the development and ongoing maintenance of this policy.

4.2 The Enterprise Security Office is responsible for compliance with this policy and may enlist other departments in the maintaining and monitoring compliance with this policy.

4.3 Any inquiries or comments regarding this standard shall be submitted to the Enterprise Security Office by sending an email to EOTSS-DL-Security Office.

4.4 Additional information regarding this document and its related policy and standards can be found at https://www.mass.gov/cybersecurity/policies.

5. COMPLIANCE

5.1 Compliance with this document is mandatory. Violations are subject to disciplinary action in accordance to applicable employment and collective bargaining agreements, up to and including the termination of their employment and/or assignment with the Commonwealth.

6. INFORMATION SECURITY OBJECTIVES

The goal of the Information Security Program is to manage risk within the Commonwealth and achieve its information security objectives through the establishment of supporting policies, processes, and functions. The information security objectives of the Commonwealth are:

6.1 Enable organizational strategy through the protection of customer data and material nonpublic information.

6.2 Comply with applicable laws, regulations, and contractual obligations with relevant stakeholders.

6.3 Establish a governance structure to effectively and efficiently manage information security risk.

6.4 Manage identified security risks to an acceptable (i.e., risk tolerance) level through design, implementation, and maintenance risk remediation plans.

6.5 Establish a culture of accountability and increasing the level of awareness of all personnel in order to meet information security requirements.

6.6 Establish responsibility and accountability for information security policies and governance across the Commonwealth.

The Commonwealth is committed to continually improving the Information Security Program to help ensure that its applicable information security objectives are met and it is able to adapt to changes in the cyber threat landscape and account for evolving organizational, legal and regulatory requirements.

7. COMMUNICATIONS

7.1. The Commonwealth's Information Security policies and standards are publicly available on the mass.gov web site. EOTSS will inform Commonwealth agencies when policies or standards are created, or when major revisions are published.

8. REPORTING REQUIREMENTS

8.1 Policy Violations

Compliance with this document is mandatory for all state agencies in the Executive Department. Violation of this document may cause irreparable injury to the Commonwealth of Massachusetts. Violations are subject to disciplinary action in accordance with applicable employment and collective bargaining agreements, up to and including the termination of their employment and/or assignment with the Commonwealth.

8.2 Reporting of Policy Violations

Any violation of this policy should be reported to a supervisor and/or the Information Security Team. Information security incidents (e.g., security breaches) shall follow the reporting requirements outlined in the Information Security Incident Management Standard.

8.3 Exceptions from Policy

The policy applies to all state agencies in the Executive Department including all executive offices, boards, commissions, agencies, departments, divisions, councils, bureaus, and offices within an executive office. In the event that a policy or procedure cannot be adhered to, a policy exception request must be submitted to and approved by the Commonwealth CISO, Deputy CISO, or delegate.

An exception may be granted only if the benefits of the exception outweigh the increased risks for the approved length of the exception, as determined by the Commonwealth CISO and the associated **Information Owner**. Compliance progress shall be validated at the exception expiration date. Exceptions may be closed if the agreed-upon solution has been implemented and the exception has been resolved. An extension may be requested if more time is required to implement the long-term solution by completing an extension request.

9. POLICY STATEMENTS

9.1 Organization of Information Security

Each organization subject to these policies shall develop, maintain and implement policies, procedures, guidelines, and standards (PSGPs) to establish and govern the Commonwealth's information security program to safeguard the confidentiality, integrity, and availability of its **information assets**, as directed by the Commonwealth's technology leadership.

9.2 Acceptable Use

Personnel are the first line of defense and have a shared responsibility to safeguard information owned or entrusted to the Commonwealth.

9.3 Access Management

Access shall be managed throughout the account lifecycle from the initial identification of a user to the granting, modifying and revoking of user access privileges to confirm that information assets are protected from unauthorized access. Accounts shall be provisioned using the least privilege access principle. Access privileges shall be monitored and reviewed periodically commensurate with their risk classification. Passwords must meet the Commonwealth's complexity requirements and changed on a regular basis.

9.4 Asset Management

Establish an information system classification schema to promote a consistent approach to risk management, business continuity and disaster recovery for information assets. Maintain an asset inventory and establish a program to manage the asset life cycle (i.e., procurement through end-ofsupport/end-of-life). Implement security controls to protect endpoints and mobile devices from malware and information leakage.

9.5 Business Continuity and Disaster Recovery

Protect mission-critical information assets, processes, and facilities from the effects of major failures or disasters by developing and implementing a business continuity strategy that is consistent with organizational objectives and priorities. Back up critical data, such as confidential information, and strive to prevent disasters and implement timely recovery from disasters as well as continue critical organizational functions during a disaster or major disruption while maintaining confidentiality.

9.6 Communication and Network Security Management

Implement network security controls such as firewalls, intrusion prevention/detection systems (IPS/IDS), virtual private networks (VPNs) and segmentation techniques so that the Commonwealth protects its information assets from compromise both from external and internal actors.

9.7 Compliance

Establish a compliance framework that will enable the Commonwealth to comply with all relevant legislative, regulatory, statutory and contractual requirements related to information security.

9.8 Cryptographic Management

Define requirements for encrypting data at rest, data in transit and data in use, commensurate with the information classification of the information requiring protection. Maintain cryptographic keys to preserve the integrity of cryptographic controls. Use of encryption controls shall be determined after a risk assessment has been performed.

9.9 Information Security Incident Management

Establish a program to effectively detect, respond and resolve incidents that affect the security of the Commonwealth's **information assets**, including establishing a Security Incident Response Team (SIRT) to manage the incident response process. Develop incident response procedures/plans and identify relevant stakeholders (both internal and external). Test incident response plans periodically for relevancy.

9.10 Information Security Risk Management

Identify and analyze information security risks that could compromise the confidentiality, integrity or availability of the Commonwealth's **information assets**, and mitigate them to an acceptable level to meet organizational objectives and compliance requirements. All relevant statutory, regulatory and contractual requirements that include security and privacy controls and the Commonwealth's approach to meet these requirements must be explicitly defined, documented and kept up to date.

9.11 Logging and Event Monitoring

Develop and implement a process to monitor and review activity on information systems. So that information system problems are identified and corrected, and operator logs and fault logging are enabled, collected and reviewed. The Commonwealth must comply with all relevant legal, regulatory and contractual requirements applicable to logging and event monitoring.

9.12 Operations Management

Develop and document standard operating procedures, change management, configuration management, capacity management and release management processes for technology environments. Back up information in a secure manner to enable the organization to restore its operational activities after a planned or unplanned interruption of service.

Establish standards to support the secure implementation of applications and services in public and private cloud environments, including Software as a Service (SaaS), Platform as a Service (PaaS) and Infrastructure as a Service (IaaS).

9.13 Physical and Environment Security

Enforce physical security controls to manage access to **information assets**. Physically protect facilities with safeguards to protect **information assets** against environmental hazards.

9.14 Secure System and Software Life Cycle Management

Perform information security reviews throughout all phases of the system and software management lifecycle to ensure risks are properly identified, addressed and mitigated in a timely and cost-efficient manner. Configure systems using security hardening standards and review configurations periodically.

9.15 Third-party Information Security

Establish a process to perform initial and ongoing due diligence of third parties that enter into formal business arrangements with Commonwealth agencies. Contractual agreements between third parties and Commonwealth agencies must address baseline information security clauses, including, but not limited to, the right to audit and adhere to data protection requirements.

9.16 Vulnerability Management

Implement security controls to manage and monitor risks to the Commonwealth's information technology environment. Vulnerability management personnel must be able to identify and respond to vulnerabilities within established and predictable timeframes. Vulnerability management activities must be reported to management periodically.

10. POLICY FRAMEWORK COVERAGE

Policy ref.	Policy/Standard name	Topics covered
IS 001	Organization of Information Security	• Information Security Organization Structure • Roles and Responsibilities • Policy Framework • Policy Life Cycle Management
IS 002	Acceptable Use of Information Technology	

(Continued)

Policy ref.	Policy/Standard name	Topics covered
IS 003	Access Management	• User and System Access Management • Account Management • Password Management
IS 004	Asset Management	• Information Asset Management • Information Protection Requirements • Information Classification • Information System Classification • Information Labeling and Handling • Endpoint Security • Information Disposal • Mobile Device Management
IS 005	Business Continuity and Disaster Recovery	• Business Continuity • Disaster Recovery
IS 006	Communication and Network Security	• Network Security Management • Remote Access Security Management • Secure File Transfer • Management of Third-party Network Access
IS 007	Compliance	• Compliance with Policies, Standards, Guidelines, and Procedures • Reporting Security Incidents and Violations • Security Compliance Reviews • External Attestation of Compliance
IS 008	Cryptographic Management	• Key Management • Approved Cryptography Techniques
IS 009	Information Security Incident Management	• Information Security Incident Management
IS 010	Information Security Risk Management	• Information Security Risk Management • Security Awareness and Training
IS 011	Logging and Event Monitoring	• Logging and Event Monitoring
IS 012	Operations Management	• Standard Operating Procedures • Change Management • Configuration Management • Capacity Management • Release Management • Data Backup and Restoration • Cloud Computing
IS 013	Physical and Environment Security	• Facility Controls and Secure Areas • Equipment and Other Media Security

(Continued)

Policy ref.	Policy/Standard name	Topics covered
IS 014	Secure System and Software Lifecycle Management	• Security in System and Software Life Cycle • Security in SDLC Support Processes • System Hardening
IS 015	Third Party Information Security	• Contractual Security Risk Identification • Third-party Selection • Contractual Security Provisions • Third-party Life Cycle Management
IS 016	Vulnerability Management	• Vulnerability and Patch Management
N/A	Glossary of Terms	N/A

11. DOCUMENT CHANGE CONTROL

Version No.	Revised by	Effective date	Description of changes
0.80	Jim Cusson	10/01/2017	Corrections and formatting
0.90	John Merto	12/18/2017	Minor corrections, wording
0.95	Sean Vinck	5.7.18	Minor corrections and formatting
0.96	Andrew Rudder	5/31/2018	Corrections and formatting
0.97	Anthony O'Neill	05/31/2018	Corrections and formatting
1.0	Dennis McDermitt	06/01/2018	Final pre-publication Review
1.0	Andrew Rudder	10/4/2018	Approved for Publication by: John Merto
1.1	Megan Perkins	7/15/2020	Annual Review; Minor corrections and formatting

The owner of this document is the Commonwealth CISO (or designee). It is the responsibility of the document owner to maintain, update and communicate the content of this document. Questions or suggestions for improvement must be submitted to the document owner.

11.1 Annual Review

This Enterprise Information Security Policy must be reviewed and updated by the document owner on an annual basis or when significant policy or procedure changes necessitate an amendment.

References

Baltimore County (n.d.). *User terms and conditions.* https://www.baltimorecountymd.gov/UserGuide/usertermsconditions.html

Bigelow, M. (2013). *Change control and change management. HIMSS publishing.* https://www.taylorfrancis.com/chapters/edit/10.4324/9781003126294-17/change-control-change-management-michelle-bigelow

Commonwealth of Massachusetts (2018, October 05). *Enterprise information security policy.* https://www.mass.gov/policy-advisory/enterprise-information-security-policy

Duncan, I., and Zhang, C. (2019, May 17). *Analysis of ransomware used in Baltimore attack indicates hackers needed "unfettered access" to city computers.* Baltimore Sun. https://www.baltimoresun.com/politics/bs-md-ci-ransomware-attack-20190517-story.html

FireEye (n.d.). *What is a zero-day exploit?* https://www.fireeye.com/current-threats/what-is-a-zero-day-exploit.html

FIRST (n.d.). *Traffic Light Protocol (TLP) FIRST Standards definitions and usage guidance — version 1.0.* https://www.first.org/tlp

Forno, R. (2015). Hack, play, win: Lessons learned running the Maryland cyber challenge. *Journal of the Advanced Computing Systems Association*, 40(6), 26–31. https://www.usenix.org/publications/login/dec15/forno

FTI (2020). *About Jack Voltaic 3.0.* https://fticybersecurity.com/2020-06/about-jack-voltaic-3-0

KrebsOnSecurity (2021, March 5). *At least 30,000 US Organizations newly hacked via holes in microsoft's email software.* https://krebsonsecurity.com/2021/03/at-least-30000-u-s-organizations-newly-hacked-via-holes-in-microsofts-email-software

Lawler, R. (2021). *The Windows update to fix "PrintNightmare" made some printers stop working.* https://www.theverge.com/2021/7/8/22569387/zebra-windows-security-update-printer-spooler-microsoft

Leyden, J. (2016). *You know how that data breach happened? Three words: EBay, hard drives.* The Register. https://www.theregister.com/2016/06/28/ebay_hard_drives_still_contain_sensitive_data_study

Miller, M. (2020). *Hackers find new target as Americans work from home during outbreak.* The Hill. https://thehill.com/policy/cybersecurity/487542-hackers-find-new-target-as-americans-work-from-home-during-outbreak

Montgomery County MD (n.d.). *Privacy policy.* https://www.montgomerycountymd.gov/mcg/privacy.html

Norris, D.F., Joshi, A., Mateczun, L., and Finin, T. (2019). *Local governments' cybersecurity crisis in 8 charts.* The Conversation. https://theconversation.com/local-governments-cybersecurity-crisis-in-8-charts-94240

Turton, W. (2021). *Hackers breach thousands of security cameras, exposing Tesla, jails, hospitals.* https://www.bloomberg.com/news/articles/2021-03-09/hackers-expose-tesla-jails-in-breach-of-150-000-security-cams

U.S. Department of Justice (n.d.) *Citizen's guide to US federal law on child pornography.* https://www.justice.gov/criminal-ceos/citizens-guide-us-federal-law-child-pornography

U.S. National Institute for Standards and Technology (NIST) (2017). *NIST special publication 800-63-3 digital identity guidelines*. https://pages.nist.gov/800-63-3

U.S. National Institute for Standards and Technology (NIST) (2018). *Cybersecurity framework version 1.1*. https://www.nist.gov/cyberframework

U.S. National Institute for Standards and Technology (NIST) (n.d.). *Risk management framework*. https://csrc.nist.gov/Projects/risk-management

U.S. National Security Agency (2010). *Defense in depth*. https://apps.nsa.gov/iaarchive/library/ia-guidance/archive/defense-in-depth.cfm

Velazco, C. and Lerman, R. (2021). *Shut down everything: Global ransomware attack takes a small Maryland town offline*. https://www.washingtonpost.com/technology/2021/07/08/kaseya-ransomware-attack-leonardtown-maryland

8

People: The Root of The Problem

8.1   Introduction

People are a critical component to cybersecurity, especially for local governments. As discussed in Chapter 2, people are one key element of cybersecurity along with technology, policies, and practices. After all, it is *people* that utilize technology and enact policies and practices to ensure high levels of local government cybersecurity. However, it is also *people* who make mistakes, either out of ignorance, negligence, or malice, and who fail to follow cybersecurity policies and procedures. So just who are the people referred to in this chapter? They include the elected officials of a local government as well as top managers, department heads, employees, vendors, contractors, and any and all others who have access to the local government's IT system. By extension, people also include those who are responsible for attacking local government information systems – including criminals and criminal organizations, although the focus of this chapter is mainly on people as internal actors.

This chapter discusses first, how people are the root of the cybersecurity problem and how they constitute perhaps the major obstacle to achieving high levels of local government cybersecurity. Second, it addresses the ways people are targeted by malicious actors. Third, the chapter covers the ways people can be assets to local government cybersecurity. Finally, it discusses the training and accountability of local government officials and staff. Last, is a brief conclusion.

8.2   People as a Problem

The results of the 2016 survey presented in Chapters 5 and 6 show that local governments generally have the technology aspect of cybersecurity under control. At the same time, it is common to hear cybersecurity officials complain that people are their biggest problem. While a perhaps obvious statement, there are many ways people can be a cybersecurity problem. First, they make mistakes. Human error can mean both unintentional actions and lack of action (e.g., not reporting a cybersecurity risk like a phishing email) that can result in an adverse cybersecurity event. If local government officials and staff are unaware of the common threats that they face or the cybersecurity policies they must

Cybersecurity and Local Government, First Edition. Donald F. Norris, Laura K. Mateczun and Richard F. Forno.
© 2022 John Wiley & Sons Ltd. Published 2022 by John Wiley & Sons Ltd.

follow, it is highly probable that they will make mistakes. For example, Shelby County, Tennessee sold what was believed to be a fully decommissioned[1] polling machine on eBay, which was used as an experimental platform at the DEFCON hacker conference and was found to have the personal information of 650,000 voters still on its hard drive, including name, address, birth date, party registration, and method of voting (Collier, 2017). Even in cases where ignorance or negligence are not in play, people can still make mistakes. After all, it only takes one click on an URL that is linked to a file containing malware for a cyberattack to succeed.

Second, people can and do act with malice. There is always the possibility that some employees may act with motives such as theft, mischief, greed, or revenge. This can be as simple as stealing a laptop with local government PII on the hard drive or as complex as altering or deleting information so it cannot be used or trusted. Disgruntled employees might even disrupt or destroy information to make systems inoperable. In 2010, a former network administrator for the City of San Francisco was found guilty of one felony count of denying computer services for refusing access to the city's passwords and declining to relinquish administrative control of the city's network (McMillan, 2010). He was ultimately sentenced to prison and ordered to pay $1.5 million in restitution (Van Derbeken, 2010). However, it is important to note that this case represents an exception and that few officials or public sector employees (17 percent) were responsible for cybersecurity incidents in the public sector in 2020 (Verizon, 2021).

Third, it is people who are responsible for engaging in attacks against local governments. As would be expected, people external to the organizations make up 83 percent of the cybersecurity incidents in the public sector (Verizon, 2021). As discussed in Chapters 3 and 12, such attacks are increasing in number as attack methods evolve and become more successful while the risk of getting caught and costs associated in launching such attacks remains low and the rewards are potentially very high. From the mythical (or perhaps not so mythical) lone hacker motivated by avarice or activism to state-sponsored or state-sanctioned cybercriminals, the types of people who attack local governments are as varied as they are numerous.

8.3 The Ways People are Targeted

People within organizations are targeted by cybercriminals in a variety of ways, with the dominant method being through social engineering. As mentioned earlier, social engineering is a technique that exploits human psychology and human error by manipulating the emotions of fear, greed, curiosity, helpfulness, and safety in the minds of the potential victim (Terranova Worldwide Corporation, 2020). For example, fear involves the threat of severe consequences if one does not respond to an email. Greed involves the possibility of potentially outsized personal gain if the victim (for example) clicks on a link included in the message. Their curiosity may be piqued by crafting an email framed in the context of a current news event like the coronavirus pandemic or a natural disaster. Or the message may play to feelings of helpfulness by asking the potential victim to provide assistance to the sender, such as to facilitate a large money transfer between bank accounts. Finally, such messages may play to the victim's sense of safety by offering them "guidance" to help ensure the security of the local government's information and assets – but in actuality, that guidance, if followed, weakens or breaks it. Emotions are a human vulnerability and make it fairly easy to use them to entice people to open an attachment or click a hyperlink connected to malware or disclose confidential or personal information like passwords.

Social engineering attacks make up about 70 percent of the cybersecurity incidents in the public sector (Verizon, 2021). Within the category of social engineering, phishing, which is explained in Chapter 3, is by far the most common method (98 percent) employed in attacks against public sector organizations (Verizon, 2021). According to Verizon, the more phishing emails an attacker sends, the more likely the campaign is to succeed – after ten emails there is more than a 90 percent chance of success (2013). Only about 2 percent of social engineering attacks in the public sector involve pretexting, and less than 1 percent involve spam. Pretexting is somewhat different from phishing and spear phishing in that it builds on the trust of the receiver by pretending to be a person with authority, like a department head or elected official. Pretexting is generally associated with what Verizon terms as a business email compromise attack. In such an attack, the cybercriminal targets employees with access to funds in order to convince them to transfer funds into an external account (Muncaster, n.d.). For example, the Clerk of Courts of Collier County, FL, paid $184,000 to a false bank account for Quality Enterprises USA, a contractor of the county, and the city of Naples, FL, paid $700,000 to someone posing as a representative of Wright Construction Group, another company contracting with the local government (Riley, 2019). When top officials, like a CEO or CFO, or elected official or top appointed official, are targeted it is known as a whaling attack because of the perceived large size and value of the target. Misrepresentation occurs in both phishing and pretexting attacks as the malicious actors pretend to be someone they are not. Finally, spam is similar to phishing but usually involves a far larger number and wider variety of targets. Attacks using spam-based techniques are all about the volume of emails sent, because someone somewhere will fall for the guise. The Collier County (FL) Mosquito Control District lost almost $100,000 in an insurance spam attack via email (Riley, 2019).

Attackers also target people in local governments using artificial intelligence (AI) and machine learning (ML) techniques with increasing frequency. As discussed in Chapter 12, these techniques and technologies can help make social engineering attacks seem more persuasive and believable. For example, AI and ML can assist attackers to automatically gather public information on local government employees in order to develop spear phishing attacks. AI and ML can also be used to write large numbers of emails in a style similar to a human, potentially even referencing personalized items that only the recipient might understand. ML and other data harvesting or analysis techniques make this process easier by finding and "mining" social media accounts and other public information on potential victims through image recognition tools to further craft more convincing phishing email messages. Voice impersonation, speech, and facial recognition and other forms of ML like "deepfakes" can be so sophisticated that they trick employees into believing they are communicating with someone they are not. An emerging phenomenon, deepfakes are synthetic images or videos that purport to be real people but are in fact hoaxes designed to trick the viewer or listener into believing what they are seeing or hearing. Of course, local governments need to understand that defenders of their IT systems can also use AI and ML to help identify cyber-attacks or even suspicious activity before an incident occurs. For example, modern email security technology utilizing AI can identify these potential attacks and either block them from delivery or prominently alert users about their potential lack of legitimacy.

Malicious actors target not only local government employees but citizens as well. The most prominent example of the targeting of citizens involves disinformation campaigns leading up to elections. Disinformation campaigns, as seen in the attempts by Russia to influence the 2016 and 2020 elections, specifically aim to lower the level of citizen trust in election administration by spreading false or misleading information online (Forno, 2020). Successful ransomware attacks against elections infrastructure, such as the 2020 attack on Hall County, Georgia's information systems, which included a voter signature database, can add fuel to the disinformation fire and effectively reduce citizen trust and potentially impact democratic participation (Forno, 2020). Although not specifically a cybersecurity concern at first glance, since 2016, many cybersecurity practitioners and technology companies have begun to examine and counter the use of cyber-related tools and techniques that seek to sow social division within local communities. And of course, ensuring the integrity of election information, systems, and results certainly falls under the purview of cybersecurity practitioners in their quest to ensure the confidentiality, integrity, and availability of information and information systems.

8.4 People as Cybersecurity Assets

People – in this case, local government employees – are central to the ability of local governments to maintain effective cybersecurity. As such, local governments should view their own people as assets and critical to their cybersecurity posture. Specifically, people can be assets in local government cybersecurity by following cybersecurity policies and practices, practicing good cybersecurity hygiene, reporting anomalies and phishing emails, and acting as cybersecurity advocates within the organization to promote good cybersecurity practices.

Officials and employees who actively follow the local government's cybersecurity policies and the cybersecurity awareness training that they receive (or should receive) are perhaps the organization's biggest assets. Doing so proactively increases the likelihood that they will not cause adverse cybersecurity events. As described earlier, it only takes one person to click one bad link to create a major cybersecurity incident. Officials and employees who are unaware of policies that, for example, prohibit sharing passwords, putting local government information on personal devices, and much more, or who know the rules governing their use of the IT system but disregard them create unnecessary risks that can easily lead to successful cyberattacks.

Practicing good cybersecurity hygiene means more than just following local government cybersecurity policies and practices. Proper cybersecurity hygiene also involves remaining vigilant and thinking through actions taken online. In some cases, it is the local government officials' and employee's responsibility to make sure the devices they are using are patched and up-to-date, whether government-provided or personally owned. It is most important that local government officials and employees as well as contractors, indeed anyone who has access to a local government's IT system, understand that security is something they must constantly keep in mind and practice responsibly. After all, cybersecurity is the responsibility of every local government official and employee, not just IT or cybersecurity staff.

Reporting suspicious activity or things like phishing emails requires awareness, attention, and motivation on the part of all users of these IT systems. Phishing and spear phishing attacks depend on employees not knowing what these attacks are and how they operate or, if they know, not paying close attention and clicking a link or responding to an email that at first glance seems legitimate. Local governments should ensure employees are able to identify phishing and spear phishing attacks as well as the proper way to deal with such attacks. At the minimum, the latter should include a written policy on about proper reporting of such attacks. Local governments should also regularly remind end users of their responsibility to be on the lookout and report potentially malicious emails or websites.

Some organizations have created a formalized role for cybersecurity advocates within individual functions or teams (Martino, 2018). People in these roles may not necessarily be technologists or cybersecurity experts but are taught cybersecurity best practices so that they can champion the cause of security within their departments. Creating and enabling proactive cybersecurity advocates in local governments can help ensure that both overall mission objectives and goals specific to cybersecurity are met. Having cybersecurity advocates in operating departments can ensure a better understanding of the department's unique organizational culture, language, and style so that cybersecurity measures can be presented in such a way to ensure wider acceptance and less resistance. Similarly, where practicable, rotating IT and cybersecurity staff among different departments can help the cybersecurity departments of larger local governments with adequate budgetary capacity better understand the nuances of each department.

8.5 Training and Accountability

As discussed in Chapters 3 and 6, the best way to ensure the people in a local government are assets to organizational cybersecurity is through training and accountability. Local governments should provide cybersecurity awareness training regularly to all end users, and local government must hold end users accountable for their cybersecurity actions and inactions. Awareness and training efforts should begin during the onboarding process and should continue throughout their time on the job. Cybersecurity awareness should never be seen as a one-off event.

Of course, cybersecurity accountability should also be emphasized from the onboarding process throughout the official or employee's career. Accountability for cybersecurity should include both rewards and punishments. Employees should be rewarded for proper cyber-hygiene and for not engaging in risky behavior or violating the local government's cybersecurity policies and regulations. Resources permitting, they could even be incentivized to follow cybersecurity best practices such as becoming recognized for reporting activity that staved off a potential cybersecurity incident. However, there should also be punishment for engaging in negligent or malicious behavior – both by senior leaders and managers and rank-and-file employees. Typical responses to employees committing a cybersecurity error include alerting managers; restricting network access; removing network access until additional training is completed; and even "naming and shaming" the employee (Help Net Security, 2020). Some of these punishments may not be appropriate for all employees and officials, but at the very least additional training should be a requirement for employees and officials making mistakes. When malicious behavior is involved, more severe punishments should be considered.

8.6   Conclusion

People are the weakest link in cybersecurity. Yet they are also essential elements to ensuring high levels of cybersecurity in organizations. Among other things, this can be accomplished through ongoing awareness training and accountability. If all end users understand that they are integral components of their local governments' cybersecurity and practice proper cybersecurity hygiene, they will be less likely to take actions, whether deliberate or not, that will expose their local government to unnecessary risks.

When thinking about cybersecurity threats, vulnerabilities, or other operational cybersecurity matters, local governments must recognize that it is ultimately *people* – not technology – that are the root of the great majority of cybersecurity problems. Developing a robust culture of cybersecurity and implementing a cybersecurity posture based on established best practices and procedures can help reduce the likelihood that people, as the weakest link in cybersecurity, will make the already-challenging task of cybersecurity for local governments even more difficult.

Note

1 Here, "decommissioned" refers to resetting a system device to erase any user data, local configurations, applications, or otherwise reset the device to its original factory condition.

References

Collier, K. (2017, August 01). *Personal info of 650,000 voters discovered on poll machine sold on eBay*. Gizmodo. https://gizmodo.com/personal-info-of-650-000-voters-discovered-on-poll-mach-1797438462
Forno, R. (2020, October 29). *Ransomware can interfere with elections and fuel disinformation – Basic cybersecurity precautions are key to minimizing the damage*. The Conversation. https://theconversation.com/

ransomware-can-interfere-with-elections-and-fuel-disinformation-basic-cybersecurity-
precautions-are-key-to-minimizing-the-damage-147531

Help Net Security (2020, August 05). *4 in 10 organizations punish staff for cybersecurity
errors*. https://www.helpnetsecurity.
com/2020/08/05/4-in-10-organizations-punish-staff-for-cybersecurity-errors

Martino, S. (2018, October 16). *Your greatest security asset: Employees*. National
Cybersecurity Alliance. https://staysafeonline.org/blog/greatest-security-asset-employees

McMillan, R. (2010, April 27). *Admin who kept SF network passwords found guilty*. Network
World. https://www.networkworld.com/article/2208076/admin-who-kept-sf-network-
passwords-found-guilty.html

Muncaster, P. (n.d.). *Social engineering attacks to watch out for*. Verizon. https://enterprise.
verizon.com/resources/articles/s/social-engineering-attacks-to-watch-out-for;

Riley, P. (2019, August 19). *Collier County scammed out of $184K in phishing scheme that
investigators say originated abroad*. Naples Daily News. https://www.naplesnews.com/
story/news/government/2019/08/19/
collier-county-scammed-out-184-k-cyber-attack-phishing-scheme/2049019001

Terranova Worldwide Corporation (2020). *How to protect your data from social engineering*.
https://terranovasecurity.com/wp-content/uploads/2020/09/White-Paper-Social-
Engineering-EN.pdf

Van Derbeken, J. (2010, August 07). *S.F. computer whiz Childs gets 4- year sentence*. SFGATE.
https://www.sfgate.com/bayarea/article/S-F-computer-whiz-Childs-gets-4-year-
sentence-3178759.php

Verizon (2013). *Verizon 2013 Data breach investigations report*. https://www.netsurion.com/
eventtracker/media/eventtracker/files/collateral/verizon-data-breach-2013.pdf

Verizon (2021). *Verizon 2021 Data breach investigations report*. https://enterprise.verizon.
com/resources/reports/2021-data-breach-investigations-report.pdf

9

The NIST Cybersecurity Framework Demystified

9.1 Introduction

Previous chapters have mentioned the NIST Cybersecurity Framework as a solid resource upon which to base local government cybersecurity programs. The purpose of this chapter is to introduce readers to the 2018 version of the framework. First, the chapter presents a brief history of the framework's development. Second, it describes overall structure and components of the framework and how local governments should use it as a continuous guide for cybersecurity improvement. The chapter concludes with an examination of each of the five functions of cybersecurity, which were previously introduced in Chapter 2, along with their categories and subcategories.

9.2 History of the Framework

NIST's original Cybersecurity Framework 1.0 (2014) was published in response to President Obama's Executive Order (EO) 13636 for improving critical infrastructure cybersecurity (U. S. National Institute of Standards and Technology, 2019). The EO directed NIST to work with private industry to create a standard of best practices for all sectors of critical infrastructure. Academics and government stakeholders were also involved in the development process. The framework is intended to be a flexible, cost-effective set of guidelines applicable to every critical infrastructure sector (Table 9.1). NIST also offers resources specific to federal organizations, small- and medium-sized businesses, state, local, tribal, and territorial (SLTT) governments, academia, assessment and auditing, and for international organizations (NIST, 2020).

Local governments can, and often are, involved in many aspects of critical infrastructure. Therefore, the framework can be adopted by organizations of all types to help them practice cybersecurity more effectively and become more cyber resilient. The framework also proposes a set of questions that local governments should ask to help

Cybersecurity and Local Government, First Edition. Donald F. Norris, Laura K. Mateczun and Richard F. Forno.
© 2022 John Wiley & Sons Ltd. Published 2022 by John Wiley & Sons Ltd.

Table 9.1 NIST Critical infrastructure sectors.

Chemical	Commercial Facilities	Communications	Critical Manufacturing
Dams	Defense industrial	Emergency services	Energy
Financial services	Food and agriculture	Government facilities	Healthcare and public health
Information technology	Nuclear reactors, materials and waste	Transportation systems	Water and wastewater systems

Source: NIST (2021a).

implement the best practices most appropriate for their size, location, budgets, and any unique cybersecurity issues they face.

The Cybersecurity Enhancement Act of 2014, which came into law almost a year after the release of version 1.0 of the framework, mandates that NIST take the lead in building consensus-based standards on an ongoing basis (NIST, 2021b). The framework was updated for the first time in 2018, and as of this writing, Version 1.1 of the framework is the most recent.

> NIST provides specific resources for SLTT governments to improve their cybersecurity including many assessment tools from peer local governments and membership organizations like MS-ISAC (NIST, 2020). NIST. (2020, May 13). State, local, tribal and territorial resources. https://www.nist.gov/cyberframework/state-local-tribal-and-territorial-resources.

9.3 Structure of the Framework and How to Use It

The NIST Cybersecurity Framework has three major components: the framework core, framework implementation tiers, and a framework profile. Adoption of the framework is a process by which local governments incorporate the standards set forth in the core into their cybersecurity risk management. Ultimately, the framework core, implementation tiers, and profiles provide local governments with a "common taxonomy and mechanism... to:

1. Describe their current cybersecurity posture [or, overall defense/readiness];
2. Describe their target state for cybersecurity;
3. Identify and prioritize opportunities for improvement within the context of a continuous and repeatable process;
4. Assess progress toward the target state; [and]
5. Communicate among internal and external stakeholders about cybersecurity risk" (NIST, 2018).

The framework core is made up of the five functions: Identify, Protect, Detect, Respond, and Recover. They are discussed individually in subsequent sections of this chapter.

The framework implementation tiers provide local governments with a simple methodology to assess how they view their overall cybersecurity risk and risk management in the context of their current practices, threat environment, mission objectives, legal requirements, and organizational constraints. The tiers are: 1) partial, 2) risk informed, 3) repeatable and 4) adaptive. The tiers assess three aspects of a local government's cybersecurity posture: its risk management process, how integrated its risk management program is, and its level of external participation.

Partial means that the local government's risk management process functions in an ad hoc or reactive fashion, with limited organizational awareness of cybersecurity risk and no external participation. Informed means that local government management approves of the risk management practices used, but that an organization-wide policy or approach is not in place, and the local government only engages in limited information-sharing activities. Repeatable means the local government's risk management practices are formalized as policy on an organization-wide level, with extensive information sharing and collaboration. Adaptive means the local government's cybersecurity risk management is adapted regularly based on previous activity and lessons learned by implementing risk-informed policies, practices, and procedures, participating and incorporating in collaborative information-sharing activities. This assessment is not intended to be a maturity model, but rather a way for local governments to better organize and prioritize their thinking around risks and objectives specific to them.

The framework profile is a document created and used by local governments to help them visualize their overall cybersecurity posture (or policies, practices, and people). To start their cybersecurity planning process, local governments should generate two profiles: a current profile reflecting the then current cybersecurity posture and a target profile representing cybersecurity goals and objectives that the local government intends to prioritize and accomplish. These profiles consist of specific cybersecurity outcomes chosen by the local government from the categories and subcategories (or outcome categories) making up the five functions. Local governments should review the categories and subcategories of each function to determine which are the most important in terms of their missions and overall levels of risk. The current profile is used to help prioritize goals and objectives to meet in order to achieve the target profile. Whatever outcome categories the local government prioritizes can then be tracked as they are implemented, which is an assessment process similar to the "as-is"/"to-be" management process in the commercial world.

Organizations can apply the NIST cybersecurity framework in various ways. However, it is important to note that the framework does not replace cybersecurity policies and practices currently in place but rather can assist local governments to identify where and how to improve and implement best practices. For example, one local government might use the framework implementation tiers to express a desired level and approach to risk management practices. Another local government might focus entirely on the framework core and profiles. A third could use the framework implementation tiers analysis to inform its profile assessment and prioritization of next-steps as identified in the categories and subcategories of the framework core. Ultimately, successful implementation of the NIST cybersecurity framework entails achieving the outcome categories chosen in the local government's target profile. Therefore, in order to make the two profiles (current and target) and implement the framework, local governments must go through each function, category, and subcategory of the framework to identify its current cybersecurity posture and to highlight what needs to be prioritized in order to achieve its desired level of cybersecurity.

Additionally, the framework also puts forth a list of seven recommended steps for establishing or improving a local government's cybersecurity program (Table 9.2). These steps should be repeated as necessary to assess and improve the local government's level of cybersecurity.

Table 9.2 NIST CSF steps to establish or improve a cybersecurity program.

Step	Description
1) Prioritize and scope	• Determine scope of cybersecurity program • Identify mission objectives and local government priorities • Determine scope of systems and assets that support the objectives and priorities • Make strategic cybersecurity implementations according to level of risk tolerance reflected in selected implementation tier
2) Orient	• Identify related systems, assets, regulatory requirements, and overall risk approach for the cybersecurity program
3) Create a current profile	• Indicating category and subcategory outcomes that are currently being achieved (even if partially so)
4) Conduct a risk assessment	• Analyze operational environment to discern likelihood of a cybersecurity event (for local governments, very high) • Identify emerging risks and utilize threat information shared internally and externally
5) Create a target profile	• Indicating category and subcategory outcomes for the local government's desired cybersecurity outcomes • Reflecting criteria within target implementation tier
6) Determine, analyze, and prioritize gaps	• Compare current and target profiles to determine gaps • Create prioritized action plan (addressing mission, costs, benefits, and risks) to achieving outcomes in target profile • Determine resources (budget and workforce) required to address gaps
7) Implement action plan	• Adjust current cybersecurity practices with the actions to take identified in the previous step • Follow suggested informative references listed in the framework by each category and subcategory

Source: NIST (2018).

The Multi-State Information Sharing & Analysis Center (MS-ISAC) provides a free tool that local governments can use annually (from October 1 to February 28) to understand and track their cybersecurity posture using NIST's Cybersecurity Framework – the Nationwide Cybersecurity Review (Center for Internet Security, n.d.). Local governments can complete the self-assessment to manage cybersecurity risk through the framework and use it as a benchmark to track year-to-year comparisons and compare to peer governments. Center for Internet Security. (n.d.). Nationwide Cybersecurity Review (NCSR). https://www.cisecurity.org/ms-isac/services/ncsr.

9.4 The Five Functions of Cybersecurity

NIST's five functions of cybersecurity are: Identify, Protect, Detect, Respond, and Recover. As previously discussed, each of the five functions of the framework contains categories and subcategories detailing the steps and methods necessary to help ensure specific cybersecurity outcomes (see Figure 9.1). These outcome categories help make actionable the priorities set forth in each function.

Five functions, 23 categories, and 108 subcategories make up the framework. Each subcategory is further distilled into specific informative references, which link to standards like NIST's Special Publications, the Center for Internet Security (CIS) Controls, ISACA's COBIT 5, and those set forth by the International Society of Automation (ISA) and the International Organization for Standardization/International Electrotechnical Commission (ISO/IEC). Although the framework can read as a nesting doll of checklists drilling down from function to category, subcategory, and informative references, many of the methods overlap to generate different desired outcomes. Table 9.2 of Version 1.1 of

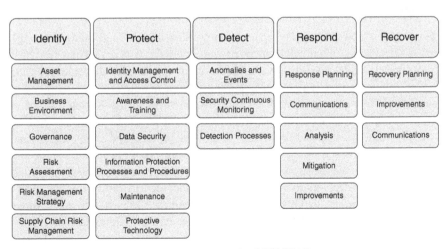

Figure 9.1 NIST CSF five functions and categories (NIST, 2018).

the cybersecurity framework provides a list of each of the functions and their related categories, subcategories, and informative references (NIST, 2018). This chapter utilizes a condensed version of the table for each function section below.

9.4.1 Identify

Identify means that local governments "develop an organizational understanding to manage cybersecurity risk to systems, people, assets, data, and capabilities" (2018, p. 7). The six identify functions are: asset management, business environment, governance, risk assessment, risk management strategy, and supply chain risk management. What this means in practice is that local governments must engage in asset management and identify aspects of their cybersecurity environment by inventorying physical hardware, software, data, and personnel. Second, local governments must assess their business environment and relate cybersecurity to organizational mission, objectives, and stakeholders. Third, local governments should establish robust cybersecurity governance by ensuring organization-wide cybersecurity policy is established and communicated to address risks and legal requirements. Fourth, instituting a risk assessment will help local governments address asset vulnerabilities and incorporate shared threat intelligence. Risk management strategies should be established and levels of organizational risk tolerance identified. Assessing the security measures used by third-party device manufacturers and application developers is an important aspect of supply chain risk management (Table 9.3).

The process of the identify function does not stop; like each of the five functions, it operates continuously. New devices, software, and applications must be included in inventories when incorporated into a local government's information systems.

9.4.2 Protect

Local governments address the protect function by "develop[ing] and implement[ing] appropriate safeguards to ensure delivery of critical services" (2018, p. 7). The six categories of protect are: identity management and access control, awareness and training, data security, information protection processes and procedures, maintenance, and protective technology. Identity management and access control involves authenticating user identities and credentials, permissions, and authorizations of which users are allowed to access the government's information systems, protecting physical and remote access and more. Staff awareness and training for all end users regardless of title, pay grade, or status in the organization is needed so that they understand their roles and responsibilities in protecting local government information systems. Data security means that the confidentiality, integrity, and availability of the local government's information, in its three states, are protected. Information protection processes and procedures involve implementing official security policies around back-ups, system configuration, physical security, and data destruction including human resources, response and recovery plans, and vulnerability management plans. System maintenance, such as replacing hardware or system updates or patches, should occur regularly and according to adopted policy. Protective technology means having technical solutions in place to help ensure system

Table 9.3 Identify categories and subcategories.

Function	Category	Subcategory
Identify	**Asset management** The data, personnel, devices, systems, and facilities that enable the organization to achieve business purposes are identified and managed consistent with their relative importance to organizational objectives and the organization's risk strategy.	**1)** Physical devices and systems within the organization are inventoried **2)** Software platforms and applications within the organization are inventoried **3)** Organizational communication and data flows are mapped **4)** External information systems are catalogued **5)** Resources (e.g., hardware, devices, data, time, personnel, and software) are prioritized based on their classification, criticality, and business value **6)** Cybersecurity roles and responsibilities for the entire workforce and third-party stakeholders (e.g., suppliers, customers, partners) are established
	Business environment The organization's mission, objectives, stakeholders, and activities are understood and prioritized; this information is used to inform cybersecurity roles, responsibilities, and risk management decisions.	**1)** The organization's role in the supply chain is identified and communicated **2)** The organization's place in critical infrastructure and its industry sector is identified and communicated **3)** Priorities for organizational mission, objectives, and activities are established and communicated **4)** Dependencies and critical functions for delivery of critical services are established **5)** Resilience requirements to support delivery of critical services are established for all operating states (e.g., under duress/attack, during recovery, normal operations)
	Governance The policies, procedures, and processes to manage and monitor the organization's regulatory, legal, risk, environmental, and operational requirements are understood and inform the management of cybersecurity risk.	**1)** Organizational cybersecurity policy is established and communicated **2)** Cybersecurity roles and responsibilities are coordinated and aligned with internal roles and external partners **3)** Legal and regulatory requirements regarding cybersecurity, including privacy and civil liberties obligations, are understood and managed **4)** Governance and risk management processes address cybersecurity risks
	Risk assessment The organization understands the cybersecurity risk to organizational operations (including mission, functions, image, or reputation), organizational assets, and individuals.	**1)** Asset vulnerabilities are identified and documented **2)** Cyber threat intelligence is received from information sharing forums and sources **3)** Threats, both internal and external, are identified and documented **4)** Potential business impacts and likelihoods are identified **5)** Threats, vulnerabilities, likelihoods, and impacts are used to determine risk **6)** Risk responses are identified and prioritized

(Continued)

Table 9.3 (Continued)

Function	Category	Subcategory
	Risk management strategy The organization's priorities, constraints, risk tolerances, and assumptions are established and used to support operational risk decisions.	**1)** Risk management processes are established, managed, and agreed to by organizational stakeholders **2)** Organizational risk tolerance is determined and clearly expressed **3)** The organization's determination of risk tolerance is informed by its role in critical infrastructure and sector specific risk analysis
	Supply chain risk management The organization's priorities, constraints, risk tolerances, and assumptions are established and used to support risk decisions associated with managing supply chain risk. The organization has established and implemented the processes to identify, assess and manage supply chain risks.	**1)** Cyber supply chain risk management processes are identified, established, assessed, managed, and agreed to by organizational stakeholders **2)** Suppliers and third-party partners of information systems, components, and services are identified, prioritized, and assessed using a cyber supply chain risk assessment process **3)** Contracts with suppliers and third-party partners are used to implement appropriate measures designed to meet the objectives of an organization's cybersecurity program and cyber supply chain risk management plan **4)** Suppliers and third-party partners are routinely assessed using audits, test results, or other forms of evaluations to confirm they are meeting their contractual obligations **5)** Response and recovery planning and testing are conducted with suppliers and third-party providers

Source: NIST (2018).

security and resilience, such as audit logs and the principle of least functionality in which non-essential system functions are prohibited (Table 9.4).

With proper protection systems and policies in place, the occurrence and impact of adverse cybersecurity events can be mitigated. Since it is impossible or nearly so to prevent cyberattacks, it is essential to be able to detect attacks when they occur.

9.4.3 Detect

Under the detect function local governments must "develop and implement appropriate activities to identify the occurrence of a cybersecurity event" (2018). The categories for detect are: anomalies and events, security continuous monitoring, and detection processes. Anomalies and events means that system activity deviating from what is normally expected is detected and analyzed to determine if it poses a danger to the local government's information system. Security continuous monitoring means that the local government's systems, networks, third-party service providers, and physical environment are constantly monitored to detect and identify potential security events that could

Table 9.4 Protect categories and subcategories.

Function	Category	Subcategory
Protect	**Identity management and access control** Access to physical and logical assets and associated facilities is limited to authorized users, processes, and devices, and is managed consistent with the assessed risk of unauthorized access to authorized activities and transactions.	**1)** Identities and credentials are issued, managed, verified, revoked, and audited for authorized devices, users and processes **2)** Physical access to assets is managed and protected **3)** Remote access is managed **4)** Access permissions and authorizations are managed, incorporating the principles of least privilege and separation of duties **5)** Network integrity is protected (e.g., network segregation, network segmentation) **6)** Identities are proofed and bound to credentials and asserted in interactions **7)** Users, devices, and other assets are authenticated (e.g., single-factor, multifactor) commensurate with the risk of the transaction (e.g., individuals' security and privacy risks and other organizational risks)
	Awareness and training The organization's personnel and partners are provided cybersecurity awareness education and are trained to perform their cybersecurity related duties and responsibilities consistent with related policies, procedures, and agreements.	**1)** All users are informed and trained **2)** Privileged users understand their roles and responsibilities **3)** Third-party stakeholders (e.g., suppliers, customers, partners) understand their roles and responsibilities **4)** Senior executives understand their roles and responsibilities **5)** Physical and cybersecurity personnel understand their roles and responsibilities
	Data security Information and records (data) are managed consistent with the organization's risk strategy to protect the confidentiality, integrity, and availability of information.	**1)** Data-at-rest is protected **2)** Data-in-transit is protected **3)** Assets are formally managed throughout removal, transfers, and disposition **4)** Adequate capacity to ensure availability is maintained **5)** Protections against data leaks are implemented **6)** Integrity checking mechanisms are used to verify software, firmware, and information integrity **7)** The development and testing environment(s) are separate from the production environment **8)** Integrity checking mechanisms are used to verify hardware integrity

(Continued)

Table 9.4 (Continued)

Function	Category	Subcategory
	Information protection processes and procedures Security policies (that address purpose, scope, roles, responsibilities, management commitment, and coordination among organizational entities), processes, and procedures are maintained and used to manage protection of information systems and assets.	**1)** A baseline configuration of information technology/industrial control systems is created and maintained incorporating security principles (e.g., concept of least functionality)
		2) A system development life cycle to manage systems is implemented
		3) Configuration change control processes are in place
		4) Back-ups of information are conducted, maintained, and tested
		5) Policy and regulations regarding the physical operating environment for organizational assets are met
		6) Data is destroyed according to policy
		7) Protection processes are improved
		8) Effectiveness of protection technologies is shared
		9) Response plans (incident response and business continuity) and recovery plans (incident recovery and disaster recovery) are in place and managed
		10) Response and recovery plans are tested
		11) Cybersecurity is included in human resources practices (e.g., deprovisioning, personnel screening)
		12) A vulnerability management plan is developed and implemented
	Maintenance Maintenance and repairs of industrial control and information system components are performed consistent with policies and procedures.	**1)** Maintenance and repair of organizational assets are performed and logged, with approved and controlled tools
		2) Remote maintenance of organizational assets is approved, logged, and performed in a manner that prevents unauthorized access
	Protective technology Technical security solutions are managed to ensure the security and resilience of systems and assets, consistent with related policies, procedures, and agreements.	**1)** Audit/log records are determined, documented, implemented, and reviewed in accordance with policy
		2) Removable media is protected and its use restricted according to policy
		3) The principle of least functionality is incorporated by configuring systems to provide only essential capabilities
		4) Communications and control networks are protected
		5) R Mechanisms (e.g., failsafe, load balancing, hot swap) are implemented to achieve resilience requirements in normal and adverse situations

Source: NIST (2018).

Table 9.5 Detect categories and subcategories.

Function	Category	Subcategory
Detect	**Anomalies and events** Anomalous activity is detected and the potential impact of events is understood.	**1)** A baseline of network operations and expected data flows for users and systems is established and managed
		2) Detected events are analyzed to understand attack targets and methods
		3) Event data are collected and correlated from multiple sources and sensors
		4) Impact of events is determined
		5) Incident alert thresholds are established
	Security continuous monitoring The information system and assets are monitored to identify cybersecurity events and verify the effectiveness of protective measures.	**1)** The network is monitored to detect potential cybersecurity events
		2) The physical environment is monitored to detect potential cybersecurity events
		3) Personnel activity is monitored to detect potential cybersecurity events
		4) Malicious code is detected
		5) Unauthorized mobile code is detected
		6) External service provider activity is monitored to detect potential cybersecurity events
		7) Monitoring for unauthorized personnel, connections, devices, and software is performed
		8) Vulnerability scans are performed
	Detection processes Detection processes and procedures are maintained and tested to ensure awareness of anomalous events.	**1)** Roles and responsibilities for detection are well defined to ensure accountability
		2) Detection activities comply with all applicable requirements
		3) Detection processes are tested
		4) Event detection information is communicated
		5) Detection processes are continuously improved

Source: NIST (2018).

cause damage. Detection processes include implementing roles and responsibilities accountable for detection, ensuring that detection processes are tested and continuously improved, and that detection information is communicated appropriately (Table 9.5).

Adverse cybersecurity events need to be detected as soon as possible. The time it takes to discover a breach can exponentially increase the amount of damage inflicted. Detecting and analyzing adverse events helps local governments respond accordingly.

9.4.4 Respond

To effectively respond to adverse cybersecurity events once they are detected, local governments should "develop and implement appropriate activities to take action regarding a detected cybersecurity incident" (NIST, 2018, p. 7). The five categories for the respond function are: response planning, communications, analysis, mitigation, and improvements. Response planning means that processes and procedures established in a response plan are executed during or after an adverse cybersecurity event. Communications involves ensuring that personnel understand and act appropriately on their roles and responsibilities when responding to an adverse event. It also means that those events are reported internally and externally according to policy. Analysis in event response means that detection notifications are investigated to understand the impact of the event, that forensics are performed, and that processes are in place to respond to vulnerabilities identified by the local government. Mitigation means that events are contained, mitigated, and that newly identified vulnerabilities are either successfully mitigated or documented as accepted risks. Improvements means that response plans incorporate lessons learned into the local government's cybersecurity posture, and that response strategies are updated (Table 9.6).

Table 9.6 Respond categories and subcategories.

Function	Category	Subcategory
Respond	**Response planning** Response processes and procedures are executed and maintained, to ensure response to detected cybersecurity incidents.	**1)** Response plan is executed during or after an incident
	Communications Response activities are coordinated with internal and external stakeholders (e.g., external support from law enforcement agencies).	**1)** Personnel know their roles and order of operations when a response is needed **2)** Incidents are reported consistent with established criteria **3)** Information is shared consistent with response plans **4)** Coordination with stakeholders occurs consistent with response plans **5)** Voluntary information sharing occurs with external stakeholders to achieve broader cybersecurity situational awareness
	Analysis Analysis is conducted to ensure effective response and support recovery activities.	**1)** Notifications from detection systems are investigated **2)** The impact of the incident is understood **3)** Forensics are performed **4)** Incidents are categorized consistent with response plans **5)** Processes are established to receive, analyze, and respond to vulnerabilities disclosed to the organization from internal and external sources (e.g., internal testing, security bulletins, or security researchers)

(Continued)

Table 9.6 (Continued)

Function	Category	Subcategory
	Mitigation Activities are performed to prevent expansion of an event, mitigate its effects, and resolve the incident.	**1)** Incidents are contained **2)** Incidents are mitigated **3)** Newly identified vulnerabilities are mitigated or documented as accepted risks
	Improvements Organizational response activities are improved by incorporating lessons learned from current and previous detection/ response activities.	**1)** Response plans incorporate lessons learned **2)** Response strategies are updated

Source: NIST (2018).

9.4.5 Recover

Finally, the recover function states that local governments should "develop and implement appropriate activities to maintain plans for resilience and to restore any capabilities or services that were impaired due to a cybersecurity incident" (NIST, 2018, p. 8). Recover has three categories: recovery planning, improvements, and communications. Recovery planning means that recovery processes and procedures are executed during and/or after an adverse cybersecurity event to ensure restoration of the local government's information systems. Improvements means that local governments incorporate lessons learned and update recovery plans. Communications for the recover function include public relations management, reputation repair, and communication of recovery activities to internal and external stakeholders, including the public (Table 9.7).

Recovery is an essential step toward ensuring local government resilience. Restoring systems and returning to normal operations in a timely manner is the ultimate goal.

9.5 Conclusion

The NIST cybersecurity framework emphasizes organizational and managerial components important in implementing the cybersecurity best practices that can be supported by appropriately configured and deployed technologies. It represents a matrix of achieving the highest level of cybersecurity attainable. Local governments can incorporate the framework into their cybersecurity planning and management in order to achieve and maintain high levels of cybersecurity.

The framework provides flexibility so that local governments can implement the best practices most appropriate for their particular risk environments. The important

Table 9.7 Recover categories and subcategories.

Function	Category	Subcategory
Recover	**Recovery planning** Recovery processes and procedures are executed and maintained to ensure restoration of systems or assets affected by cybersecurity incidents.	**1)** Recovery plan is executed during or after a cybersecurity incident
	Improvements Recovery planning and processes are improved by incorporating lessons learned into future activities.	**1)** Recovery plans incorporate lessons learned **2)** Recovery strategies are updated
	Communications Restoration activities are coordinated with internal and external parties (e.g., coordinating centers, internet Service Providers, owners of attacking systems, victims, other CSIRTs, and vendors).	**1)** Public relations are managed **2)** Reputation is repaired after an incident **3)** Recovery activities are communicated to internal and external stakeholders as well as executive and management teams

Source: NIST (2018).

numbers to remember about the NIST cybersecurity framework are *three* and *five*: three major components involved in adopting the framework (framework core, framework implementation tiers, and framework profiles) and five cybersecurity functions that identify cybersecurity outcomes to be prioritized by local governments (identify, protect, detect, respond, recover). The framework presents a cyclical process through which organizations can continuously improve their cybersecurity outcomes. This cycle of continuous improvement can help local governments achieve high levels of cybersecurity by identifying current gaps and the steps to take to reach the state of best practice and to ensure this process is repeated to continuously to identify new gaps. By going through each function, category, and subcategory of the framework, local governments can prioritize their most important areas for improvement based on the risks they face and their available resources.

References

U.S. National Institute of Standards and Technology (2014, February 12). *Framework for improving critical infrastructure cybersecurity version 1.0*. https://www.nist.gov/system/files/documents/cyberframework/cybersecurity-framework-021214.pdf

U.S. National Institute of Standards and Technology (2018, April 16). *Framework for improving critical infrastructure cybersecurity version 1.1*. https://nvlpubs.nist.gov/nistpubs/CSWP/NIST.CSWP.04162018.pdf

U.S. National Institute of Standards and Technology (2019, November 21). *History and creation of the framework*. https://www.nist.gov/cyberframework/online-learning/history-and-creation-fraamework

U.S. National Institute of Standards and Technology (2020, May 13). *State, local, tribal, and territorial resources*. https://www.nist.gov/cyberframework/state-local-tribal-and-territorial-resources

U.S. National Institute of Standards and Technology (2021a, March 2). Critical infrastructure resources. https://www.nist.gov/cyberframework/critical-infrastructure-resources

U.S. National Institute of Standards and Technology (2021b, May 12). *Evolution of the framework*. https://www.nist.gov/cyberframework/evolution

10

Cybersecurity Law and Regulation for Local Government

10.1   Introduction

This chapter addresses the growing field of cybersecurity law. Cybersecurity law, for the purposes of this book, is made up of the laws and regulations concerning the proper management of a local government's information assets in order to support the confidentiality, integrity, and availability of those assets. Some, mainly larger local governments, maintain robust legal departments. However, they may contract out for certain types of specialized legal services, cybersecurity among them. Some, perhaps many smaller local governments, however, do not have the resources to support legal departments and must contract out for most or all of their legal services.

Lawyers working in government practice have expertise in many different areas from administrative, criminal, and environmental law to tax, banking, transactional law, and consumer protection. Practice types also vary from bill drafting and regulatory work to litigation and negotiation. These lawyers represent the interests of the local government itself, as well as its citizens. The legal responsibilities facing local governments are plentiful, and they continue to grow. Like almost any organization, local governments must now consider hiring legal counsel with cybersecurity expertise, or "Privacy Officers" who have knowledge and expertise in the areas of information privacy laws and compliance.

This chapter presents an overview of the laws and regulations relevant to local government cybersecurity so that local officials and others are at least aware of potential compliance requirements. These laws directly impact local government cybersecurity postures by mandating specific security standards, technologies, and policies that staff must implement. First, it covers federal policies applicable to local governments including: the Health Insurance Portability and Accountability (HIPAA) Act; IRS Publication 1075; the Federal Information Security Modernization Act (FISMA); the Family Education Rights and Privacy Act of 1974 (FERPA); among others. Second, the chapter covers sector specific security standaards such as the Payment Card Industry (PCI) and North American Electric Reliability Corporation (NERC) standards. Third, the chapter reviews a variety of typical state laws including: state and local cybersecurity legislation; security breach notification laws; data security and data disposal laws; and data protection and privacy laws. Fourth is an introduction of the European Union General Data

Cybersecurity and Local Government, First Edition. Donald F. Norris, Laura K. Mateczun and Richard F. Forno.
© 2022 John Wiley & Sons Ltd. Published 2022 by John Wiley & Sons Ltd.

Protection Regulation (GDPR) and its potential relevance to local government. Fifth, is a brief discussion of proposed federal cybersecurity legislation that would impact local government, like the America COMPETES Act. Conclusions and recommendations close the chapter.

For local governments, many of the laws and regulations discussed in this chapter are not merely suggestions. They contain rules that local governments are mandated to adopt and implement. It is important to be aware of them, not only to ensure no laws are being broken, but also to implement best practices that can help local governments comply with federal and state mandates. Failing to comply with these mandates, in some situations, can be punishable by fines and even jail time (e.g., when protected health, cardholder, tax, or other information described below is willfully exposed).

10.2 Federal Policies

The following federal policies largely deal with protecting the confidentiality, integrity, and availability of various types of sensitive personal data, from health information to tax and cardholder information. The aim of these laws is to balance the interests of privacy, and the flow of information necessary for efficient and effective service provision. Local governments, depending on the services they provide and federal programs they administer, can find themselves subject to one or more, if not all of these regulations.

10.2.1 Health Insurance Portability and Accountability (HIPAA) Act

HIPAA governs how organizations protect the healthcare information of their employees and the electronic storage of protected health information. In 2009 the Healthcare Information Technology for Economic and Clinical Health (HITECH) Act expanded HIPAA's enforcement and breach notification rules. Some local governments agencies are considered "covered entities" and are thus subject to HIPAA and HITECH regulations, for example, by administering Medicaid or operating healthcare clinics. The Affordable Care Act and expansions to Medicare and Medicaid increased local government responsibility for information security. Public health agencies must implement measures to meet two major cybersecurity objectives in order to comply with these regulations: protect individually identifiable health information from unauthorized access and allowing for authorized access to protected health information consistent with the Privacy Rule. HIPAA's Privacy Rule sets forth the specific standards by which this information must be protected, with the intent of balancing the interests of patient privacy and the flow of information necessary to ensure the provision of quality care (US Department of Health & Human Services, 2013). Local governments must adopt and implement the proper identity and access management measures to prevent unauthorized access to protected patient information. These access control measures require proper documentation and periodic review in order to be successful. If a breach does occur, HIPAA requires organizations to notify individuals who are affected (e.g., because of compromised PII), as well as the media.

10.2.2 (IRS) Publication 1075 Tax Information Security Guidelines

IRS Pub. 1075 is the *Tax Information Security Guidelines for Federal, State and Local Agencies* (Internal Revenue Service [IRS], 2016). It aims to protect federal tax information and tax returns, both digitally and physically, from unauthorized access and disclosure. Specifically, federal tax information should be restricted on a need-to-know basis, in that employees should only have access if the information is necessary to perform their duties. Protecting the privacy of tax and taxholder information is essential to maintaining citizen confidence in government.

These guidelines are based on the security standards set forth in NIST Special Publication 800-53 on security and privacy controls for information systems (2020a). Yet again, access control and identity management requirements are major components of IRS Pub. 1075 compliance. In order to receive tax information from the IRS, local governments must create an account with the agency's Secure Data Transfer program, which encrypts the data during transmission. Local government agencies must be prepared to show that they have the ability to protect the confidentiality of federal tax information by securely storing the data on their IT systems. They must also maintain updated safeguard reports and certain related communications. The IRS Safeguards Program provides further technical assistance and resources for protecting federal tax information (Internal Revenue Service, 2021).

10.2.3 Federal Information Security Modernization Act (FISMA)

FISMA was enacted in 2002 to protect information used by federal agencies and stored on federal networks. It has since been expanded to cover state and local governments administering and participating in federal programs like Medicaid, Medicare, veteran's health, and federal student loans (Taylor, 2013). There is some overlap with HIPAA standards and IRS Pub. 1075, but FISMA compliance accomplishes more than HIPAA and IRS Pub 1075 alone. While NIST SP 800-53 (2020a) is relevant here, so are other standards set forth in the NIST SP 800 series focused on computer security, particularly SP 800-171 (2020b) on protecting unclassified information, and 800-63 (2017) on digital identity guidelines. Additionally, Federal Information Process Standards (FIPS) Publications 199 (standards for security categorization) and 200 (minimum security requirements for federal information systems) also discuss how agencies can meet FISMA requirements (Federal Information Processing Standards Publication, 2004, 2006). In lay terms, due diligence under FISMA means that local governments covered by the act must take the following steps: 1) categorize and inventory information systems; 2) select and implement privacy and security controls to meet the local government's mission; 3) assess the effectiveness of the controls in place; 4) authorize the information systems for operation; and 5) continuously monitor the information systems (NIST, 2020a).

10.2.4 Family Educational Rights and Privacy Act of 1974 (FERPA)

FERPA governs the rights of parents and children to access and amend children's education records, as well as how personally identifiable information (PII) in those records can be disclosed (Family Educational Rights and Privacy Act (FERPA), 2011). FERPA provides students and parents rights to review and correct education records kept by their school and allows for schools to disclose records in certain situations. Student education records include report card information, transcripts, class schedules, disciplinary records, and contact and family information. Schools can disclose such records to other school officials within the same institution or agency, contractors the agency has hired, another institution in which the student seeks to enroll, or in connection with financial aid, etc. without parental consent. Otherwise, written consent is required in order to disclose these records.

Under FERPA, educational and other institutions must protect student education records. This applies to all local government organizations receiving federal funds from Department of Education programs, like public schools, school districts, vocational and technical schools, and postsecondary institutions. While FERPA does not impose specific security controls for individual institutions, cybersecurity breaches that result in student records being illegally disclosed can ultimately lead to FERPA violations. Specifically, the law states "an educational agency or institution that does not use physical or technological access controls must ensure that its administrative policy for controlling access to education records is effective and that it remains in compliance with the legitimate educational interest requirement" of record disclosure (34 CFR §99.31, p. 265). Institutions subject to FERPA should follow NIST's SP 800 series, particularly 800-171 on protecting unclassified information (2020b), which can help to prevent any such violations. The Department of Education's Privacy Technical Assistance Center also provides helpful resources such as its data security checklist (2015).

10.2.5 Criminal Justice Information Services (CJIS) Security Policy Compliance

CJIS is a division of the FBI that serves the law enforcement community by providing tools, services, and sharing criminal justice information. The CJIS Security Policy regulates how local governments utilizing CJIS services protect sensitive criminal background and fingerprint information (Criminal Justice Information Services [CJIS], 2020). These services include the National Instant Criminal Background Check System (NICS); the National Crime Information Center (NCIC), which is an electronic clearinghouse of crime data such as mug shots and crime records used by almost every criminal justice agency in the country; the National Data Exchange (N-DEx), which is an online tool for sharing information across jurisdictions; the Law Enforcement Enterprise Portal (LEEP) that allows for real-time multi-agency collaboration during high-profile events; Identity History Summary Checks, fingerprints, other biometrics, and more (Federal Bureau of Investigation, n.d.).

All local government agencies with access to, or that operate in support of, the CJIS division's services and information, such as local police departments, are subject to the security policy. The policy applies to how the criminal justice information (CJI) and other PII is created, viewed, modified, transmitted, disseminated, stored, and destroyed. It is the minimum standard that local governments must meet, but additional measures can also be incorporated. Specifically, the security policy sets forth standards covering 13 policy areas (Table 10.1). The requirements set forth in each of these policy areas include user agreements, information exchange agreements, security training for employees, the reporting of security incidents, access control and account management, password strength and multi-factor authentication, data encryption, wireless networking, physical and remote access, Virtual Private Networks (VPNs) and mobile devices and more. Additionally, these policy areas correspond with NIST SP 800-53 on security and privacy controls (2020a).

Table 10.1 CJIS security policy: policy areas.

Policy Area	Covers
1) Information exchange agreements	• Information exchange – handling; user agreements; outsourcing standards • Monitoring, review, and delivery of services • Secondary dissemination
2) Security awareness training	• Basic security awareness training (levels 1–4) • Local agency security officer (LASO) training • Security training records
3) Incident response	• Reporting security events – reporting structure and responsibilities • Management of security incidents – incident handling and collection of evidence • Incident response training • Incident monitoring
4) Auditing and accountability	• Auditable events and content • Response to audit processing failures • Audit monitoring, analysis, and reporting • Time stamps • Protection of audit information and audit record retention
5) Access control	• Account management • Access enforcement • Unsuccessful login attempts • System use notification • Session lock • Remote access
6) Identification and authentication	• Identification policy and procedures • Authentication policy and procedures • Advanced authentication
7) Configuration management	• Access restrictions for changes • Security of configuration documentation
8) Media protection	• Media storage and access • Media transport • Digital media sanitization and disposal • Disposal of physical media

(Continued)

Table 10.1 (Continued)

Policy Area	Covers
9) Physical protection	• Physically secure location • Controlled area
10) System and communications Protection and information integrity	• Information flow enforcement • Facsimile transmission of CJI • Partitioning and virtualization • System and information integrity policy and procedures
11) Formal audits	• Audits by CJIS • Audits by state CJIS systems agency • Special inquiries and audits • Compliance subcommittees
12) Personnel security	• Personnel screening requirements for individuals Requiring unescorted access to unencrypted CJI • Personnel termination • Personnel transfer • Personnel sanctions
13) Mobile devices	• Wireless communications technologies • Mobile device management • Wireless device risk mitigations • System integrity • Incident response • Access control • Identification and authentication

Source: Criminal Justice Information Services (2020).

As is the case for each of the federal policies discussed in this section, the intent of the CJIS security policy is to balance public safety and civil liberties as much as possible. Without the sharing of CJI across jurisdictions, local law enforcement agencies would struggle to succeed in finding those engaging in violent and criminal behavior and holding them accountable. We do not need to return to the days of fugitives moving on to a different state, whose law enforcement is unaware of an individual's criminal history. However, there are profound privacy and civil liberties concerns if unfettered access to this information were provided. Vigilante justice and mob thinking make misidentifications all the more likely, and remove all constitutional protections afforded to those suspected of criminal activity. National security concerns also arise if this information is not protected.

10.2.6 Computer Fraud and Abuse Act (CFAA)

CFAA, perhaps the premier federal computer crime law, was first enacted in 1986 and has since been amended several times. The act prohibits "intentionally access[ing] a computer without authorization or exceed[ing] authorized access," and obtaining information from a protected computer, which includes information from any federal department or agency, or financial institution, damaging said devices or information, or otherwise hacking into these systems and causing at least $5,000 in damages (Computer Fraud and Abuse Act, 1986). "Without authorization" has been interpreted as widely as to include violating a website's terms of service or employment acceptable use policy. For example, the Supreme Court recently determined that a law enforcement officer's use of the government's license plate database for information requested and paid for by a civilian did not "exceed authorized access" because he was authorized to access the system despite accessing it for an unauthorized purpose (*Van Buren v. United States,* 2021). The CFAA provides an important tool for prosecutors to seek recourse against those who have caused an adverse cybersecurity event in a local government's information system that "raises concerns pertaining to national security, critical infrastructure, public health and safety, market integrity, international relations, or other considerations having a broad or significant impact on national or economic interests" (US Department of Justice, 2020). Violations of this act are punishable with up to 20 years in prison if a prior offense has been committed.

10.2.7 Electronic Communications Privacy Act (ECPA)

ECPA, also enacted in 1986, covers restrictions on how local governments and law enforcement officers can access the stored communications of businesses and residents in their jurisdiction (Electronic Communications Privacy Act, 1986). The law extended restrictions on telephone wire-taps to electronic communications on computers and was last updated by the USA PATRIOT Act. Local governments and their officers may not attempt to intercept such communications unless they have obtained judicial authorization, or a warrant, to do so. The warrant must be supported by probable cause, and can last up to 30 days (Bureau of Justice Assistance, n.d.). If a warrant is not obtained, any evidence gathered will not be admissible as evidence in court.

10.3 Sector Specific Security Standards

The following are security standards set by professional organizations within specific sectors of the economy that also pertain to local governments. These standards are not established by federal policy, but must be followed by all organizations involved in these particular sectors and activities.

10.3.1 Payment Card Industry (PCI) Data Security Standard

The PCI Data Security Standard regulates how organizations protect cardholder data or "any information contained on a customer's payment card...printed on either side of the card [or] contained in the digital format on [the card's] magnetic stripe" (PCI Security Standards Council, 2008, p. 1). The standard was first established in 2004 to help govern the transition to digital transactions and help protect against payment fraud. The PCI standard was one of the first of such cybersecurity regulatory requirements faced by most local governments (Chabrow, 2009).

Table 10.2 PCI data security standard goals and requirements.

Goals	PCI DSS Requirements
Build and maintain a secure network	1. Install and maintain a firewall configuration to protect cardholder data
	2. Do not use vendor-supplied defaults for system passwords and other security parameters
Protect cardholder data	3. Protect stored cardholder data
	4. Encrypt transmission of cardholder data across open, public networks
Maintain a vulnerability management program	5. Use and regularly update anti-virus software or programs
	6. Develop and maintain secure systems and applications
Implement strong access control measures	7. Restrict access to cardholder data by business need-to-know
	8. Assign a unique ID to each person with computer access
	9. Restrict physical access to cardholder data
Regularly monitor and test networks	10. Track and monitor all access to network resources and cardholder data
	11. Regularly test security systems and processes
Maintain an information security policy	12. Maintain a policy that addresses information security for employees

Source: PCI Security Standards Council LLC (n.d.).

Local governments are subject to follow the PCI standard if they process or handle debit, credit, or EBT (Electronic Benefit Transfer) card transactions. The wide array of services provided by local governments necessitate that they follow the PCI security standard in order to protect cardholder data received from online and in-person transactions like tax, water bill, permit, and other payments.

The PCI standard sets forth 12 major requirements to help meet six overarching goals that are aligned with good cybersecurity practices: 1) build and maintain a secure network; 2) protect cardholder data; 3) maintain a vulnerability management program; 4) implement strong access control measures; 5) regularly monitor and test networks; and 6) maintain an information security policy (see Table 10.2). In brief, the standards include restricting physical access to cardholder data, restricting access on a need-to-know basis, and not using system default passwords. The PCI standard also requires that robust identity and access management measures be in place. Cardholder information must be received, processed, stored, and transmitted securely. Local governments can defer PCI compliance responsibilities by working with a third-party merchant service provider.

10.3.2 North American Electric Reliability Corporation Critical Infrastructure Protection (NERC CIP) Standards

The NERC CIP Standards were developed by the North American Electric Reliability Corporation in 2008 to regulate the cybersecurity of bulk electric system (BES) owners and operators in North America, including state and local government electric utilities (North American Electric Reliability Corporation [NERC], n.d.). A BES includes the systems for electrical generation, transmission lines, and connections with neighboring systems. Some local government BES owners include the Alameda Bureau of Electricity in California, the Columbus Division of Electricity in Ohio, the Long Island Power Authority in New York, and the Los Alamos County Utilities Department in New Mexico (The Utility Connection, n.d.). As of this writing, there are 12 control families in the standards, with four more subject to future enforcement (Table 10.3). These "control families" are similar to the CJIS policy areas described above and govern the types of security

Table 10.3 NERC CIP control families.

Status	Control Family	Requirements
Required	BES cyber system Categorization (CIP 2-5.1a)	1) Implement process that considers assets for low-medium-high impact BES cyber systems: a. Control centers b. Transmission stations and substations c. Generation resources d. Systems critical to system restoration e. Special protection systems f. Protection systems of distribution providers
	Security management controls (CIP 3-8)	1) CIP senior manager approval every 15 months for documented security policies
	Personnel & training (CIP 4-6)	1) Security awareness program 2) Cybersecurity training program 3) Personnel risk assessment program 4) Access management program 5) Access revocation
	Electronic security perimeter(s) (CIP 5-6)	1) Electronic security perimeter 2) Remote access management
	Physical security of BES cyber systems (CIP 6-6)	1) Physical security plan 2) Visitor control program 3) Physical access control system maintenance and testing program
	System security management (CIP 7-6)	1) Ports and services 2) Security patch management 3) Malicious code prevention 4) Security event monitoring 5) System access control
	Incident reporting and response planning (CIP 8-6)	1) Cybersecurity incident response plan specifications 2) Cybersecurity incident response plan implementation and testing 3) Cybersecurity incident response plan review, update, and communication 4) Notifications and reporting for cybersecurity incidents

(Continued)

Table 10.3 (Continued)

Status	Control Family	Requirements
	Recovery plans for BES cyber systems (CIP 9-6)	1) Recovery plan specifications 2) Recovery plan implementation and testing 3) Recovery plan review, update, and communication
	Configuration change management and vulnerability Assessments (CIP 10-3)	1) Configuration change management 2) Configuration monitoring 3) Vulnerability assessments
	Information protection (CIP 11-2)	1) Information protection 2) BES cyber asset reuse and disposal
	Supply chain risk management (CIP 13-1)	1) Develop documented supply chain cybersecurity risk management plan 2) Implement the plan 3) Obtain CIP senior manager approval of plan
	Physical security (CIP 14-2)	1) Transmission owners must perform initial and subsequent risk assessment of transmission stations and substations 2) Unaffiliated third party must verify risk assessment 3) Notify transmission operator if they have control of primary control center 4) Evaluate potential threats and vulnerabilities of physical attack on transmission stations 5) Develop documented physical security plans 6) Unaffiliated third party must verify security plan
Future	Electronic security perimeter(s) (CIP 5-7)	1) Electronic security perimeter 2) Remote access management 3) Vendor remote access management
	Configuration change management and vulnerability Assessments (CIP 10-4)	1) Configuration change management 2) Configuration monitoring 3) Vulnerability assessments
	Communications between control centers	1) Implement plan to mitigate risks of unauthorized disclosure or modification of real-time assessment and real-time monitoring data while transmitted between control centers
	Supply chain risk management (CIP 13-2)	1) Develop documented supply chain cybersecurity risk management plan 2) Implement the plan 3) Obtain CIP senior manager approval of plan

Source: NERC (n.d.).

controls required for each area. The NIST SP 800 series help meet the myriad of standards set forth in these control families.

Each control family sets forth the purpose of the control, who it applies to, the facilities involved, exemptions to the CIP, effective dates, background information for the control, the requirements and measures of the control, and how to comply with the control. For example, CIP 4-6 on personnel and training entails five requirements, or in this case, programs that BES owners must implement: 1) a security awareness program; 2) a cybersecurity training program; 3) a personnel risk assessment program; 4) an access management program; and 5) a program for access revocation. Each of the requirements are then broken down into parts and examples of measures taken that would provide evidence of fulfilling the requirement. Here again, these requirements echo what has been repeatedly discussed in this book as effective cybersecurity best practices.

10.4 State Laws

This section explores state and local cybersecurity legislation including security breach notification laws, data security and data disposal laws, and data protection and privacy laws. Local governments should examine their state's laws in order to determine what rules they are subject to follow.

10.4.1 State Cybersecurity Legislation

The National Conference of State Legislatures (NCSL), which tracks cybersecurity legislation annually, found that at least 45 states considered over 250 measures focusing on cybersecurity in 2021 (2021a). At the time of writing, 58 of the bills or resolutions have been enacted. This count does not include all cybersecurity appropriations enacted during the year. Clearly, there has been some state level movement and response to ongoing cybersecurity threats. The NCSL found four common issues that received the most legislative activity: mandating that government agencies implement formal security policies; conduct cybersecurity training and plan and test for incident response; regulating cybersecurity insurance; creating commissions or task forces to study cybersecurity issues; and supporting cybersecurity training and education programs. The first specifically deals with local government cybersecurity. Ongoing legislative activity around what local governments must implement and establish in terms of their cybersecurity is a welcome sign of needed attention and support. The remaining three issues receiving the most attention all indirectly impact local governments, as well. For example, local governments are purchasers of cybersecurity insurance. Task forces will likely study the impact of cyberattacks on the public sector. And assistance for cybersecurity education can only help address the skills gap facing the industry at large, and local governments more acutely.

10.4.2 Security Breach Notification Laws

According to the NCSL, all 50 states, DC, Puerto Rico, Guam, and the Virgin Islands have implemented security breach notification laws (2021b). Breach notification laws require organizations to notify individuals, government entities, and sometimes the media of cybersecurity breaches that expose citizen or customer PII. These laws vary depending on the size and type of organization affected, the number of records impacted, and the type of information exposed. Definitions of "breach," notice requirements, and exemptions vary as well. The types of organizations subject to these laws typically include governmental entities, educational institutions, businesses, and other organizations that collect and sell information. Not every law covers all types of organizations, so local governments must closely examine the security breach notification laws enacted in their state. Another aspect of breach notification laws that varies includes the types of records the laws govern, such as account numbers, identification numbers, drivers license information, name combined with social security number (SSN), user names and passwords, biometric information, medical information, and more. Additionally, the timing and method of notification can vary, as well as who must be notified and what information must be included in the notice. Exemptions generally provide "safe harbor" for data that is redacted, encrypted, unreadable, or unusable.

California's data breach notification law was passed in 2002 and was the first of its kind enacted in the country. It has become a model for many other state laws and provides a good example for what local governments are required to do when they experience a breach (Cal. Civil Code § 1798.25 – 1798.29). In California, if a local government experiences a breach and PII stored on its IT system is illegally acquired, the local government must notify the individuals whose PII has been exposed. The notification must be made "in the most expedient time possible and without unreasonable delay" unless law enforcement determines it will impede a criminal investigation. The law also requires written or electronic notice of the breach and provides a model notification form that local governments can follow (Table 10.4).

In addition to providing victims with meaningful information about the breach, the local government also has the discretion to provide information about what it has done to protect individuals whose information has been breached or provide advice on steps those individuals can take to protect themselves. If the breach impacts more than 500 California residents, the local government must notify the Attorney General, as well.

Table 10.4 Model breach notification form.

[Name of Local Government/Logo] Date: [insert date]	
NOTICE OF DATA BREACH	
What happened?	
What information was involved?	
What are we doing?	
What you can do.	
Other important information	
For more information:	Call [telephone number] or go to [internet website]

Source: Cal. Civil Code § 1798.25 – 1798.29

10.4.3 Data Security and Data Disposal Laws

According to the NCSL, 32 states have adopted some form of data security laws that require state agencies, and in some situations, local governments, to implement certain types of data security measures. Many of these laws were enacted in the two to three years prior to the publication of the NCSL report in 2020 (National Conference of State Legislatures, 2020). Data security laws govern how local governments protect the PII that they maintain and control how PII is protected, destroyed, disclosed, used, or modified. Data security laws in Alabama, Maryland, Nevada, and Utah explicitly include local governments. More states may include local governments in their definition of "public agency" or "state agency."

Some state data security laws cover specific types of information like, SSNs, health information, and financial or tax information. Others establish positions like information security and privacy officers, CIOs and CISOs, and set forth the roles of those officials. Still more require adoption of strategic policies, mandate annual assessments, and establish record keeping and training requirements and more.

Data destruction and retention rules cover when and how local governments destroy and dispose of personally identifiable information or make it unreadable. Sixteen states have instituted data disposal laws applicable to government (NCSL, 2019). Generally, these laws require that local governments take steps to protect against unauthorized access or use of the PII when it is being destroyed, considering the sensitivity of the information, the local government agency involved, and types of available destruction methods. Some of these laws are enforced through fines. HIPAA also mandates specific rules around the disposal of electronic health information.

10.4.4 Data Protection and Privacy Laws

Data protection and privacy laws are a recent trend in state-level cybersecurity legislation. These laws specifically deal with how organizations use, store, and destroy information they gather on individuals. They also provide certain rights to individuals in determining how they wish their data to be used, and whether they wish to have their data processed or tracked. Organizational obligations and consumer rights make up the bulk of these laws. These laws often also include rules on disposal of PII, protection of PII, and security breach notifications.

The International Association of Privacy Professionals (IAPP) follows state-level privacy legislation and of the 27 bills considered in 2021, two were enacted, six are still active, and 19 failed (Rippy, 2021a). As of this writing, three states have enacted data protection and privacy laws: California, Virginia, and Colorado. California's privacy law does not apply to governmental agencies (Office of the California Attorney General, n.d.). Virginia's law explicitly exempts political subdivisions of the Commonwealth, as well (Virginia General Assembly, 2021). However, the most recent addition to the group of states with a comprehensive privacy rights law, Colorado, explicitly includes governmental entities (Colorado Attorney General, n.d.). All of these laws are similar to one another and are modeled in whole or in part on the European Union's General Data Protection Regulation (GDPR).

The Colorado Privacy Act (CPA) applies to any organization that maintains, owns, or licenses PII or personal information on Colorado residents. The law primarily requires three things: that said organizations establish policies governing disposal of PII; that they take reasonable steps to protect PII; and that they notify residents and the Attorney General of breaches. The act contains many of the same rights and obligations set forth in the GDPR. These include: the right of access (to the personal data being stored); the right of rectification (or to correct inaccuracies in the personal data); the right of deletion (of personal data); the right of portability (or to obtain personal data in a usable format); the right to opt-out of certain automated decision-making (e.g., targeted advertisements, sale of personal data, or profiling in furtherance of significant decisions); and the right to appeal business denials (Rippy, 2021b). Local governments have seven duties they must meet in terms of data collection and processing (Table 10.5). These include notice and

Table 10.5 Rights and duties under the CPA.

Rights	Description
Right to opt out	Of processing of personal data for: • Targeted advertising • The sale of personal data • Profiling in decisions that produce "legal or similarly significant effects"
Right of access	To confirm whether their personal data is being processed, and gain access to the data
Right to correction	To correct inaccuracies in the personal data
Right to deletion	To delete personal data concerning the consumer
Right to data portability	To obtain personal data in a portable and readily usable format to transmit to another entity without hindrance

Duty	Description
Duty of transparency	Provide consumers with reasonably accessible, clear and meaningful privacy notice including: • The categories of personal data being collected/processed • Purposes for which they are processed • How and where consumers can exercise rights
Duty of purpose Specification	Specify the express purposes for which personal data are collected/processed
Duty of data minimization	"Collection of personal data must be adequate, relevant and limited to what is reasonably necessary to the specified purposes for which the data are processed"
Duty to avoid secondary use	Prohibits the processing of personal data for purpose not reasonably necessary or compatible with the specified purposes
Duty of care	Take reasonable measures to secure personal data in storage and use from unauthorized acquisition
Duty to avoid unlawful discrimination	Prohibits the processing of personal data in violation of laws prohibiting unlawful discrimination against consumers
Duty regarding sensitive data	Consent/parental consent required to process sensitive data

Source: Colorado General Assembly (2021).

transparency requirements, stated purpose and processing limitations for the personal data, protecting the data from unauthorized access, and consent for the processing of sensitive information. Enforcement of this law lies with the Colorado Attorney General's Office, as well as district attorneys, giving 60 days for organizations to cure violations.

10.5   European Union General Data Protection Regulation (GDPR)

Adopted in 2016 and implemented in 2018, the GDPR has set the global standard for comprehensive data protection and privacy laws (European Data Protection Supervisor, n.d.). The law establishes privacy and security regulations for organizations processing data on people residing in the EU, not necessarily EU citizens, but traffic from any person in the EU. It applies to organizations offering goods or services targeted to people in the EU or those that process and monitor data generated by those in the EU, including local governments in the US. Any organization processing or monitoring internet traffic from the EU technically falls under the purview of the GDPR. The GDPR's own explanation of the applicability of these rules state that it is unclear whether one-off visits to certain narrowly targeted websites by EU citizens would place an organization "in the crosshairs of European regulators? It's not likely. But technically you could be held accountable for tracking these data" (Wolford, 2021a). Applicability of the GDPR to local governments outside of the EU has generally been interpreted around whether the government is "targeting" EU residents when providing services (Kawamoto, 2018). For example, EU residents paying a water bill on a local government website might not fall under the GDPR, but local government tourism websites and advertisements targeted to those in the EU would (Kawamoto, 2018).

The GDPR sets forth seven principles of data protection including: lawfulness, fairness and transparency; purpose limitation; data minimization; accuracy; storage limitation; integrity and confidentiality; and accountability (Wolford, 2021b). Some of these mirror provisions of the Colorado Privacy Act discussed above. Lawfulness, fairness, and transparency around data processing means that it should be clear to the consumer that their data is processed in such a fashion. Purpose limitations specify that the data is processed for legitimate purposes that are explicitly stated to the consumer. Data minimization means only the data required should be collected and processed for the specified purposes. Accuracy involves keeping the information up-to-date, storage limitation means the data is stored for only as long as it is needed, integrity and confidentiality means that processing should be done with encryption so that it is secure, and accountability means organizations are able to demonstrate compliance with the GDPR.

GDPR also establishes eight innovative, if not at times controversial, privacy rights for EU citizens, including: the right to be informed; the right of access; the right of rectification; the right to erasure; the right to restrict processing; the right to data portability; the right to object; and rights in relation to automated decision-making and profiling. Again, the rights of information, access, rectification, erasure, to restrict processing (or opt out), to data portability, and to object are all parallel to the rights afforded by the CPA. Rights related to automated decision-making and profiling is reflected in the CPA's duty to avoid unlawful discrimination.

Last, American local governments should be aware that although the GDPR has yet to be enforced against them, GDPR regulations technically would apply to local governments tracking data from the EU. Therefore local governments should keep the GDPR regulations in mind as similar data security and privacy rules continue to be introduced in legislatures in the US.

10.6 Federal Legislation

Since FISMA was enacted in 2002, there has been no major cybersecurity legislation passed by the US Congress and signed into law. Despite many attempts at passing such comprehensive legislation, only Presidential Executive Orders have been issued in the interim. See, for example: President Obama's EO 13636 on Improving Critical Infrastructure Cybersecurity (2013), which established the NIST Cybersecurity Framework (covered in Chapter 9); President Trump's EO 13800 on Strengthening the Cybersecurity of Federal Networks and Critical Infrastructure (2017), which encouraged modernization of federal IT and partnerships with industry; and President Biden's EO 14028 on Improving the Nation's Cybersecurity (2021) focused on bolstering the software supply chain (discussed in Chapter 12).

10.6.1 Recently Enacted

The recently enacted Infrastructure Investment and Jobs Act, also known as the Bipartisan Infrastructure Framework, created a $1 billion state, local, tribal and territorial (SLTT) cybersecurity grant program to be administered by the Federal Emergency Management Agency in consultation with CISA (Infrastructure Investment and Jobs Act, 2021). The Act's other cybersecurity measures include authorizing the Department of Homeland Security to declare that a significant cybersecurity incident has occurred or is likely to occur and to provide voluntary assistance to non-federal entities in responding to and recovering from the incident, and creating a Cyber Response and Recovery Fund to assist in recovery from such incidents. Additionally, the Act regulates other aspects of infrastructure cybersecurity including: promoting the creation of public-private partnerships to enhance the security of the electric grid; creating the Energy Cyber Sense program to test the cybersecurity of products and technologies used in the energy sector; creating incentives for advanced cybersecurity technology investment in the electric grid; establishing the Rural and Municipal Utility Advanced Cybersecurity Grant and Technical Assistance Program; and more. Cybersecurity measures are also included for highways, water systems, and research and innovation.

10.6.2 Pending Legislation

As of this writing, at least 13 bills concerning cybersecurity have been introduced in the 117th Congress (2021–2023). Many of these bills attempt to address issues around cyber workforce training, supply chain security, and international competitiveness with China (Hecht and Fjeld, 2021). They also attempt to reinvigorate federal abilities to address cybersecurity by forming new departments, such as the proposed Bureau of International Cyberspace Policy or International Technology Partnership Office at the Department of State, or granting additional authority to other agencies, such as the Federal Trade Commission (FTC). Some have proposed directing the FTC to open a bureau to investigate security and privacy issues in the organizations that the agency oversees (Shepardson and Bartz, 2021).

The Cyber Incident Notification Act would require that federal agencies, government contractors, and critical infrastructure operators notify CISA of a detected breach within 24 hours and would grant reporting organizations limited immunity (Office of Senator Mark Warner, 2021). While some local government agencies are undoubtedly considered critical infrastructure, such as water treatment or electricity distribution, not all local governments would be subject to this reporting requirement. A federal privacy bill, similar to the CPA and the GDPR, has also been introduced although it is unclear whether sufficient political will to pass such a bill currently exists (Information Transparency and Personal Data Control Act, 2021).

Two particularly comprehensive bills, the Senate's United States Innovation and Competition Act and the House of Representative's more expansive response bill, The America COMPETES Act, would establish regional cybersecurity hubs partnering government, private, and academic stakeholders (United States Innovation and Competition Act, 2021; The America COMPETES Act, 2022). Additionally, they would award strategy development and strategy implementation grants to eligible regional technology and innovation hubs. The bill would also establish a Directorate for Science and Engineering Solutions in the National Science Foundation. The main purpose of both bills is to attempt to address supply chain gaps, vulnerabilities in critical infrastructure, and to boost the standing of the US as a global leader in AI and high performance computing and manufacturing. While its unclear what, if any, standards either version would create for local governments, if reconciled and passed the legislation, and others like it would undoubtedly impact local government cybersecurity down the line.

10.7 Conclusions and Recommendations

This chapter presents a representation of the matrix of federal, state, and international cybersecurity regulations facing American local governments. Cybersecurity compliance is complex and requires expertise in the form of cybersecurity counsel, privacy officers, or compliance officers. For many local governments, this function may need to be outsourced to third-party vendors offering services that help local governments comply with the wide variety of federally mandated security measures.

Local government officials should, at the very least, be aware that such compliance requirements exist. It is up to the CIO, CISO, and IT staff to implement the necessary measures to protect the local government's information systems and assets from unauthorized access or use. They must be given the tools and resources required to do so. Without such awareness and support, the local government and its officials might very well be at risk of violating the law and be subject to fines or other punishments for unauthorized data disclosure. Following these policies and regulations means implementing high-level cybersecurity standards and controls that will best help protect the local government. Specifically, implementing security measures from NIST's Special Publication 800 series helps meet many of these various requirements.

Proposed cybersecurity legislation from the 117th Congress indicates a new willingness and push at the US federal level to regulate cybersecurity in the face of constant cyberattacks and increased international competition. Local governments should anticipate federal and/or state level requirements for breach notifications and threat-information sharing (with CISA and other federal agencies) in the not too distant future. There may also be opportunities for grant funding to help boost local government cybersecurity. However, until then, local governments must navigate the plethora of federal, state, and international cybersecurity regulations to which they are subject without much guidance and assistance from higher levels of government.

References

Bureau of Justice Assistance, US Department of Justice. (n.d.). *Electronic Communications Privacy Act of 1986 (ECPA).* https://bja.ojp.gov/program/it/privacy-civil-liberties/authorities/statutes/1285

California Civil Code § 1798.25 – 1798.29 et sec.

California Office of the Attorney General (n.d.). *California consumer privacy act (CCPA).* https://oag.ca.gov/privacy/ccpa#:~:text=No.,nonprofit%20organizations%20or%20government%20agencies

Chabrow, E. (2009, September 24). *PCI: A vital standard for government.* GovInfoSecurity. https://www.govinfosecurity.com/blogs/pci-vital-standard-for-government-p-311

Colorado Attorney General (n.d.). *Colorado's consumer data protection laws: FAQ's for businesses and government agencies.* https://coag.gov/resources/data-protection-laws

Colorado General Assembly (2021). Colorado Privacy Act, S.B. 21-190, http://leg.colorado.gov/sites/default/files/documents/2021A/bills/2021a_190_rer.pdf

Computer Fraud and Abuse Act of 1986, 18 USC § 1030 (1986).

Criminal Justice Information Services, US Federal Bureau of Investigation (2020, June 01). *Criminal justice information service (CJIS) security policy version 5.9.* https://www.fbi.gov/file-repository/cjis_security_policy_v5-9_20200601.pdf/view

Electronic Communications Privacy Act of 1986, 18 USC Chapter 119 (1986).

European Data Protection Supervisor (n.d.). *The history of the general data protection regulation.* https://edps.europa.eu/data-protection/data-protection/legislation/history-general-data-protection-regulation_en

Exec. Order No. 13636, 78 Fed. Reg. 11737 (February 12, 2013).

Exec. Order No. 13800, 82 Fed. Reg. 22391 (May 11, 2017).

Exec. Order No. 14028, 86 Fed. Reg. 26633 (May 12, 2021).

Family Educational Rights and Privacy Act (FERPA) of 1974, 34 CFR § 99 *et seq.* (2011).

Federal Information Processing Standards Publication (2004, February). *FIPS Pub. 199: Standards for security categorization of federal information and information systems.* https://nvlpubs.nist.gov/nistpubs/FIPS/NIST.FIPS.199.pdf

Federal Information Processing Standards Publication (2006, March). *FIPS Pub. 200: Minimum security requirements for federal information and information systems.* https://nvlpubs.nist.gov/nistpubs/FIPS/NIST.FIPS.200.pdf

Hecht, A., and Fjeld, C.T. (2021, May 05). *Cyber policy legislative tracker.* Mintz. https://www.mintz.com/insights-center/viewpoints/2236/2021-05-04-cyber-policy-legislative-tracker

Information Transparency and Personal Data Control Act, H.R. 1816, 117th Congress (2021). https://www.congress.gov/bill/117th-congress/house-bill/1816

Infrastructure Investment and Jobs Act, H.R. 3684, 117th Congress (2021). https://www.congress.gov/bill/117th-congress/house-bill/3684

Internal Revenue Service, US Department of the Treasury (2016, September 30). *Publication 1075 Tax information security guidelines for federal, state and local agencies.* https://www.irs.gov/pub/irs-pdf/p1075.pdf

Internal Revenue Service, US Department of the Treasury (2021, March 4). *Safeguards program.* https://www.irs.gov/privacy-disclosure/safeguards-program

Kawamoto, D. (2018, May 2). *Will GDPR rules impact states and localities?* Government Technology. https://www.govtech.com/data/will-gdpr-rules-impact-states-and-localities.html#:~:text=%E2%80%9CFederal%2C%20state%20and%20local%20governments,are%20not%20exempt%20under%20GDPR.%E2%80%9D

National Conference of State Legislatures (2019, January 4). *Data disposal laws.* https://www.ncsl.org/research/telecommunications-and-information-technology/data-disposal-laws.aspx

National Conference of State Legislatures (2020, February 14). *Data security laws state government.* https://www.ncsl.org/research/telecommunications-and-information-technology/data-security-laws-state-government.aspx

National Conference of State Legislatures (2021a, June 22). *Cybersecurity Legislation 2021.* https://www.ncsl.org/research/telecommunications-and-information-technology/cybersecurity-legislation-2021.aspx#:~:text=2021%20Introductions&text=Requiring%20government%20agencies%20to%20implement,industry%20or%20addressing%20cybersecurity%20insurance

National Conference of State Legislatures (2021b, April 15). *Security breach notification laws.* https://www.ncsl.org/research/telecommunications-and-information-technology/security-breach-notification-laws.aspx

North American Electric Reliability Corporation (n.d.). *Critical infrastructure protection.* https://www.nerc.com/pa/Stand/Pages/CIPStandards.aspx

Office of Senator Warner, M.R. (2021, July 21). *Following solarwinds and colonial hacks, leading national security senators introduce bipartisan cyber reporting bill* [press release]. https://www.warner.senate.gov/public/index.cfm/2021/7/following-solarwinds-colonial-hacks-leading-national-security-senators-introduce-bipartisan-cyber-reporting-bill

PCI Security Standards Council LLC (n.d.). *Maintaining payment security.* https://www.pcisecuritystandards.org/merchants/process

PCI Security Standards Council LLC (2008). *PCI data storage do's and don'ts.* https://www.pcisecuritystandards.org/pdfs/pci_fs_data_storage.pdf

Rippy, S. (2021a, July 08). *US state privacy legislation tracker.* International Association of Privacy Professionals. https://iapp.org/resources/article/us-state-privacy-legislation-tracker

Rippy, S. (2021b, July 08). *Colorado privacy act becomes law.* International Association of Privacy Professionals. https://iapp.org/news/a/colorado-privacy-act-becomes-law

Shepardson, D. and Bartz, D. (2021, September 10). *US lawmakers seek $1 bln to fund FTC privacy probes.* Reuters. https://www.reuters.com/business/retail-consumer/us-lawmakers-seek-1-bln-fund-ftc-privacy-probes-2021-09-10

Taylor, L.P. (2013). FISMA trickles into the private sector. In Patricia Moulder, Technical Editor, *FISMA Compliance handbook.* Syngress.

The America COMPETES Act of 2022, H.R. 4521, 117th Congress (2022). https://docs.house.gov/billsthisweek/20220131/BILLS-117HR4521RH-RCP117-31.pdf

The Utility Connection (n.d.). *251 Publicly owned electric and gas utilities (US).* http://www.utilityconnection.com/page2e.asp

United States Innovation and Competition Act of 2021, Pub. L. No. 117-58, 135 Stat. 429 (2021). https://www.congress.gov/bill/117th-congress/senate-bill/1260

U.S. Department of Education Privacy Technical Assistance Center (2015, July). *Data security checklist.* https://studentprivacy.ed.gov/sites/default/files/resource_document/file/Data%20Security%20Checklist_0.pdf

U.S. Department of Health and Human Services (2013, July 26). *Summary of the HIPAA privacy rule.* https://www.hhs.gov/hipaa/for-professionals/privacy/laws-regulations/index.html

US Federal Bureau of Investigation (n.d.). *Criminal justice information service (CJIS).* https://www.fbi.gov/services/cjis

US National Institute of Standards and Technology (NIST) (2017, June). *NIST Special Publication 800-63-3: Digital identity guidelines.* https://nvlpubs.nist.gov/nistpubs/SpecialPublications/NIST.SP.800-63-3.pdf

US National Institute of Standards and Technology (NIST) (2020a, September). *NIST special publication 800-53 Revision 5: Security and privacy controls for information systems and organizations.* https://nvlpubs.nist.gov/nistpubs/SpecialPublications/NIST.SP.800-53r5.pdf

US National Institute of Standards and Technology (NIST) (2020b, February). *NIST Special publication 800-171 Revision 2: Protecting controlled unclassified information in nonfederal systems and organizations.* https://nvlpubs.nist.gov/nistpubs/SpecialPublications/NIST.SP.800-171r2.pdf

Van Buren v. United States, No. 19-783, 2021.

Virginia General Assembly (2021). *Virginia consumer data protection act, S.B. 1392,* https://lis.virginia.gov/cgi-bin/legp604.exe?211+ful+SB1392

Wolford, B. (2021a). *Does the GDPR apply to companies outside of the EU?* GDPR.eu. https://gdpr.eu/companies-outside-of-europe

Wolford, B. (2021b). *What is GDPR, the EU's new data protection law?* GDPR.eu. https://gdpr.eu/what-is-gdpr

11

Important Questions to Ask

11.1 Introduction

This chapter, perhaps more than any other, is directed especially toward the top elected and appointed officials in local governments, although it will also be valuable to all staff regardless of pay grade or position. The chapter presents and provides brief answers to a number of questions that top local government officials should ask themselves and their cybersecurity teams. Asking should not be a simple one-off action, but rather an ongoing process. It is not sufficient, for example, for officials to ask the cybersecurity team what IT assets are being protected (Section 11.2) only once, because the number and types of assets change over time. Likewise, it is not sufficient to ask only once about the principal cyberthreats the local government is facing (Section 11.3) because the nature and severity of those threats change over time, just as does the underlying technology.

However, local officials need not pester cybersecurity staff with relentless and unnecessary questioning (after all, these staff members have important work to do!) Ideally, top officials should require regularly scheduled briefings by their governments' cybersecurity leadership to ensure that these and presumably other questions are asked and answered.

The questions discussed in this chapter are based upon industry experience, best practices, and recent academic research regarding local government cybersecurity. Presented in no particular order, they are intended to serve as a solid, although not a comprehensive or exhaustive starting point to highlight some of the most important cybersecurity issues about which top local officials should inquire.

11.2 What Should My Local Government Be Protecting?

The first step in information protection is knowing what actually needs protecting. As discussed in Chapter 2, the goal of cybersecurity is to protect a local government's "networks, devices, and data from unauthorized access" and to "ensur[e] confidentiality, integrity, and availability of information" (US Cybersecurity Infrastructure and Security Agency [CISA], 2019). This includes local government systems, platforms, data repositories, workflows, computers, cellphones, modems, servers, routers, and more. Local

Cybersecurity and Local Government, First Edition. Donald F. Norris, Laura K. Mateczun and Richard F. Forno.
© 2022 John Wiley & Sons Ltd. Published 2022 by John Wiley & Sons Ltd.

government IT or cybersecurity staff must first develop an inventory of these systems and devices, as well as any processes and procedures currently in effect. Additionally, the staff should work to understand where any points of vulnerability – both technical and operational – might exist by conducting a formal risk-analysis process. This will help identify everything that needs protection.

For example, a local government comptroller or tax office might deem the ability to collect tax payments a critical local service. However, it is not simply the website that citizens and businesses pay taxes through that must be protected. The computer servers (web servers, databases, etc.) in the tax office and any external connections to payment processors, internet providers, or other government entities across the locality must be considered part of the tax collection workflow. Taken together, this one government service actually reflects a comprehensive and potentially complicated information environment that must be evaluated and protected, and demonstrates how cybersecurity considerations are so pervasive across modern organizations in ways that may not often be considered if you only protect individual computers. The NIST Cybersecurity Framework (Chapter 9) and specifically the NIST Risk Management Framework can help local governments identify cybersecurity assets and vulnerabilities, and guide plans and activities that make the best use of the often scarce financial and personnel resources available for this monumental task (NIST, n.d.).

Due to the often federated and decentralized nature of local governments it is frequently difficult to obtain a complete view of everything within the IT organization's purview. However, at the minimum, IT and cybersecurity staff should know the critical systems, resources, and workflows within their local government environment to have a clear understanding of what it is they are being charged with protecting. Just as in the five functions of cybersecurity cycle discussed in Chapters 2 and 9, local governments must continuously identify the information systems and assets that make critical service delivery possible.

11.3   What are the Biggest Cybersecurity Threats Facing My Local Government?

As this book heads to press in late 2021, the biggest cybersecurity threat is almost undoubtedly ransomware attacks. These attacks have increased in number considerably during the COVID-19 pandemic and are expected to continue to become even more frequent in number and severe in nature. This is partly because they are so profitable and there is so little risk to the attackers that they will be caught and prosecuted (see Chapters 1, 3, and 12). Phishing and spear phishing attacks (which are often used to deliver ransomware and other types of malware) are also increasing and pose a significant threat to local governments.

In addition to the prominence of ransomware, various sources suggest that there are additional threats that make the list of top cybersecurity concerns, including attacks on IoT devices, credential harvesting, zero day exploits, insider threats, attacks on third parties and cloud providers, DoS and DDoS attacks, and more (e.g., GDATA, 2021; Goddard, 2021; Gurinaviciute, 2021).

It is fair to say that regardless of the threat, all pose serious risks, and all require strong cybersecurity defenses. Just like preparing for power outages or weather events, local governments must adopt appropriate plans and make adequate preparations to take the necessary actions to keep their operations functioning during and after attacks. In some cases, additional funding or staffing capabilities may be required to accomplish this necessary task.

11.4 Who is in Charge of Cybersecurity in My Local Government?

Typically, the answer is the CISO or other staff member formally assigned this responsibility. However, who is in charge varies in practice. Larger, more well-funded local governments are likely to have experienced and well-trained CISOs and more extensive cybersecurity capabilities and staffing. Smaller jurisdictions, on the other hand, are likely to have smaller budgets, fewer staff, and the smallest may not only lack a CISO but also one or more full-time, trained staff members to address cybersecurity, if not routine IT matters.

Additionally, the degree of responsibility assigned to the CISO or other staff person in charge of cybersecurity (hereafter, just CISO) will also vary by having more or less authority. In some local governments the CISO will have total responsibility for cybersecurity across the organization. For example, the 2020 CISO survey found that nearly two-thirds of CISOs had total responsibility while in just over one-third responsibility was divided. In one of the cities with divided cybersecurity responsibility, San Francisco, the CISO has to deal with 52 separate departments that are semi-autonomous (Norris, 2021).

In every local government, ultimate responsibility for all functions rests with the chief elected official or officials and/or the top appointed manager. This is not to say that these officials will be as knowledgeable about or as fluent in cybersecurity as cybersecurity professionals, although some might well be. Rather, the top officials will look to their cybersecurity staff to advise them. However, the final decision-making authority on cybersecurity issues remains theirs. Yet, when something goes wrong, the proverbial *buck* – as Harry Truman wryly noted – stops with the top elected officials. This said, the buck may pause elsewhere on its way to the top, as it did in Baltimore after the 2019 ransomware attack when the CIO who had warned officials about cybersecurity weaknesses was essentially fired (see Chapter 1).

Finally, and to no one's surprise, who is really in charge in at least some few jurisdictions, may not be who actually is listed on the organization chart. It may be someone (elected or appointed) behind the scenes or perhaps someone not part of the local government at all (such as a major donor or vendor) with sufficient knowledge or influence to affect decision-making around and administration of this vital function. Large "P" politics may also play a role in cybersecurity in some local governments where, for example, political ideology drives or at least influences outsourcing decisions and vendor awards. Needless to say, these exceptions are never in the best interests of good local government administration and should be scrupulously avoided, and, if identified, firmly remedied to the extent possible.

Local governments should always have a clear cybersecurity chain of command, at the head of which is a trained, experienced CISO who is formally invested with sufficient authority and responsibility to manage this function. There should be no question in any official or staff member's mind about who is in charge. If there is (especially if it is widespread within the organization), surely problems will follow, especially during adverse cybersecurity events.

11.5 Is Cybersecurity Properly Staffed in My Local Government?

There is no easy way to answer whether your local government cybersecurity function is properly staffed. The 2020 CISO survey that one of the authors conducted (mentioned in Chapters 5 and 6) addressed this question and found considerable variation in cybersecurity staffing among the local governments in the survey (Norris, 2021). For example, one city reported no in-house cybersecurity staff, and one reported 24. The number of cybersecurity staff was not exactly proportional to local government population, although larger governments generally had more cybersecurity staff. Among the smaller jurisdictions in the survey (less than 700,000 residents), the number of in-house cybersecurity staff ranged from zero to 12. Among the mid-size larger jurisdictions (between 700,000 and 1 million), one had zero, one had five, one eight, and one 14. Among the larger jurisdictions (between one million and nearly four million), one had seven, one nine, one 12, and one 24.

Some sources suggest that cybersecurity staffing should be a percentage (usually in the range of 5 to 10 percent) of an organization's IT staff (e.g., Fimlaid, 2019; Mehravari and Allen, 2016). This may not be the best advice because IT staffing may be quite small or unusually large, so a percentage guideline may not produce satisfactory staffing results for every local government. A better approach might be to examine the types and range of cybersecurity functions that must be performed in a local government and then estimate the number of staff and skill sets required for those functions. A second, and complementary approach might be to determine the number of cybersecurity personnel in similarly sized local governments whose cybersecurity functions are similar. Whatever approach is taken, top local officials should carefully examine what is needed to ensure that cybersecurity is adequately staffed and then, within budgetary limitations, authorize the CISO to advertise, recruit, and hire the appropriate number of qualified staff.

11.6 Does My Local Government Budget Adequately for Cybersecurity?

As noted at various points in this book, studies have repeatedly found that inadequate funding is the top barrier to cybersecurity in American local governments. The 2016 nationwide survey found that the top four barriers to cybersecurity were inability to pay competitive salaries, insufficient number of cybersecurity staff, lack of funds, and lack of adequately trained personnel. And each of these barriers is linked to funding (Norris et al., 2019). So, it is likely that many local governments may not be funding cybersecurity adequately, either.

The IT research and advisory firm Gartner found that average spending by US businesses on cybersecurity is between 5 and 8 percent of companies' IT budgets (Nash, 2019). Among the local governments in the 2020 survey, the average amount of cybersecurity spending was 4 percent of the IT budget, and the range was between zero and 10 percent. Just over half of these governments spent less on cybersecurity (as a percentage of their IT budgets) than Gartner found among US businesses, while one-third were within or greater than Gartner's estimate (Nash, 2019).

One way for local officials to learn if the cybersecurity budget is sufficiently adequate is to regularly ask their CISOs this question, although the answer provided may not be totally objective. One complaint often heard from business executives and local government officials is that IT departments are always asking for more money. Therefore, it is important to obtain a more objective picture of cybersecurity funding needs versus funds actually budgeted. This can be accomplished by comparing available cybersecurity resources against similarly sized local governments in the region, conducting a risk analysis to help determine the likely scope of an appropriately sized cybersecurity capability, or engaging with consultants and other third parties to provide management analysis and advice on how to balance necessary cybersecurity requirements with current or projected funding availability.

11.7 Does My Local Government Follow Cybersecurity Best Practices?

For nearly thirty years, government, industry, and academic experts have developed and promulgated many best practice recommendations regarding how to build and sustain effective cybersecurity in organizations. This book contains an entire chapter (9) about the NIST Cybersecurity Framework, a document that epitomizes current cybersecurity best practices, and Chapter 7 discusses essential cybersecurity policies. If local governments follow cybersecurity best practice recommendations like these, they will be able to provide acceptable, if not high, levels of cybersecurity for their information assets. Properly implemented, many of these recommendations (known as cyber-hygiene) can reduce the chances of both accidental and malicious cybersecurity incidents.

Unfortunately, studies have shown that, on average, local governments do not practice cybersecurity effectively. The results of the 2016 survey, discussed in Chapter 6, make this strikingly clear. Only 55 percent of respondents said that their local government's cybersecurity *technology* was at the level of best practice, only 43 percent said their *practices* were at that level, and less than one-third said that their policies were at that level with one-quarter saying that their policies were one generation behind (Norris et al., 2020).

But how can local officials know if their governments are following best practices? Perhaps the best way is to task the CISO with reporting at least annually to top officials about which best practices have been implemented, whether they are fully or only partially implemented, whether there have been any implementation problems, whether all relevant personnel, elected and otherwise, have been trained in cybersecurity awareness and hygiene and are practicing it properly and more. Officials in larger local governments (and those with sufficient funding) may want to periodically hire security firms or seek assistance from other security experts (e.g., local universities, the National Guard cyber units, CISA, etc.) to conduct independent audits of their governments' cybersecurity policies, procedures, and practices to ensure that they are following best practices. The bottom line is to ask and then to verify and, as has been noted elsewhere in this chapter, make sure that this is an ongoing process and not a one-off exercise.

11.8   Do My Local Government's Cybersecurity Policies and Procedures Match What is Happening in Practice?

This is an easy one to answer. Following the recommendations of the previous section, ask, keep asking, and verify. Then ask again. Use independent external organizations to conduct audits as needed. Additionally, local government cybersecurity and IT organizations should engage in an internal process of continual self-assessment and improvement to ensure not only effectiveness of their cybersecurity program and activities, but that it remains effective against an ever-changing threat and vulnerability landscape.

11.9   How Does My Local Governments Ensure Continuous Improvement for Cybersecurity?

Effective cybersecurity is a journey, not a destination. Cybersecurity should also be considered a process of continuous improvement (e.g., Gelnaw, 2019; Interactive.com, 2021). A continuous improvement process is needed because the threat landscape is constantly changing and evolving. As a result, local governments must continuously adapt to the changing cybersecurity environment. This can be accomplished through a process of continuous improvement in which local governments constantly monitor for threats, identify and examine risks, and make any adjustments needed in their cybersecurity program to counter the threats and mitigate the risks identified in the monitoring process.

   One reason for the failure of so many organizations, in both the public and private sectors, to follow a continuous improvement process is that many of their top executives think in terms of models that emphasize cybersecurity in fortification terms – building firewalls, etc. "The problem with these mental models is that they treat cybersecurity as a finite problem that can be solved, rather than the ongoing process that it is" (Lohrmann, 2019).

   To ensure that their governments engage in continuous improvement, local officials should task their CISOs to conduct regular briefings on how the continuous cybersecurity improvement process works in their governments, if one exists, and what are the results of that process. If a continuous improvement process does not exist, or has only been partially implemented, these officials should task their CISOs with establishing one or fully implementing one.

11.10 Do All Officials and Employees in My Local Government Receive Adequate Cybersecurity Training?

To answer this question, top local officials need to ask their cybersecurity leadership what training is offered, how frequently it is offered, whether it is mandatory or optional, and whether any means are employed to periodically test if end users are practicing proper cybersecurity hygiene. Answers to the first two will provide information about whether the right training is being provided and whether it is offered frequently enough. At a minimum, local governments should provide cybersecurity awareness training for all officials, staff, contractors, indeed all parties who use their governments' IT systems and networks. The training must be mandatory for all, and accountability mechanisms should be developed in order to ensure that all users practice proper cybersecurity hygiene (see Chapter 8).

Some of the more important components of cybersecurity awareness training include: ensuring users understand the local government's rules concerning computer, email, internet, and social media usage; password rules; how to identify and what to do about social engineering (phishing and more); rules concerning BYOD, and the rules concerning working remotely, among other items.

It is helpful to conclude the training with quizzes or scored games to find out if users actually learned what was taught in the trainings. If it appears that learning did not occur satisfactorily, then perhaps re-training is needed or maybe the training itself needs to be re-tooled or some combination of both.

Additionally, cybersecurity staff should run periodic tests to determine if end users are practicing what they have learned from the training. This could be something as simple as a phishing email designed to trick unwary users into opening an attachment or clicking on a URL or dropping USB drives around the facility to see if users connect them to their computers (thus potentially launching a malware attack) or bring them to IT instead. Perhaps consider contests to recognize employees who demonstrate sound cybersecurity practices. Those who fail tests should be required to attend further trainings. Repeated failures could result in the loss of some or all computer use privileges and in extreme cases result in termination of employment. It's important to remember that cybersecurity training activities can be as innovative, creative, and even as fun as imagination or budgets allow, which in turn can facilitate greater participation and learning by turning an otherwise boring required task into something interesting and even rewarding.

11.11 Is My Local Government Able to Detect Cyberattacks?

As discussed earlier in this book, it is essential that local governments are able to detect attacks, incidents, and breaches. If they cannot, they are essentially operating blind. The 2016 survey found that fewer than half of local governments were prepared to detect attacks – 42 percent, incidents – 38 percent, and breaches – 36 percent (Norris et al., 2019). These capabilities have almost certainly improved since the survey was conducted at least among larger and more well-funded local governments. Unfortunately, it is questionable if others have improved substantially. Therefore, local officials should task their CISOs to brief them periodically on measures being taken to ensure that their local governments are taking all the means necessary to detect attacks, incidents, and breaches, to explain those measures, and describe their effectiveness.

Detection of attacks, incidents, or suspicious activity comes in many forms. Most frequently, the proper deployment of sensors such as firewalls and intrusion prevention systems that monitor networks, along with security tools on individual computers like antimalware software, is the first step, as is subscribing to third-party threat monitoring services. Data from these sensors can be fed into a Security Information and Event Management (SIEM) system that provides IT and cybersecurity staff an aggregated top-down picture of the activity on their networks to allow them to identify and respond to potentially malicious activity more quickly. Additionally, the IT help desk can be a source of incident detection based on what type of inquiries are received from users reporting problems or other anomalies happening on their computers. Unfortunately, some incidents (including data breaches) are only discovered through third party and media reports after the fact.

11.12 Is My Local Government Able to Respond Effectively to Adverse Cybersecurity Events?

The 2016 survey found that only 27 percent of local governments were prepared to recover from breaches, 25 percent to recover from exfiltration of data, and 48 percent to recover from ransomware attacks (Norris et al., 2019). As mentioned above, this has no doubt improved among at least some local governments, but among those without adequate resources and staffing it probably remains unsatisfactory.

In order to be able to recover from adverse cybersecurity events, it is essential that local governments adopt and implement at least the following policies: acceptable use policy, information security policy, privacy policy, identity and access management policy, incident handling policy, and disaster recovery/business continuity policy, which will help them to understand the actions that must be taken to respond to cybersecurity incidents. Chapter 7 describes these policies – and others – in greater detail.

11.13 Should My Local Government Try to Build Cybersecurity Partnerships and, if So, with What Organizations?

The answer to this question is a resounding yes. First, local governments should develop proactive relationships with local, state, and federal law enforcement organizations that handle cybersecurity investigations. For example, the FBI facilitates industry-specific Information Sharing Analysis Centers (ISACs) that have local government affiliates, as do the Department of Justice's Joint Terrorism Task Forces (JTTFs). Perhaps the largest ISAC related to local governments is the Multi-State Information Sharing and Analysis Center (MS-ISAC), which has at least 10,706 local governments and local government agencies and organizations as partners (MS-ISAC, n.d.). MS-ISAC membership comes with access to threat advisories, a cyber alert map, incident response services, education materials, and tabletop cybersecurity exercises, a 24/7 security operation center, a Malicious Code Analysis Platform (MCAP), a Vulnerability Management Program (VMP), and more. Regional information sharing organizations like the New York City Cyber Critical Service and Infrastructure (CCSI) Project, which has 282 members, also offer the opportunity to share threat intelligence (Manhattan District Attorneys Office, n.d.; Paul, 2021). The Coalition of City CISOs is a smaller, more targeted organization for cybersecurity operations leaders of larger municipalities to network, and share best practices and threat information (Coalition of City CISOs, n.d.).

In addition to the FBI and MS-ISAC, local governments should consider forming relationships with CISA, which provides assistance in incident response through the National Cybersecurity and Communications Integration Center (CISA, 2021). CISA has 10 regional offices throughout the country which provide services to critical infastructure providers and state and local governments, and whose Regional Directors are excellent points of contact for relationship building and in times of emergency (CISAc, n.d.) CISA also offers a range of assessment tools such as: vulnerability scanning; phishing campaign assessment; risk and vulnerability assessment; cyber resilience review; external dependencies management assessment; cyber infrastructure survey; remote penetration testing; web application scanning; Cyber Security Evaluation Tool (CSET®); and validated architecture design review (CISAa, n.d.).

Local government cybersecurity departments should seek out, join, and participate in local, regional, national, and/or global working groups, task forces, associations, training events, infrastructure providers, utilities, hospitals, etc. to gain professional and operational networking opportunities, share information about threats and risks, learn, and otherwise mutually support the cybersecurity community. Professional organizations such as the International City/County Management Association, the National Association of Counties, and the Public Technology Institute all provide up-to date cybersecurity resources and recommendations for local governments.

In an ideal world, such professional and personal relationships should be established and developed *before*, not during or after, a cybersecurity incident occurs. Doing so frequently provides those involved a "running start" as they begin preparing the response. If relationships with law enforcement organizations that can assist with cybersecurity investigations are already formed, the built trust and familiarity can help with a more quick and efficient process of incident response and mitigation. Information-sharing organizations, like MS-ISAC, help local government cybersecurity departments keep abreast of the latest threats and trends in order to better identify an incident when it occurs, and to address known vulnerabilities.

Local governments might also consider forming relationships with regional academic institutions, like universities, community colleges, and technical schools for cybersecurity internships, job placements, and more. For example, the Center for Advanced Red Teaming at the University at Albany works with organizations in the public (and private) sector to help anticipate, prevent, and mitigate cybersecurity incidents (The Center for Advanced Red Teaming, n.d.). Red Teaming is a process by which a team of people tests an organization's information systems to identify any vulnerabilities in practice, which also helps train the team of testers. Such partnerships can help address the skills gap in local government cybersecurity by creating a pipeline to employment for local, trained cybersecurity practitioners.

11.14   Does My Local Government Follow the NIST Cybersecurity Framework's Standards?

The answer to this question can be relatively straightforward as a yes or no. However, as discussed in Chapter 9, there is not exactly a clear line or point when a local government can say, "yes, the NIST Cybersecurity Framework has been fully implemented." The more correct answer would be, "yes, the local government cybersecurity department has incorporated the NIST Cybersecurity Framework into its cybersecurity program and planning, which we follow to the best of our ability and available resources."

   The framework provides a process and tool through which local governments can identify and assess its current cybersecurity posture, and plan for where it wishes to be in the future. The framework's categories and subcategories describe the steps a local government must take in order to meet a specific desired outcome regarding an aspect of the organization's cybersecurity. Depending on the unique characteristics of the local government and the services it provides, different areas of the framework may be more robustly followed than others. They also directly link to the specific industry standards and NIST special publications that set forth the technical requirements for meeting those outcomes. Following the NIST Cybersecurity Framework as closely as possible will ensure the local government has implemented current cybersecurity best practices and standards and have a high level of cybersecurity protection.

11.15   Does My Local Government Need Cybersecurity Insurance?

Cybersecurity insurance can help protect local governments against losses related to cyberattacks and breaches. Although policies can vary widely, covered expenses typically include the cost of notifying individuals and providing credit-monitoring services for those whose PII has been affected by a breach, as well as costs related to recovering data and restoring systems to a functioning state. Legal costs related to litigation subsequent to a breach, or regulatory proceedings can also be covered by cybersecurity insurance. Crisis management, forensics, and loss of income might also be included. These costs are generally not included in general liability insurance policies. Local governments considering cybersecurity insurance can experience many benefits, such as undergoing a formal cybersecurity risk assessment in order to receive coverage. Undergoing such a review can identify and highlight vulnerabilities and encourage adoption of cybersecurity best practices.

   There are exemptions to cybersecurity insurance policies, including the war and terrorism exemption, which raise questions about coverage of attacks stemming from state-sponsored organizations. It is unclear how the war and terrorism exemption affects cybersecurity insurance coverage in practicality. In 2017, Mondelez International, a large multinational food corporation housing brands like Chips Ahoy, Oreo, Halls, and Cadbury suffered at least $100 million in damages caused by the NotPetya cyberattack (Bateman, 2020). The US, UK, Lithuania, Estonia, Canada, Australia, New Zealand, and others jointly attributed the NotPetya attack to the Russian government (Corcoran, 2019). Zurich American Insurance denied Mondelez International's claim on the sole ground that "hostile or warlike action...by any government or sovereign power... or agent or authority [thereof]" was excluded under the policy (Bateman, 2020). Mondelez brought suit in 2018, and litigation remains ongoing as of this writing.

Cybersecurity insurance can also create perverse incentives for attackers if it covers ransomware payments. If successful attacks against organizations with cybersecurity insurance frequently result in payment, it encourages further attack. Additionally, as seen in the attack against Colonial Pipeline, ransom payment does not ensure system restoration, let alone speedy recovery (Turton et al., 2021). While it is not specifically illegal to make ransomware payments, the US Department of the Treasury issued an advisory highlighting the risk of sanctions against those making or facilitating such payments to "malicious cyber actors" (US Department of the Treasury, 2020). Moreover, some state governments are moving in the direction of adopting legislation to prohibit state agencies and local governments from paying ransom (Bergal, 2021). This is likely a growing trend.

Because attribution of who conducted a cyberattack can be incredibly difficult and take an extensive amount of time to accomplish, and because ransom payments are often made using anonymous cryptocurrencies (making it that much more difficult to know who is on the receiving end), it is almost impossible to know whether the payment is made to a designated "malicious cyber actor." Despite the potential for quick system restoration as the result of paying the ransom demand, it is probably best that local governments not make or authorize ransomware payments regardless of whether such payments are covered by cybersecurity insurance.

Local governments should consider the numerous benefits of cybersecurity insurance coverage, including the process of applying for coverage itself. The New York State Department of Financial Services (NYDFS) issued industry guidance to insurers in the form of a cybersecurity insurance risk framework in 2021 (New York State Department of Financial Services, 2021). The framework directs cybersecurity underwriters to implement seven best practices. Local governments must therefore understand specifically what is and is not covered by their cybersecurity insurance policies. Despite the current uncertainties in the cybersecurity insurance market, the benefits and services provided by coverage are considerable, especially for local governments with limited resources. Looking ahead, it is also unclear if cybersecurity insurance policies will continue providing coverage for ransomware attacks and how future ransomware policy riders might be structured.

11.16 What Would an Attacker Do Against Our Local Government, and Would We Be Prepared?

Attackers will utilize known vulnerabilities and threats in the hopes that some local governments or third parties have not yet patched or upgraded their systems, or that a user will fall prey to a social engineering attack like a phishing email. Attackers will try robust measures to gain access to government systems. System access allows adversaries to sit, wait, and watch activity on government networks, to capture and potentially expose or sell PII and other government data, or to encrypt, destroy, or expose said data and systems unless a ransom is paid. Defenders must be prepared to detect a breach as soon as possible, to mitigate the effects of a breach, and to improve local government systems so similar attacks will not succeed in the future.

One of the best ways for local governments to understand what an attacker can do against their information systems is by engaging in a Red Team/Blue Team review and training process. As discussed in Section 11.13 above, a red team is a group of individuals testing a government's systems in a campaign as if they were legitimate attackers. The red team emulates common attack tools and methodologies and goes through the attack lifecycle as a typical hacker might. Blue teams act as the government's proactive network defenders. These defenders try to divert the adversary's efforts by precluding them from having an effect and impeding their actions, limiting the effectiveness of the attack, and exposing the adversary. These two groups take combined lessons learned and integrate improvements into the government's information systems. Frequently, the red teams are third-party experts who specialize in penetration testing and other types of adversarial behavior practiced by cyberattackers.

Engaging in red team/blue team exercises can help local governments identify and remediate cybersecurity vulnerabilities. Tabletop cybersecurity exercises are also a great option to help local government leaders – especially managers – understand the threats they face, how they might respond to them, and otherwise get a sense of how adverse cybersecurity events are experienced in reality. CISA offers tabletop exercises (CISAb, n.d.) as well as remote penetration tests, phishing campaign assessments, web application scanning, and vulnerability scanning (CISAa, n.d.). And, as mentioned earlier, cybersecurity awareness activities and training can help local governments understand their level of preparedness – especially as pertaining to individual end-users.

> CISA provides free cybersecurity tabletop exercises that local governments should utilize in order to practice real-life scenarios, spot areas for improvement and incorporate lessons learned into policy and practice (CISA, n.d.). Tabletop exercises provide the opportunity for relationship building across departments, which is essential in the event of a emergency, and for employee training and development more generally. https://www.cisa.gov/publication/cybersecurity-scenarios

11.17 Conclusion

This chapter has raised and endeavored to answer a number of important cybersecurity related questions that local government leaders should be asking of themselves and their IT and cybersecurity professionals. But these are not the only questions that can and should be asked! Again, local government officials must understand that cyber threats continually change and evolve so asking questions like these must not become a one-and-done task on a management checklist. Rather, such data collection, reflection, and self-assessment should be a continuous process that leads to the development of specific insights and recommendations that can guide day-to-day cybersecurity activities and craft an understanding of the cybersecurity culture within the local government.

This analysis also can be presented to top elected and appointed officials not only to provide updates on local government cybersecurity matters, but also to help justify management decisions and policies as well as requested additional budget or staffing resources for cybersecurity. Ultimately, cybersecurity is an iterative process and a continuous cycle – asking questions like those presented in this chapter can help make implementing and managing the process of effective local government cybersecurity a smoother one for all concerned.

References

Bateman, J. (2020, October 05). *War, terrorism, and catastrophe in cyber insurance: Understanding and reforming exclusions.* Carnegie Endowment for International Peace. https://carnegieendowment.org/2020/10/05/war-terrorism-and-catastrophe-in-cyber-insurance-understanding-and-reforming-exclusions-pub-82819

Bergal, J. (2021, July 26). *States consider legislation to ban ransomware payments.* Government Technology. https://www.govtech.com/policy/states-consider-legislation-to-ban-ransomware-payments

Center for Advanced Red Teaming (n.d.). *The global focal point for Red Teaming research, training and practice.* https://www.albany.edu/cehc/cart

Coalition of City CISOs (n.d.). *About us.* https://cityciso.org/about-us

Corcoran, B. (2019, March 08). *What Mondelez v. Zurich may reveal about cyber insurance in the age of digital conflict.* LawFare. https://www.lawfareblog.com/what-mondelez-v-zurich-may-reveal-about-cyber-insurance-age-digital-conflict

Cybersecurity Infrastructure and Security Agency (CISA), US Department of Homeland Security a (n.d.). *Cyber resource hub.* https://www.cisa.gov/cyber-resource-hub

Cybersecurity Infrastructure and Security Agency b (CISA), US Department of Homeland Security (n.d.). *CISA tabletop exercise package.* https://www.cisa.gov/publication/cisa-tabletop-exercise-package

Cybersecurity Infrastructure and Security Agency (CISA), US Department of Homeland Security c (n.d.). *CISA Regions.* https://www.cisa.gov/cisa-regions

Cybersecurity Infrastructure and Security Agency (CISA), US Department of Homeland Security (2019, November 14). *Security Tip (ST04-001) What is cybersecurity?* https://us-cert.cisa.gov/ncas/tips/ST04-001

Cybersecurity Infrastructure and Security Agency (CISA), US Department of Homeland Security (2021, February 25). *Cyber incident response.* https://www.cisa.gov/cyber-incident-response

Fimlaid, J. (2019, March 5). *Information security staffing guide.* NuHarbor Security. https://www.nuharborsecurity.com/information-security-staffing-guide

GDATA (2021, May 3). *11 Biggest cyber security threats in 2021.* https://www.gdatasoftware.com/blog/biggest-security-threats-2021

Gelnaw, A. (2019, March 22). *The importance of continuous improvement in security performance management.* BitSight. https://www.bitsight.com/blog/importance-continuous-improvement-security-performance-management

Goddard, W. (2021, May 18). *Top 25 cyber security threats.* IT Chronicles. https://itchronicles. com/information-security/top-25-cyber-security-threats

Gurinaviciute, J. (2021, February 3). *5 biggest cybersecurity threats.* Security Magazine. https://www.securitymagazine.com/articles/94506-5-biggest-cybersecurity-threats

Interactive.com (2021). *A framework for continuous cyber security improvement.* https://www.interactive.com.au/
insights/a-framework-for-continuous-cyber-security-improvement

Lohrmann, D. (2019, February 23). *Why so many organizations still don't understand security.* Government Technology. https://www.govtech.com/blogs/lohrmann-on-cybersecurity/why-many-organizations-still-dont-get-security.html. In this blog post, Lohrmann cites the following: Alex Blau. 2017. The Behavioral Economics of Why Executives Underinvest in Cybersecurity. *Harvard Business Review.*

Manhattan District Attorneys Office (n.d.). *NYC cyber critical service and infrastructure (CCSI) project.* https://www.manhattanda.org/ccsi

Mehravari, N. and Allen, J. (2016, February 22). *Structuring the chief information security officer (CISO) organization.* SEI Blog. https://insights.sei.cmu.edu/blog/structuring-chief-information-security-officer-ciso-organization

Multi-State Information Sharing & Analysis Center (MS-ISAC) (n.d.). *MS-ISAC local governments.* https://www.cisecurity.org/partners-local-government

Nash, K.S. (2019, December 30). *Tech chiefs plan to boost cybersecurity spending.* The Wall Street Journal. https://www.wsj.com/articles/tech-chiefs-plan-to-boost-cybersecurity-spending-11577701802

New York State Department of Financial Services (2021, February 04). *Insurance circular letter no. 2 (2021).* https://www.dfs.ny.gov/industry_guidance/circular_letters/cl2021_02

Norris, D.F. (2021) A new look at local government cybersecurity 2020. *Public Management/ Local Government Review,* pp. 15–20. Washington. D: International City/County Management Association.

Norris, D.F., Mateczun, L., Joshi, A., and Finin, T. (2019). Cyberattacks at the grassroots: American local governments and the need for high levels of cybersecurity. *Public Administration Review,* 79 (6), 895–904. https://doi.org/10.1111/puar.13028

Norris, D.F., Mateczun, L., Joshi, A., and Finin, T. (2020). Managing cybersecurity at the grassroots: Evidence from the first nationwide survey of local government cybersecurity. *Journal of Urban Affairs,* 43 (8), 1173–1195. https://doi.org/10.1080/07352166.2020.1727295

Paul, D. (2021, July 08). *New York City opens cyberattack defense center.* The Wall Street Journal. https://www.wsj.com/articles/new-york-city-opens-cyberattack-defense-center–11625778530

Turton, W., Riley, M., and Jacobs, J. (2021, May 13). *Colonial Pipeline paid hackers nearly $5 million in ransom.* Bloomberg. https://www.bloomberg.com/news/articles/2021-05-13/colonial-pipeline-paid-hackers-nearly-5-million-in-ransom

U.S. Department of the Treasury (2020, October 01). *Advisory on potential sanctions risks for facilitating ransomware payments.* https://home.treasury.gov/system/files/126/ofac_ransomware_advisory_10012020_1.pdf

U.S. National Institute of Standards and Technology (NIST) (n.d.). *About the risk management framework (RMF).* https://csrc.nist.gov/Projects/risk-management/about-rmf

12

The Future of Local Government Cybersecurity

12.1   Introduction

This chapter discusses a number of cybersecurity issues that local governments are likely to confront in the near future, as well as many years down the line. Indeed, local governments are faced with addressing many of these issues today, although the issues will certainly evolve over time, presenting these governments with new and ever more difficult challenges. These issues are not listed in any particular order and certainly not in order of importance (which would be highly subjective and likely quite controversial). Readers should draw their own judgments regarding the relative importance of each of them. Readers should understand, too, that what the authors have written in 2021 is likely to change over time and present quite differently in a few years.

To give but a few examples, the contents of this chapter include discussions of more hackers and more hacking, more ransomware attacks, the proliferation of IoT devices, and the impacts of Bring Your Own devices. In addition, the chapter covers continuing cybersecurity challenges related to working remotely, legacy technologies, artificial intelligence (AI), and much more.

12.2   The Cloud

The "cloud" is a term used to refer to information resources stored by third-party organizations separate from the firms or local governments using those resources. Think of outside providers such as Amazon Web Services (AWS), Microsoft Azure, IBM, Google Oracle, and others. Although the cloud can be perceived as data storage floating in the sky, this metaphor is not literally true. There is no actual cloud, just server farms and data centers on terra firma. The cloud is the use of information services, like data storage and software, over the internet. Local government information resources, thus, can be stored not only on local government computers or networks, but instead reside with one or more cloud providers. Most local governments that use the cloud employ cloud-based products and services through third-party contractors such as Dell, CDW, Carahsoft Technology Corp. and SHI (some of which do not receive as much name recognition but are among the top cloud contractors based on numbers of contracts and dollar value),

Cybersecurity and Local Government, First Edition. Donald F. Norris, Laura K. Mateczun and Richard F. Forno.
© 2022 John Wiley & Sons Ltd. Published 2022 by John Wiley & Sons Ltd.

rather than contract directly with major providers like Amazon and Google (Pittman, 2017a).

> Remember, the cloud is a fancy term for someone else's computer – Richard Forno.

Some local governments may choose to create a private cloud, which is a cloud service solely for that local government and not shared by any other entities. Private cloud environments can be located either on site at the local government or hosted by a third party such as those mentioned above. The City of San Diego runs a private cloud in which it controls and operates almost 400 applications such as: permitting; its open data portal DataSD with performance analytics; the city's mobile app to connect with citizens Get It Done; StreetsSD which allows residents to examine current street conditions and repairs; OpenGov which visualizes the city's annual budget; and PerformSD which visualizes data for residents to better understand how the city is performing (Pittman, 2017b). Local governments can also choose to use public clouds, which are entirely maintained by third parties, or hybrid clouds, which are a part private and part public cloud. Cloud technologies, whether public or private, provide local governments increased flexibility in providing public-facing services and conducting internal business.

Adoption of cloud technologies by local governments has both benefits and limitations. Major benefits of cloud adoption, as found by a 2021 MeriTalk survey of state and local IT leaders, include: improved data availability and interoperability of systems (37 percent); improved flexibility and agility (37 percent); and improved cybersecurity (36 percent) (2021). In some situations, cloud-based services can provide cost savings to local governments by improving the manageability of information resources and reducing system maintenance costs.

The Center for Digital Government's 2018 Digital Counties Survey, administered annually to all US counties in conjunction with the National Association of Counties, found four major hurdles to migrating to the cloud including: the presence of legacy, or existing and sometimes outdated, systems; human resource issues; understanding security in the cloud; and determining how to calculate cost savings (Government Technology News Staff, 2021). Almost half of the counties in the survey noted that current and ongoing investments in legacy systems made migrating to the cloud less appealing (Government Technology News Staff, 2021). Human resource issues include ensuring local government IT and cybersecurity employees have the skills necessary to manage a cloud-based environment. Many local governments, or almost a third of respondents to the Digital Counties Survey, did not fully understand how security in the cloud actually works (Government Technology News Staff, 2021). One way to alleviate concerns that the cloud is less secure than keeping IT infrastructure in-house is to utilize vendors rated by StateRAMP, a nonprofit that assesses cloud vendors to ensure they meet certain security measures for state and local governments (Kanowitz, 2021). Finally, IT has historically been classified as a capital expense in local government budgets. Shifting to the cloud also means shifting cloud-related IT costs to the operating budget, which can cause issues in funding availability and support.

Local governments must understand that the cloud does not eliminate their cybersecurity risks. Rather, it shifts them to the cloud services providers who are charged with protecting their clients and their data. The SolarWinds attackers specifically sought access to cloud-based service providers through the software supply chain by targeting the authentication systems of cloud providers, like Microsoft 365. This affected downstream users of Microsoft's services, such as the US Treasury Department and other federal, state, and local agencies (Budd, 2020).

According to the MeriTalk survey, 57 percent of state and local governments feel they are not getting the most out of their investments in the cloud (2021). Yet, a large majority (79 percent) believed the hybrid cloud is ideal for a resilient government (i.e., one that is prepared to continue operations even if breached), and a slightly larger majority (83 percent) report improvements in their ability to meet the mission. Local governments must now incorporate security of cloud-based services, providers, and third-party contractors into their overall cybersecurity posture.

The future of the cloud for local governments requires strategic planning and risk management. As a result, they should strategically prioritize which systems and applications would be better managed via the cloud and which should remain within the purview and control of the local government itself. Of course, local governments must also ensure they have the connectivity, workforce, and procurement capabilities needed to successfully migrate to a cloud environment and effectively manage their cloud applications.

12.3 Hackers...More of Them and More Hacking

In recent years, there has been an enormous increase in the number of cybercriminals and others who attack information systems. This was especially true during the COVID-19 pandemic, largely because of so many people working remotely. As a result, breaches of information systems have also increased a great deal – since 2018 by 11 percent and since 2014 by 67 percent (Bissell et al., 2019). Last, there has been a reported 300 percent increase in cybercrimes between when the pandemic began in early 2020 and early 2021 (Walter, 2020).

There are at least six major reasons for the growing number of cybercriminals and cyberattacks. First, cybercrime is a business, and at least at the moment it pays well (e.g., Nakashima and Lerman, 2021). Indeed, more than eight in ten cyberattacks are financially motivated (Verizon, 2020). In other words, cybercriminals attempt to steal money or something else valuable or to blackmail organizations for a price. The latter is especially true of ransomware attacks. In the 2021 ransomware attack against Colonial Pipeline, the company reportedly paid their attackers $4.4 million in bitcoin (Bussewitz, 2021). As a result of the large rewards of ransomware attacks, more people of a less-than-ethical inclination are attracted to this field of endeavor.

Second, it is increasingly easy to enter the cybercrime business. In the early days of cybercrime, hackers had to the have technical skills needed to conduct attacks. Today, almost anybody can do it because of the widespread availability on the internet of inexpensive and easy to use do-it-yourself hacking kits and even attack tools that can be rented for a certain period of time (e.g., Patterson, 2018; Stevens, 2018).

Third, many organizations, especially local governments, do a poor job securing their IT systems. The 2016 UMBC-ICMA survey clearly showed how poorly local governments defended against cyberattacks and managed their cybersecurity (Norris et al., 2019). Another survey found that more than three-quarters of organizations had not even developed and implemented incident response plans to improve their ability to respond to cybersecurity emergencies (Milkovich, 2020). This is an especially egregious example of cybersecurity malpractice. If such an organization is breached and is shut down in part or in whole, it would have no guidance or roadmap about how to continue operations or recover from the breach. Think about the Baltimore and Atlanta breaches discussed in Chapter 1.

Fourth, cybercriminals are rarely apprehended and/or punished for their crimes. According to security expert Roger Grimes (2012): "Rob a bank and face a one-in-four or one-in-five chance of doing hard time. Steal someone's identity and your odds of being caught are almost infinitesimal." There are various reasons for law enforcement's lack of success tracking down and punishing cybercriminals, but they all add up to the same result. For the attackers, cybercrime is a fairly low-risk activity today.

Fifth, cybercriminals target people. As discussed in Chapter 8, people are the weakest link in the cybersecurity equation. The great majority of breaches occur because a person, most often accidentally, opens an attachment or clicks on a URL that he or she should not. According to one source, 95 percent of breaches are the result of errors people make (Milkovich, 2020). Cybercriminals know people make mistakes, and this is why, more often than not, they employ phishing or spear phishing attacks, betting that someone somewhere will make that mistake. More than two-thirds of attackers use phishing as the primary method of getting past cyber defenses, with eight in ten security incidents involving phishing (Varonis, 2021).

Sixth, cybercrime constantly evolves, and cybercriminals evolve along with it. Perhaps the best recent example of this evolution occurred during the COVID-19 pandemic when cybercriminals targeted people working remotely, hospitals, pharmaceutical companies, personal protective equipment (PPE) manufacturers, people and organizations seeking to purchase PPE, and COVID-19 vaccine manufacturers, among others. As history shows, cybercriminals constantly evolve alongside emerging technologies to devise newer and more effective ways of targeting and attacking their victims.

Cybercrime and cyberattacks are here to stay. Cybercriminals are neither stupid nor lazy. They research what they are about to attack, use the best tools they can find, and are relentless in their malicious activities. Their cost of entry to the world of cybercrime is rather low and there is a low probability of discovery, capture, and prosecution. Making their life easier is that unlike traditional criminals, cybercrime activities can be launched or conducted from anywhere in the world against any target in the world, which also creates a challenging legal environment in which to attempt prosecution (e.g., Sjouwerman, 2019).

In all, these reasons explain why the numbers of attackers and attacks continues to increase. They also suggest that the world is unlikely to see a reduction in the numbers of either one anytime soon. Last, they also suggest that laws and law enforcement are not up to the task of preventing cybercrime or catching and punishing cybercriminals.

12.4 Best Practices...Always Follow Them

To ensure that local governments practice the highest levels of cybersecurity possible they must always follow time-tested best practices. There are many reasons why local governments should do so, not the least of which is that deploying anything less than best practices leaves them open to unnecessary cyber risk. Consequently, it is essential that local governments make the adoption and use of cybersecurity best practices a high priority.

Best practices are critical. Although cyber threats constantly evolve, these simple and widely adopted solutions are essential elements in the defense against the constant cyberattacks confronting local governments. NIST's Cybersecurity Framework, discussed in Chapter 9, provides direction and guidance for local governments to help determine the most appropriate best practices to follow (2018).

Recent trends in cybersecurity best practices include: improvements in identity and password management like multi-factor and biometric authentication; the need to protect increasing numbers of workers operating remotely (e.g., remote access and the cloud); third-party vendor security (e.g., software, applications, cloud providers, etc.); and artificial intelligence (AI) and machine learning (ML) applied to detection and security technologies (Gartner, 2021; Panetta, 2021). Local governments can anticipate these trends affecting them in the future if they haven't yet already experienced them at some level.

Other future best practices that will likely impact local governments include ensuring security of Internet of Things connected devices, especially those used in smart city initiatives, monitoring users who are authorized to access sensitive systems, especially subcontractors and remote employees, and more. Following the guidance from NIST, CISA, and membership organizations like the International City County Management Association, the National League of Cities, National Association of Counties, and the Public Technology Institute will help local governments stay abreast of and more effectively respond to changes in the field.

> The Town of Oldsmar, Florida's water treatment facility was breached in 2021 because multiple users shared the same password for remote access to the system. Additionally, the facility was utilizing the Windows 7 operating system, which Microsoft no longer supported.

> The City of Baltimore did not patch its systems in a timely manner which led to a successful ransomware attack in 2019. The patch had been made available at least two years before the breach.

12.5 Skilled Cybersecurity Worker Shortage

It should come as no surprise to anyone who has been paying attention to cybersecurity over the past several years that there is a large and growing worldwide shortage of trained personnel to fill cybersecurity jobs. According to CyberSeek (n.d.), a website supported by funding from NIST that provides information about the cybersecurity job market, as of 2021 there were more than 956,000 cybersecurity workers in the US. In August of 2021, the *Washington*

Post reported that there were almost 465,000 cybersecurity jobs nationwide that were vacant, which is a deficit of nearly 49 percent. Among federal, state, and local governments, there was a deficit of approximately 36,000 cybersecurity positions. US Department of Homeland Security, which houses CISA, had 1700 cybersecurity vacancies (Marks, 2021).

It gets worse because no available source suggests that much can be done in the short (or possibly even in the long) run to rectify this situation. Experts in the field (e.g., Hospelhorn, 2020; Morgan, 2017, among many others) suggest that the principal causes of the shortage are: the constantly increasing numbers of cyberattacks; the younger generation not being interested (which is thought to be largely because K-12 education does not expose children to cybersecurity, at least from middle school onward); universities are not training and graduating sufficient numbers of students in cybersecurity; organizations failing to cross-train IT employees in cybersecurity; the apparent false hope that the shortage can be solved by the application of artificial intelligence technologies to cybersecurity problems; some IT and cybersecurity leaders not taking the shortage seriously; and burnout – a 2018 survey found that 39 percent of cybersecurity professionals said they were very satisfied with their current job, but, nearly half were only somewhat satisfied and 14 percent were either not very satisfied or not satisfied at all (Oltsik, 2019).

While it appears that there is not a great deal that local governments can do about the shortage, here are a few suggestions that may help, if only on the margins. First, cross-train current IT staff in cybersecurity where practicable and relevant to their duties. However, be aware that if these staff transition into full time cybersecurity work, their IT jobs will need to be filled, and there is also currently a shortage of IT workers (English, 2021). Partnering with K-12 school systems, community colleges, and colleges and universities in their catchment areas might present novel ways to expand the pool of available cybersecurity workers. Perhaps consider engaging with state officials to draw upon the expertise of any National Guard cyber units (in states that have them) to help improve local government cybersecurity practice and readiness and, in the event of a breach, ask the Guard cyber unit to assist in recovery.

Additionally, consider partnering with organizations representing minorities and women because both groups are underrepresented in tech fields, especially in cybersecurity, to increase their presence in local government. Local governments could consider outsourcing some or all of the cybersecurity activities to qualified vendors under appropriate supervision. Perhaps explore partnering with other local governments to share the burden of cybersecurity and share information and best practices. This could be especially useful for small local governments with limited cybersecurity staffing. Finally, within budgetary limits, consider increasing the salaries of cybersecurity staff and new hires and provide incentives and bonuses.

12.6 Ransomware

Chapter 3 contains a discussion of ransomware – what it is, how it works, and what local governments should and should not do if they are on the receiving end of a ransomware attack. This section does not repeat earlier discussions but rather focuses on the likely future trajectory of ransomware as a local government cybersecurity concern. To begin with, readers should know that there is little or no research from any source, popular, professional, or scholarly, that to date has provided any evidence-based projections of the future of ransomware. Most projections simply state that things "are likely to get worse." Sadly, that is the projection of this section as well, although this section also discusses the rationale for its projection. This is certainly not good news for local governments let alone any other organizations.

At least in the foreseeable future, the number of ransomware attacks and the number of cybercriminals conducting ransomware attacks will increase; the cost of ransom will increase; attacks will escalate during troubled times (as was the case during the COVID-19 pandemic); and while effective governmental regulation is needed, government action will be slow to follow.

What factors support this likely future? The first and perhaps most important is that ransomware attacks are successful and are financially rewarding to cybercriminals. Ransomware is highly profitable, a $1.4 billion business in the US and a $10.4 trillion business globally (Morgan, 2020; Tinianow, 2020). Such profits, in turn, entice more people to join the ranks of this particular variant of cybercrime. And as mentioned earlier, cybercrime, including ransomware, is very low risk for the attacker (see Section 11.2). The sheer number of cybersecurity events in the news further contributes to "breach fatigue," which reduces the motivation of individuals and organizations to act to combat adverse cybersecurity events (e.g., Sloan, 2020).

Additionally, cryptocurrencies, such as bitcoin and its cousins, enable cybercriminals to escape detection by hiding financial transactions, such as receiving ransom payments, from law enforcement. According to the ransomware incident response and recovery firm Coveware, 99 percent of ransomware payments were made in bitcoin in 2019 (2019).

Phishing attacks have risen 667 percent since the pandemic started and 90 percent of ransomware attacks use phishing (Shi, 2020). Fifth, cybercrime, including ransomware, is easier than ever and newbies with virtually no technical skills can buy pre-packaged attack kits and run attacks.

Finally most organizations, and this is especially true of local governments (see the 2016 survey), do a really poor job protecting their IT assets. Ransomware is a great example of how failure to implement basic IT practices can wreak havoc. Chapter 7 identifies actions that are necessary to help make attacks like ransomware less effective for criminals and less costly for victims, but those tools must be in place *before* the attack.

Thankfully, there is, perhaps, one trend that is not as grim as those discussed above. According to a Pew survey conducted in October of 2020, 71 percent of workers said that they were working at home most or all of the time (Parker et al., 2020). As work moves back to the office, and other potentially more cyber-secure environments, while the number of ransomware attacks may not decline, there may be fewer successful attacks. Only time will tell.

12.7 IoT Proliferation

Chapter 1 discussed the Internet of Things (IoT) in some detail. This section examines its future. First, a reprise of the numbers. According to Statistica, there are currently 13.8 billion IoT and non-IoT units connected to the internet. That is expected to increase to

30.9 billion by 2025 (Vailshery, 2021). By comparison, there were only 7.9 billion inhabitants of the Earth in May of 2021!

Most of the trade and popular publications envision a rosy future for the IoT (which could be because much of that material is from firms trying to sell services). Indeed, one source flatly states: "The future of IoT has the potential to be limitless" (Ericsson, n.d.) while many others are equally optimistic about various potential uses of the IoT such as in agriculture, smart cities, smart homes, wearable devices, and industrial applications, especially when 5G (fifth-generation mobile networks) and artificial intelligence fully arrive. Rosy scenarios, indeed.

The security company Norton made ten predictions about the future of the IoT (Norton, 2019). Seven of them followed the rosy scenario and were quite optimistic: continued increase of the number of devices on the IoT; growth of smart cities; growth of smart cars; growing importance of AI; 5G leading to more IoT devices; development of more secure and smarter routers; and privacy and security issues leading to legislative and regulatory action. Three of Norton's predictions addressed security: cybercriminals will use IoT to engage in DDOS attacks, and such attacks will be increasingly dangerous (two points); and the IoT will produce privacy and security concerns. This was a somewhat more balanced view of the future of the IoT, but, like so many other predictions, it was overly influenced by "Rosy" and did not give the dark side (security concerns) of IoT sufficient attention.

For others, while the IoT does, indeed, have such potential, there is a darker side. As the IoT grows and more and more devices have been and will be added, security (or the lack thereof) has been and will continue to be a major concern. Smart doorbells can be taken over, as can sensors that control a variety of important functions such as traffic lights, water filtration and distribution systems, and various electronic gizmos that control the electrical grid and oil and gas pipelines. As the CBS program *60 Minutes* demonstrated in 2015, a talented adversary can even commandeer automobiles remotely.

What is the IoT's likely future? First, there is little doubt that it will continue to grow, possibly astronomically. Second, there will almost certainly be innovative, possibly even game-changing applications of the IoT (e.g., driverless cars that do not crash or hit pedestrians, for example). No one, however, can know the precise directions of the growth or its impacts. Third, there are serious security concerns about the IoT: a) the IoT expands the attack surface of all organizations (including our homes) that deploy IoT devices; and b) adequate security is not built into either the internet or many (perhaps most or close to all) of the devices that are and will be connected to it. As long as this pattern continues, there will be security events (e.g., shutting down the electric grid or a substantial a portion of it, just to mention one possibility). As a result, this seems to be a case of being careful what you wish for. As "limitless" as the IoT may (or may not) be, without adequate security, there inevitably will be problems, possibly some of catastrophic proportions. All one has to do to get a sense of how bad things could be is to run a Google search of "The Dark Side of the IoT" (e.g., Kranz, 2018; Miles, 2019; Richard, n.d.; just to mention a few). Unfortunately, the negative consequences (the dark side of the IoT) are rarely found in the literature discussion of its future.

12.8   BYOD

Chapter 3 discusses the status (at the time this book was completed) of the use of personal devices in local governments, and BYOD policies are further explored in Chapter 7. This section addresses the future of "bring your own device" rules and strategies in local governments.

The use of personal devices can be more efficient, flexible, and provide cost savings in some situations, but such use also inherently raises the level of cybersecurity risk facing local governments. The issue of BYOD may seem passé at this writing in 2021, but the shift towards hybrid offices and working remotely means concerns remain regarding the use of personal devices for work. As discussed throughout the book, personal devices increase a local government's attack surface because of the increasing number of, often insecure, devices that are added to the government's IT systems and networks. These personally owned, insecure devices also have access to more websites and apps than governmentally managed devices.

The BYOD market was valued at $186 billion in 2019, and is expected to grow to $430 billion by 2025, up from only $30 billion in 2014 (Global Market Insights, Inc, 2016; MarketWatch, 2021). This is a direct shift from what was a declining market in 2018 (Research and Markets, 2018). While the future of work remains uncertain, both BYOD and working remotely will remain a part, possibly a growing part (at least as compared to pre-pandemic times), of the overall work environment. BYOD policies almost certainly will need to be updated to reflect a hybrid work environment, detailing which devices are accepted and how to be compliant with desired security standards. Local governments can expect policy and compliance changes as the balance of the hybrid office is established and local government and employee expectations are refined. NIST Special Publication 800-124 Rev. 2 (draft) deals with mobile device security within organizations and can be a helpful resource for local government cybersecurity professionals (2020b).

In a 2021 report, Lookout, a cloud security provider, examined the data of their federal, state, and local clients for threats facing US governments (2021). This report is a helpful predictor of future BYOD threats and trends beyond the pandemic. Lookout found that close to 25 percent of state and local government employees use personal devices when teleworking. This can expose local governments to mobile phishing attempts, which can be sent via text message or in a phone call, as well as threats from insecure applications downloaded and used on those devices. Phishing exposure rates for unmanaged devices used by state and local government employees exceed that of managed devices (11 percent versus 6 percent). The purpose of these phishing attempts has shifted from malware delivery (69 percent in 2019 and 31 percent in 2020) to credential harvesting (56 percent in 2019 and 80 percent in 2020), which allows attackers to pose as legitimate users and gain "authorized" access to systems that system administrators may not catch. Threats to mobile apps surged 20-fold during this same period, as well.

Perhaps the most concerning issue with BYOD usage is that many employee devices have outdated operating systems (99 percent of government Android users are exposed to hundreds of vulnerabilities). Unlike desktops and laptops, mobile devices, including tablets, often do not have endpoint security, which protects devices that connect to a network so that they are secure from malicious activity (McAfee, 2021). When 62 percent of workers believe mobile devices aid in productivity, and 36 percent say their use of mobile devices for work has increased during 2020, the potential security implications associated with those devices are profound (Hein, 2021).

12.9 Working Remotely

Telework (working from home, the hybrid office, and all of the ways working remotely is now described) raises a number of concerns for local government cybersecurity such as: the use of insecure personal devices for government business; connecting devices to insecure Wi-Fi networks; and the security of the cloud and third-party vendors used by remote workers. As mentioned in the BYOD section above, the future of the local government office is unclear. However, it is safe to say that in general, work arrangements are unlikely to return to how they were pre-pandemic and local governments can expect to see an increase in telework. The almost overnight shift to telework accelerated many trends, from telework itself, to AI (e.g., facial recognition, automated decision-making, intelligent traffic systems, etc.), online service delivery, and cloud adoption. Many local governments understand the growing pains, benefits, and limitations to working remotely by now and the transition back to the office has shown that, for some, hybrid offices, in which employees can work remotely part time and be in office part time, may be here to stay (Keegan and Greenberg, 2021).

The 2020 State and Local Government Workforce Survey found that telework among state and local government employees was at its peak in 2020 (Center for State & Local Government Excellence [SLGE], 2020). More than one in five governments increased the number of employees eligible to participate in flexible work in 2020, and another one in five increased the range of flexible work arrangements offered. Local government respondents to an ICMA survey found that larger governments are more apt to utilize telework, because smaller governments tend to have more direct interactions with citizens (Vinchesi, 2020). Over half (56 percent) of state and local governments with more than 10,000 employees offer regular telework for eligible positions (SLGE, 2020). The ICMA survey found that some positions are more appropriate for telework than others, such as finance and planning, economic development, and inspectional services (Vinchesi, 2020). Departments typically excluded from allowing at least some of their employees to use flexible work arrangements (meaning flexible schedules, work hours, and telework) include public safety, public works, parks and recreation, public health, social services, and libraries (SLGE, 2020).

Working remotely may be a perk that can help recruit talent to local government, which is especially needed due to existing skill gaps in the IT and cybersecurity workforce. It can also be more efficient for certain positions. But it may also cause less frequent collaboration, where it might have otherwise occurred in office. Local governments must find the appropriate balance of remote and in person work to balance these and other interests.

All local governments, no matter the size, should now expect to adopt and implement security and risk management plans for employees working remotely. Telework agreements for employees are also now necessary. The Municipal Research and Services Center, a nonprofit assisting local governments in the state of Washington, provides an extensive list of example telecommuting policies and other resources that can be adapted by most local governments (2021).

12.10 Defense in Depth

Defense in depth is a time-tested strategic concept in cybersecurity management, where layers of defensive protocols are put in place to protect sensitive data and systems through redundant fail-safes that attempt to counter attacks at each level of penetration. As discussed earlier in the book, these layers protect the confidentiality, integrity, and availability of the local government's information assets. Each measure is intended to address various vectors of attack, such as: firewalls to block network attacks; intrusion detection and prevention systems to alert officials to suspicious network activity; network segmentation to split and organize networks by the level of security required; and more. Multiple layers of security are required to effectively address the plethora of attack styles and methods seen today. Ideally, when one defensive layer or tool fails to counter the attack, a different measure established at another attack vector might succeed, with each successive layer helping further secure the network.

Defense in depth is organized into three categories: physical, technical, and administrative. Physical controls, which are discussed in Chapters 7 and 10, help protect information systems at the physical point of entry, such as access control systems, video surveillance, and locks to a server room. Technical controls include the local government's methods of user authentication, and how data is stored (e.g., encrypted). The principle of least privilege, that users are assigned to only the systems that are required for them to perform their duties, is a recommended component of defense in depth. Finally, administrative controls deal with the local government's cybersecurity policies like those discussed in Chapter 7.

This defensive approach was created by the National Security Agency (NSA) and is an established requirement for federal agencies set forth in NIST Special Publications 800-161 (2015), and 800-53 Rev. 4 (2014). It was originally a military strategy of delaying the advancement of attackers by giving up space on the battlefield to buy time to respond. The layers help stall the attacker's momentum. Many companies offering cybersecurity products and services advertise their defense in depth methods, indicating that employing the strategy as a single organization is costly, which may very well be the case for many local governments. The first step is to understand the baseline status quo of the local government's information systems, policies, and strategies to see which layers may need to be addressed or refined.

With the documented increase in cyberattacks and attackers and the direct and collateral damage they cause, local governments should incorporate a defense in depth strategy in their cybersecurity policies and strategies now and maintain it as strongly as possible well into the future. Local governments may also anticipate that aspects of this approach may be mandated by the federal or state governments at some point in the future. Federal agencies are already required to do so.

The defense in depth strategy is itself future-oriented, in that the true purpose of employing it is to be able to scale, as each layer of defense (physical, technical, and administrative) is adaptable and can be adjusted to address threats in the future. The strategy is frequently cited as a recommendation to addressing the ongoing plague of ransomware attacks (PhishLabs, 2021; Sophos, 2021). Sophos found that local governments are the most likely of all sectors to have its data encrypted in a ransomware attack (2021). Defense in depth and layered security measures can help local governments address emerging threats like these by having trained IT staff capable of defending against attacks and various technologies and policies in place to enable them to do so.

However, given the evolution of cybersecurity risks, the defense in depth concept, while still extremely useful, is being enhanced by a new form of security thinking that doesn't even trust the people and devices within that trusted enclave, as discussed next.

12.11   Zero Trust

In today's age of increasing technological complexity, local governments are likely to have multiple information systems and networks that connect multiple locations and end users; employ mobile devices and allow users to connect their own devices to their network(s); and employ cloud technology. Configurations with these and greater levels of complexity vastly expand the attack surface of local government information systems and greatly increase the vulnerability of these governments' systems and data. Consequently, according to many sources, all organizations, including local governments, should look beyond traditional methods of securing systems and networks (e.g., password protection) and adopt what is known as a Zero Trust (ZT) approach to network and data security (e.g., NIST, 2020a; NSA, 2021; Warner, 2021).

Zero Trust means what it says – no user and no device should be trusted to connect to a device or network until fully and continually authenticated. In the words of the NSA: "The Zero Trust security model eliminates implicit trust in any one element, node or service and instead requires continuous verification...The Zero Trust security model assumes that a breach is inevitable or has already occurred, so it constantly limits access to only what is needed and looks for anomalous malicious activity" (NSA, 2021, p. 1).

NSA further states that under a ZT "mindset," organizations should assume that "all requests for critical resources and all network traffic may be malicious"; and that "all devices and infrastructure may be compromised" (NSA, 2021, p. 3). In other words, trust nothing and no one until they are fully verified.

In 2020, NIST issued Special Publication 800-207 entitled *Zero Trust Architecture*, in which the agency described Zero Trust this way (p. 1): "A ZT approach is primarily focused on data and service protection but can and should be expanded to include all enterprise assets (devices, infrastructure components, applications, virtual and cloud components) and subjects (end users, applications and other non-human entities that request information from resources)" (Rose et al., 2020). In other words, and as NSA and numerous others have said, every person, device, application, etc., that attempts to connect to an organization's IT system or network must be verified, and verified each and every time they attempt to connect. Under EO 14028, CISA has also begun developing guidance documents for a federal government Zero Trust architecture (CISA, n.d.).

Implicit in this approach is the understanding that, for end users, simple password verification is insufficient, and, for devices and applications, the fact that they may be owned or "rented" by the organization is insufficient as well. More complex methods of verification are essential. These may and should include multi-factor authentication (MFA) and other advanced methods such as biometrics (e.g., facial scans, retina scans, fingerprints). Multi- factor means that two or more items must be verified before a user is allowed access. For example, when one signs into a remote account with a password, the account holder will ask one or more security questions (What is your Mother's maiden name? In what town did you grow up?) and/or send a code to the user which the user must enter to complete the sign in process. MFA and biometrics make authentication a bit more complicated for end users but much more secure for the organizations and their networks and data.

> There is no need to provide accurate answers to these questions. A user might say his or her mother's maiden name might be "tennis" and the pet dog's name might be "Kentucky." When answering these questions, the only thing that matters is providing a correct response, not whether the answer actually makes sense. Taking a more creative approach to these questions can make it more difficult for attackers to commandeer accounts via the lost-password feature.

Simply put, Zero Trust should be the future of cybersecurity for all organizations, local governments included, that are serious about protecting their information assets.

12.12 Increased Governmental Regulation of Cybersecurity

Currently, neither the federal government nor states engage in much, if any, regulation of local government cybersecurity (or, indeed, of the cybersecurity practices of most organizations). However, this can be expected to change, although perhaps slowly, in coming years, and local governments can expect to face a much more rigorous regulatory environment. As more and more local governments and agencies dealing with critical infrastructure are breached, a stronger federal response is likely. Indeed, this has already begun with President Biden's Executive Order on Improving the Nation's Cybersecurity, which is discussed further later in Section 12.15 of this chapter. Hopefully, increased attention will also come with increased support for funding for cybersecurity, including employee training as well as actions to expand the pool of qualified cybersecurity workers. At the very least, as issues of local government cybersecurity become more politically salient and, if they remain nonpartisan or bipartisan, increased support for cyber is made all the more possible. Major policy areas concerning local government cybersecurity that are likely to see increased regulation include: information sharing with external organizations; public notice requirements; federal grant funding to incentivize state and local government cybersecurity spending; prohibiting ransomware payments; the use of artificial intelligence; and privacy and data protection.

First, information sharing and public notice requirements. Outside of industry-specific laws discussed in Chapter 10, the federal government does not require that local governments share information about breaches to agencies like the FBI or CISA, let alone disclose breaches to the public. To be clear, all 50 states do have security breach and PII disclosure notification laws covering private and some governmental entities, meaning that some local governments do have public notice requirements (see Chapter 10). However, local government notification to and engagement with the FBI and CISA occurs on an entirely voluntary basis.

In the future, local governments can expect to be required to maintain closer relationships with these and other federal agencies involved in cybersecurity, and to notify them and potentially the public of breaches. Notification of breaches to other local governments may also be prioritized. Information sharing about cybersecurity threats with organizations such as the Multi-State Information Sharing & Analysis Center (MS-ISAC) will likely also be a priority. Ultimately, a federal strategy of providing and sharing resources with local governments may be created. At least one can hope!

Second, federal and state grants to local governments to improve cybersecurity can help incentivize adequate and consistent spending for cyber by these governments. The federal government can also mandate that local governments adopt specific policies and standards and meet other requirements in order to receive said funds. Third, local governments can expect increased regulation around whether and when they are allowed to pay ransom in the event of ransomware attacks. As of this writing, legislatures in New York, North Carolina, and Pennsylvania are considering banning state and local agencies from paying ransoms (Bergal, 2021). As seen in the 2021 hack of Colonial Pipeline, the company paid a hefty $4.4 million ransom and still needed to rebuild systems and reboot from back-ups after the decryption tool provided by the hackers was too slow (Bussewitz, 2021; Eaton and Volz, 2021). However, the FBI was able to trace and identify a virtual currency wallet used by the hackers in the blockchain and recover the ransom, which had reduced in value to $2.3 million (US Department of Justice, Office of Public Affairs, 2021). Many local government police departments and 911 centers have chosen to make ransomware payments in order to restore critical systems as quickly as possible and to protect against disclosure of sensitive or life-threatening information. At least 11 law enforcement agencies have been impacted since 2020 (Suderman, 2021). This said, paying ransom may no longer be an option for local governments under either state and/or federal law in the not-too-distant future.

Fourth, local governments may also find an increase in regulation of the use of AI and ML. Typical uses of AI include facial recognition, helping to better understand the data already generated by local governments, automated decision-making based on that data, intelligent traffic systems, and other systems management. As discussed in this chapter's sections on Increased Automation (12.14) and AI and ML (12.17), local governments can boost their cybersecurity by using AI for network traffic analysis and data encryption. Perhaps the most discussed application of AI by local governments is the use of facial recognition by law enforcement. After the tragic death of George Floyd in 2020, many local governments and private providers such as Amazon and Microsoft reassessed the use of facial recognition in response to the movement to address police violence. The state of Maine banned the government use of facial recognition in most situations, with an exception for when police have probable cause that an unidentified person committed a serious crime, or in order to prevent fraud (Gershgorn, 2021). Yet, rules around storage and use of body camera and other footage generally remain unclear in many situations. The European Union has been more aggressive than the US in its discussion and planning around accepted uses of artificial intelligence in general, and by governments, especially in terms of automated decision-making (see European Location Interoperability Solutions for e-Government (ELISE), 2021). While most regulation of US local government use of AI and ML may take place further down the road, it should still be on the radar of local government officials and managers.

Finally, local governments can also anticipate potential regulations around data privacy, monitoring, and management as seen in the EU's General Data Protection Regulation (GDPR), which is further discussed in Chapter 10. Although data privacy and protection may not immediately seem to be cybersecurity issues, they are in terms of local government compliance. The GDPR has been replicated and modified in the recently adopted Colorado Privacy Act. These laws cover how organizations maintain and secure the information they gather on visitors to their websites, and govern rights consumers have over their information. The data must be stored and processed for specific purposes, in a specific way, and for only certain periods of time. While it is unlikely that the federal government will implement such wide sweeping regulations (at least in the near future), legislation may be considered and adopted in other American states that is similar to that adopted by Colorado and the EU.

It is important to remember that technology and how it is used evolves much more quickly than law, policy, and regulation.

12.13 Building Cybersecurity Into All New Hardware, Software, and Anything that is Connected to the IT System

Planning in governments at all levels and in all fields must deliberately and purposively include cybersecurity. This includes, for example, planning for physical systems like elevators and Heating, Ventilation and Air Conditioning (HVAC) systems, developing databases or loading information onto public-facing websites, implementing new technologies like body cameras, contracting with a new organization for services, and more. Including cybersecurity in planning processes is a best practice for organizations with distributed and diverse responsibilities such as local governments. It is a foundational element of each of the five functions of NIST's Cybersecurity Framework discussed in Chapter 9 (2018). Without continual planning, which must be followed by regular assessments, the critical framework functions are not likely to be achieved, meaning that local governments will fail to provide high levels of cybersecurity.

Cybersecurity should be included in all aspects of local government activities, especially when new services, procedures, operations, and technologies are being considered for adoption or existing ones are being modified. Indeed, before any new or modified services, procedures, operations, and technologies are permitted to go live, all aspects of their cybersecurity must be assessed and addressed. Similarly, when any unit within a local government considers creating such things as web portals, developing or acquiring apps, or storing sensitive information on the government's IT system, the unit must involve the IT or cybersecurity department (preferably both). In this way, IT and cyber staff will be able to lend their expertise in the planning process to ensure that cybersecurity concerns are addressed, and that local government cybersecurity policies and procedures are followed.

If these steps are not taken prior to developing or implementing new services, procedures, operations, and technologies, local governments will be blind to areas of risk associated with those services. Including cybersecurity in organizational planning at the earliest point in the decision-making process is key to effective cybersecurity management. And, incorporating cybersecurity in the planning and development of local government services, procedures, operations, and technologies can help address potential future threats as they evolve.

Local governments should anticipate that, at some point in the future, they will likely be required to include cybersecurity in all areas of planning. This is true regardless of whether mandates come from the state or federal governments or from local government leaders as part of a process of developing and maintaining a culture of cybersecurity.

In 2021, the Office of Inspector General of the US Defense Department reported that the operating systems used by 75 percent of the Pentagon's 3D printers were out of date. Incorporating cybersecurity in the planning into the 3D printer project could have ensured a policy of regular updates and patches, making this a completely avoidable threat (DOD Office of Inspector General, 2021). Although not a local government example, such entities would be wise to learn from this incident to ensure they are not caught in a similar situation themselves by making sure cybersecurity is part of all technology deployment plans.

12.14   Increasing Automation

Automation of cybersecurity involves implementing security tools and technologies that help local governments monitor traffic on their networks and protect the data and information within their control. These technologies can help remove the need for human intervention in the monitoring and detection processes, reducing employee workload and potential for human error in often repetitive, time-consuming tasks. Rather than have employees analyze threats and comparing it to threat intelligence, deciding how to respond and then individually resolving the issue, the entire process can be automated. Considering the number of threat alerts facing organizations like local governments, it would be nearly impossible to address every threat by hand, especially with limited cybersecurity staff. With automation, staff can be redeployed to other high priority tasks. While not every cybersecurity task can be automated, automation can provide cost savings, improve efficiency, and reduce error in local government cybersecurity.

Many tools of automation utilize AI and ML to boost ease of analysis. Local governments can automate aspects of their cybersecurity utilizing Robotic Process Automation (RPA) to engage in automatic: threat detection; triage decision-making/workflows; response determination; and threat resolution. Local governments can create standardized incident response processes and workflow logics that can quarantine devices, block URLs, geolocate IP addresses, and delete suspected malware (Splunk, n.d.). This can be accomplished by using two related automation technologies: security information and event management (SIEM), and security orchestration, automation, and response (SOAR). SIEM technologies are tuned to collect and aggregate event data to differentiate between anomalous and normal activity, whereas SOAR systems combine this data from all platforms with automated workflows into one location for ease of analysis, investigation, and automated response (Kirtley, 2020). Typical aspects of these technologies include: alert triage and prioritization; orchestration and automation (coordinating workflows); case management and collaboration; dashboard and reporting; and threat intelligence and investigation.

The future of automation in cybersecurity involves continued automation of detection, decision-making, and response to anomalous events. The most common use for SOAR technologies is to triage suspected phishing emails. However, these automation technologies are most commonly utilized by larger organizations with mature security operations centers, traits that are not common among most local governments. It is expected that by 2022, 30 percent of organizations will utilize these tools, compared to only 5 percent in 2019 (Neiva et al., 2019). Local governments will likely follow this same trend, and shift towards incorporating automation technologies into their cybersecurity in the coming years. As with other aspects of cybersecurity that organizations outsource, SIEM and SOAR technologies are becoming embedded with other products offered by security vendors. Local governments can anticipate further development in the use of AI/ML in automation technologies so that devices can learn to defend themselves.

12.15 Software Supply Chain Risks

Two of the most notable successful cyberattacks in recent years, SolarWinds (2020) and Kaseya (2021), highlight the growing risk of downstream cyberattack through the software supply chain. Both SolarWinds and Kaseya offer different software and services to thousands of organizations around the world. Unfortunately, these software and platforms suffered vulnerabilities that allowed the attackers to access the systems of the users of the software (SolarWinds) and send out ransomware to the company's customers and subsequently those customer's clients (Kaseya). The CISA labeled the Kaseya attack as a "supply-chain ransomware attack" (CISA, 2021a). The Kaseya attack ultimately affected more than 1500 organizations, including US local governments such as Leonardtown and North Beach, Maryland whose computers and networks were disabled (Freed, 2021). Often these attacks hijack software updates, undermine the integrity of the software's code, or compromise open-source code (CISA, 2021b).

President Biden's 2021 Executive Order 14028 on improving the nation's cybersecurity specifically addresses these risks by directing NIST to develop standards and best practices to enhance the security of the software supply chain (NIST, n.d.). NIST then published guidance outlining security measures for critical software, and guidelines recommending minimum standards for vendors' testing of their software source code. Among other things, when using critical software, local governments should apply practices of least privilege, network segmentation, and proper configuration to limit access to sensitive information resources and systems to those who need access to fulfill the responsibilities of their job (NIST, 2021). Network segmentation is the process by which networks are split into different networks according to the level of sensitivity, and therefore security, involved. Proper configuration of the networks means that the networks, and the protocols involved in their operation, are configured appropriately for their intended use.

As local governments continue to utilize software offered by third parties, outsource to security vendors, and move to the cloud, they will continue to face risks imposed by the software supply chain. Dependence on these products and services means that, unfortunately, it is almost impossible to avoid these risks. Risks in the software supply chain are only slated to grow in the future, as it is an efficient mode of attack to reach many potential victims. Instituting a defense in depth strategy and incorporating the supply chain into local government risk management are helpful tools to guard against the effects of such an attack.

12.16 Legacy Technology

Think of legacy technology as the old stuff, such as hardware, devices, software, and systems that are outdated and obsolete (or nearly so). For example, a local government in 2022 should not be running computers or other devices based on Microsoft Windows 98, an operating system long since deprecated by Microsoft that is now unsupported and rife with security and stability problems. Many organizations, local governments included, have and still use legacy technologies, some going back many years, and those systems perform important tasks within the organizations.

Moreover, because of the rapid pace of technological change, technologies that were acquired only a few years ago could be made obsolete by newer technologies that far outpace their dated cousins and/or because manufacturers no longer support the older technologies rendering them obsolete. Organizations continue to use legacy systems for various reasons including the fact that many legacy systems are or appear to be doing exactly the jobs for which they were purchased and also because of the cost and difficulty of upgrading them (e.g., Be Informed, 2021; Sawant, 2020).

There are good reasons, however, for local governments to consider replacing legacy systems or legacy components of their information systems, especially for reasons of cybersecurity. Legacy systems are likely not well-enough equipped to withstand modern cyberattacks, and they may not be capable of being upgraded or adapted to defend against such attacks (e.g., Synchrony, n.d).

This produces a conundrum of what local governments should do regarding legacy systems. The best advice is for these governments to seriously examine the pros and cons, including costs, of upgrading (if possible) or replacing all of the legacy systems that they operate in order to ensure the highest levels of cybersecurity for their information systems. Doing so will require careful and thorough analysis of the risks posed by legacy systems as well as identification of reasonable and cost-effective alternatives to them.

> During the COVID-19 pandemic, 19 states suffered extensive delays in processing unemployment claims due to legacy systems, often dating from the 1980s, many of which were incompatible with federal unemployment IT systems (Charette, 2020).

12.17 Artificial Intelligence and Machine Learning

One definition of artificial intelligence (AI) is "the ability of a digital computer or computer-controlled robot to perform tasks commonly associated with intelligent beings. The term is frequently applied to the project of developing systems endowed with the intellectual processes characteristic of humans, such as the ability to reason, discover meaning, generalize, or learn from past experience" (Copeland, n.d.). Although there are many definitions of AI, this one does a very good job of capturing the key elements of AI and showing that its purpose is the use of computers to mimic some of the most important functions of the human brain, which will then provide the device the ability to act autonomously or independently (in whole or in part) of humans.

In the world of cybersecurity, AI can be used by attackers as well as defenders of computer systems. Moreover, whichever group is more proficient at using AI will have definite advantages over the other. Hackers will use AI in the future to penetrate IT systems more easily, and defenders will use AI to anticipate and to identify and ward off attacks more effectively. As one might imagine, the payoffs for both sides are considerable. Success for attackers means money and other valuables while success for defenders is measured by identifying and defeating attackers.

AI properly used by attackers can make social engineering attacks much more powerful and successful. AI can be used to "to spot patterns in behavior, understanding how to convince people that a video, phone call or email is legitimate and then persuading them to compromise networks and hand over sensitive data" (Durbin, 2020). AI can also be used to more rapidly and effectively search for new vulnerabilities in information systems and digital devices and then exploit those vulnerabilities.

Defenders, on the other hand, can use AI to improve the automated monitoring of systems and networks to identify anomalies and attacks in progress more quickly and to shut down attacks. Defenders can also use AI to improve anti-virus software and to model user behavior to identify unusual or suspicious patterns (Shakeel, 2021). The AI battle will likely continue well into the future, and local governments need to be aware of it and make plans to incorporate AI into their cybersecurity defenses.

Machine learning (ML) can be defined as "an application of artificial intelligence (AI) that provides systems the ability to automatically learn and improve from experience without being explicitly programmed. Machine learning focuses on the development of computer programs that can access data and use it to learn for themselves" (Expert.ai Team, 2020). Contemporary examples of ML include such things as image recognition (e.g., facial recognition), medical diagnosis (e.g., reading digital exams such as X-rays and MRI results), speech recognition (e.g., Amazon's Alexa, Apple's Siri, and Google's Nest devices) and more.

According to one source, "Today, it's impossible to deploy effective cybersecurity technology without relying heavily on machine learning. At the same time, it's impossible to effectively deploy machine learning without a comprehensive, rich and complete approach to the underlying data." Machine learning also requires massive amounts of data and the data must be accurate and comprehensive. ML is used to analyze the data in order, among other things, to learn patterns and from those patterns make decisions to assist in quickly identifying cyberattacks and stopping them. ML, thus, "can make cybersecurity simpler, more proactive, less expensive and far more effective" (Perlman, n.d.).

In short, AI and ML have the potential to be an extraordinary tool for improving operational cybersecurity. Unfortunately, as with many other information technology developments, they also provide new capabilities for adversaries to develop innovative and potentially more dangerous and successful attacks.

12.18   Conclusion

This chapter has presented a number of evidence-based predictions about the future of local government cybersecurity in order to make local government officials and their cybersecurity staff aware of impending trends. These predictions, however, are likely to have a short shelf life. This is because, at this writing, and no matter where the evidence has pointed, one thing is certain: cybersecurity is a discipline that is changing constantly, often in unpredictable ways.

New threats will almost certainly arise, and cybercriminals will devise new and more ingenious ways to ply their trade. However, defenders will develop and deploy new and more effective ways of protecting against these threats. IoT expansion will not be stopped (or possibly even slowed down), but perhaps software and device developers (on their own or under governmental pressure) will begin to build cybersecurity into their products. Working remotely will continue but perhaps at a considerably reduced rate once the COVID-19 pandemic has passed. And perhaps organizations and governments of all sizes will be able to identify, train, teach, fund, hire, and manage enough qualified cybersecurity professionals to make a positive impact on local government cybersecurity going forward.

These are just a few of the reasons why local government officials and their cybersecurity staffs must constantly scan the cybersecurity horizon to identify new threats, methods of defense, and opportunities to improve their government's practice of cybersecurity. The future is always uncertain, but the best way to meet the challenges of tomorrow is through effective planning today. For local governments, their citizens and businesses, this is their most important task.

References

Be Informed (2021). *Legacy technology: 5 most asked questions*. https://www.beinformed.com/blog/legacy-technology-5-most-asked-questions

Bergal, J. (2021, July 26). *States consider legislation to ban ransomware payments*. Government Technology. https://www.govtech.com/policy/states-consider-legislation-to-ban-ransomware-payments

Bissell, K., LaSalle, R.M., and Cin, P.D. (2019, March 6). *Ninth annual cost of cybercrime study*. Accenture. https://www.accenture.com/us-en/insights/security/cost-cybercrime-study

Budd, C. (2020, December 23). *How the SolarWinds hackers are targeting cloud services in unprecedented cyberattack*. GeekWire. https://www.geekwire.com/2020/solarwinds-hackers-targeting-cloud-services-unprecedented-cyberattack

Bussewitz, C. (2021, May 19). *Colonial Pipeline confirms it paid $4.4M to hackers*. Associated Press. https://apnews.com/article/hacking-technology-business-ed1556556c7af6220e6990978ab4f745

Center for State & Local Government Excellence (2020, April). *State and local government workforce: 2020 survey*. https://www.slge.org/assets/uploads/2020/04/workforcesurvey2020.pdf

Charette, R.N. (2020, August 28). *Inside the hidden world of legacy IT systems*. IEEE Spectrum. https://spectrum.ieee.org/inside-hidden-world-legacy-it-systems

Copeland, B.J. (n.d.). *artificial intelligence*. Britannica. https://www.britannica.com/technology/artificial-intelligence

Coveware (2019, November 1). *Ransomware payments rise as public sector is targeted, new variants enter the market*. https://www.coveware.com/blog/q3-ransomware-marketplace-report

Cybersecurity and Infrastructure Security Agency (CISA), US Department of Homeland Security (n.d.). *Moving the US government towards Zero Trust cybersecurity principles*. https://zerotrust.cyber.gov

Cybersecurity and Infrastructure Security Agency (CISA), US Department of Homeland Security (2021a, July 02). *Kaseya VSA supply-chain ransomware attack* [press release]. https://us-cert.cisa.gov/ncas/current-activity/2021/07/02/kaseya-vsa-supply-chain-ransomware-attack

Cybersecurity and Infrastructure Security Agency (CISA), US Department of Homeland Security (2021b, April). *Defending against software supply chain attacks*. https://www.cisa.gov/sites/default/files/publications/defending_against_software_supply_chain_attacks_508_1.pdf

CyberSeek (n.d.). *Heat map*. https://www.cyberseek.org/heatmap.html

Durbin, S. (2020, October 13*). How criminals use artificial intelligence to fuel cyber attacks*. Forbes. https://www.forbes.com/sites/forbesbusinesscouncil/2020/10/13/how-criminals-use-artificial-intelligence-to-fuel-cyber-attacks/?sh=7fcbc2955012

Eaton, C., and Volz, D. (2021, May 19). *Colonial Pipeline CEO tells why he paid hackers a $4.4 million ransom*. Wall Street Journal. https://www.wsj.com/articles/colonial-pipeline-ceo-tells-why-he-paid-hackers-a-4-4-million-ransom-11621435636

English, L. (2021, June 01). *The tech talent war has no end insight: Here's what you need to know.* Forbes. https://www.forbes.com/sites/larryenglish/2021/06/01/the-tech-talent-war-has-no-end-in-sight-heres-what-you-need-to-know/?sh=22e627005f2d

Ericsson (n.d.). *Future IoT.* https://www.ericsson.com/en/future-technologies/future-iot#:~:text=The%20future%20of%20IoT%20has,diverse%20use%20cases%20at%20hyperscale

European Location Interoperability Solutions for e-Government (ELISE) (2021, June 10). *Artificial intelligence in the public sector.* https://joinup.ec.europa.eu/collection/elise-european-location-interoperability-solutions-e-government/artificial-intelligence-public-sector

Exec. Order No. 14028, 86 Fed. Reg. 26633 (2021, May 12).

Expert.ai Team (2020, May 6). *What is machine learning? A definition.* https://www.expert.ai/blog/machine-learning-definition

Freed, B. (2021, July 08). *Maryland towns impacted in Kaseya ransomware breach.* StateScoop. https://statescoop.com/kaseya-revil-ransomware-leonardtown-north-beach-maryland

Gartner (2021, May 17). *Gartner forecasts worldwide security and risk management spending to exceed $150 billion in 2021* [press release]. https://www.gartner.com/en/newsroom/press-releases/2021-05-17-gartner-forecasts-worldwide-security-and-risk-management

Gershgorn, D. (2021, June 30). *Maine passes the strongest state facial recognition ban yet.* The Verge. https://www.theverge.com/2021/6/30/22557516/maine-facial-recognition-ban-state-law

Global Market Insights, Inc. (2016, March 22). *Bring your own device (BYOD) market size worth USD 366.95 billion by 2022: Global Market Insights Inc.* [press release]. https://www.globenewswire.com/news-release/2016/03/22/822021/0/en/Bring-Your-Own-Device-BYOD-Market-size-worth-USD-366-95-Billion-by-2022-Global-Market-Insights-Inc.html

Government Technology News Staff (2021, June 02). *The state of cloud in state and local governments.* Government Technology. https://www.govtech.com/cloud-different/the-state-of-cloud-in-state-and-local-governments

Grimes, R. (2012, January 10). *Why Internet crime goes unpunished: Until we make the Internet secure, cyber criminals will continue to pull off high-value, low-risk offenses.* CSO Magazine. https://www.csoonline.com/article/2618598/why-Internet-crime-goes-unpunished.html

Hein, D. (2021, February 08). *Employees believe mobile devices play a key role in productivity.* Mobility Management Solutions Review. https://solutionsreview.com/mobile-device-management/employees-believe-mobile-devices-play-a-key-role-in-productivity

Hospelhorn, S. (2020, March 29). *Solving the cybersecurity skills shortage within your organization.* Varonis. https://www.varonis.com/blog/cybersecurity-skills-shortage

Kanowitz, S. (2021, March 02). *StateRAMP: How state and local governments accelerate cloud adoption.* GCN. https://gcn.com/articles/2021/03/02/stateramp-readies.aspx

Keegan, M.J., and Greenberg, S. (2021, April 13). *The future of work in local governments post pandemic.* IBM Center for The Business of Government. https://www.businessofgovernment.org/blog/future-work-local-governments-post-pandemic

Kirtley, E. (2020, July 09). *What is SIEM? What is SOAR? How are they different?* Swimlane. https://swimlane.com/blog/siem-soar

Kranz, M. (2018, September 28). *Overcoming the dark side of IoT.* Cisco. https://blogs.cisco.com/innovation/overcoming-the-dark-side-of-iot

Lookout (2021). *US government threat report: Telework exposes government to high mobile risk.* https://www.lookout.com/info/government-threat-report-lp

MarketWatch (2021, April 12). *Bring-your-own-device (BYOD) market size, share, industry, analysis, price, trends, growth, report and forecast 2020–2025* [press release]. https://www.marketwatch.com/press-release/bring-your-own-device-byod-market-size-share-industry-analysis-price-trends-growth-report-and-forecast-2020-2025-2021-04-12

Marks, J. (2021, August 2). *The cybersecurity 202: The government is facing a severe shortage of cyber workers when it needs them the most.* https://www.washingtonpost.com/politics/2021/08/02/cybersecurity-202-governments-facing-severe-shortage-cyber-workers-when-it-needs-them-most

McAfee (2021). *What Is Endpoint Security?* https://www.mcafee.com/enterprise/en-us/security-awareness/endpoint.html

MeriTalk (2021). *Hybrid at hyperspeed: Cloud strategy for the new reality of government.* https://www.meritalk.com/wp-content/uploads/2021/01/hybrid-at-hyperspeed-report.pdf

Miles, S. (2019, February 14). *Cybercriminals take aim: The dark side of IoT.* IoT For All. https://www.iotforall.com/cybercriminals-take-aim-dark-side-iot

Milkovich, D. (2020, December 23). *15 Alarming cyber security facts and stats.* Cybint. https://www.cybintsolutions.com/cyber-security-facts-stats

Morgan, S. (2017, December 11). *5 reasons the cybersecurity labor shortfall won't end soon.* Dark Reading. https://www.darkreading.com/risk/5-reasons-the-cybersecurity-labor-shortfall-wont-end-soon/a/d-id/1330575

Morgan, S. (2020, November 13). *Cybercrime to cost the world $10.5 trillion annually by 2025.* Cyber Crime Magazine. https://cybersecurityventures.com/hackerpocalypse-cybercrime-report-2016/#:~:text=A%202017%20report%20from%20Cybersecurity,figure%20rose%20to%20%2411.5%20billion

Municipal Research and Services Center (2021, May 19). *Telecommuting.* https://mrsc.org/Home/Explore-Topics/Management/HR-Management/Telecommuting.aspx

Nakashima, E. and Lerman, R. (2021, May 15). *Ransomware is a national security threat and a big business: And it's wreaking havoc.* Washington Post. https://www.washingtonpost.com/technology/2021/05/15/ransomware-colonial-darkside-cyber-security

Neiva, C., Lawson, C., Bussa, T., and Sadowski, G. (2019, June 27). *Market guide for security orchestration, automation and response solutions.* Gartner. https://www.gartner.com/en/documents/3942064/market-guide-for-security-orchestration-automation-and-r

Norris, D.F., Mateczun, L., Joshi, A., and Finin, T. (2019). Cyberattacks at the grassroots: American local governments and the need for high levels of cybersecurity. *Public Administration Review*, 79(6), 895–904. https://doi.org/10.1111/puar.13028

Norton (2019, August 28). *The future of IoT: 10 predictions about the Internet of Things.* https://us.norton.com/internetsecurity-iot-5-predictions-for-the-future-of-iot.html

Oltsik, J. (2019, April). *The life and times of cybersecurity professionals, 2018*. Enterprise Strategy Group. https://cdn.ymaws.com/www.members.issa.org/resource/resmgr/surveys/esg-issa-2018-survey-results.pdf

Panetta, K. (2021, April 05). *Gartner top security and risk management trends for 2021*. Gartner. https://www.gartner.com/smarterwithgartner/gartner-top-security-and-risk-trends-for–2021

Parker, K., Horowitz, J. M., and Minkin, R. (2020, December 9). *How the coronavirus outbreak has – and hasn't – changed the way Americans work*. Pew Research. https://www.pewresearch.org/social-trends/2020/12/09/how-the-coronavirus-outbreak-has-and-hasnt-changed-the-way-americans-work

Patterson, D. (2018, September 26). *The dark web is where hackers buy the tools to subvert elections*. CBS News. https://www.cbsnews.com/news/campaign-2018-election-hacking-the-dark-web

Perlman, A. (n.d.). *The growing role of machine learning in cybersecurity*. Security Roundtable. https://www.securityroundtable.org/the-growing-role-of-machine-learning-in-cybersecurity

PhishLabs (2021). *Ransomware playbook: Defense in depth strategies to minimize impact*. https://www.phishlabs.com/blog/ransomware-playbook-defense-in-depth-strategies-to-minimize-impact-2

Pittman, E. (2017a, May 31). *Cloud players: Who's who in the government market*. Government Technology. https://www.govtech.com/biz/Cloud-Players-Whos-Who-in-the-Government-Market.html

Pittman, E. (2017b, May 31). *How should IT strategies evolve to capitalize on the cloud's potential today?* Government Technology. https://www.govtech.com/computing/how-should-it-strategies-evolve-to-capitalize-on-clouds-potential-today.html

Research and Markets (2018, April 04). *Global mobile device management (MDM) market 2018–2023: Decline of bring your own device (BYOD) devices expected to act as the restraining factor for the growth of the market* [press release]. https://www.globenewswire.com/news-release/2018/04/04/1460141/0/en/Global-Mobile-Device-Management-MDM-Market-2018-2023-Decline-of-Bring-Your-Own-Device-BYOD-Devices-Expected-to-Act-as-the-Restraining-Factor-for-the-Growth-of-the-Market.html

Richard, C. (n.d.). *What is the dark side of ioT?* Security Informed. https://www.securityinformed.com/insights/dark-side-of-internet-of-things.1578417703.html

Rose, S., Borchert, O., Mitchell, S., and Connelly, S. (2020, August). *Zero trust architecture*. National institute for Standards and Technology (NIST).

Sawant, V. (2020, December 28). *A brief guide to legacy system modernization*. Rackspace Technology. https://www.rackspace.com/blog/brief-guide-legacy-system-modernization

Shakeel, I. (2021, April 6). *Use AI to fight AI-powered cyber-attacks*. AT&T Business. https://cybersecurity.att.com/blogs/security-essentials/use-ai-to-fight-ai-powered-cyber-attack

Shi, F. (2020, March 26). *Threat spotlight: coronavirus-related phishing*. Barracuda Networks. https://blog.barracuda.com/2020/03/26/threat-spotlight-coronavirus-related-phishing

Sjouwerman, S. (2019, December 23). *Seven reasons for cybercrime's meteoric growth*. Forbes. https://www.forbes.com/sites/forbestechcouncil/2019/12/23/seven-reasons-for-cybercrimes-meteoric-growth/?sh=2641e0415fa2

Sloan, K. (2020 March 12). *The problem with data breach fatigue*. Cybintsolutions. https://www.cybintsolutions.com/the-problem-with-data-breach-fatigue

Sophos (2021). *The state of ransomware in government in 2021.* https://secure2.sophos.com/en-us/medialibrary/Gated-Assets/white-papers/sophos-state-of-ransomware-in-government-2021-wp.pdf

Splunk (n.d.). *What is security automation?* https://www.splunk.com/en_us/data-insider/what-is-security-automation.html#overview

Stevens, G. (2018, December 7). *Dark web phishing kits: Cheap, plentiful and ready to trick you.* Security Boulevard. https://securityboulevard.com/2018/12/dark-web-phishing-kits-cheap-plentiful-and-ready-to-trick-you

Suderman, A. (2021, May 09). *Ransomware gangs get more aggressive against law enforcement.* Associated Press. https://apnews.com/article/ransomware-gangs-hacking-police-cybercrime-pipeline-3a38c27c4fafe0c39461fb71bf91a42a

Synchrony Systems, Inc. (n.d.). *5 Ways your legacy systems may add to cybersecurity risks.* https://sync-sys.com/5-ways-your-legacy-systems-may-add-to-cybersecurity-risks

Tinianow, A. (2020, July 1). *Bitcoin demand drives $1.4 billion ransomware industry in the U.S.* Forbes. https://www.forbes.com/sites/andreatinianow/2020/07/01/bitcoin-demand-drives-14-billion-ransomware-industry-in-the-us/?sh=601541f532d8

U.S. Department of Defense, Office of Inspector General (2021, July 01). *Audit of the cybersecurity of department of defense additive manufacturing systems (DODIG-2021-098).* https://www.dodig.mil/reports.html/article/2683843/audit-of-the-cybersecurity-of-department-of-defense-additive-manufacturing-syst

U.S. Department of Justice, Office of Public Affairs (2021, June 07). *Department of Justice seizes $2.3 million in cryptocurrency paid to the ransomware extortionists darkside* [press release].https://www.justice.gov/opa/pr/department-justice-seizes-23-million-cryptocurrency-paid-ransomware-extortionists-darkside

U.S. National Institute of Standards and Technology (NIST) (2014). *Special Publication 800–53 Rev. 4.* https://nvlpubs.nist.gov/nistpubs/SpecialPublications/NIST.SP.800-53r4.pdf

U.S. National Institute of Standards and Technology (NIST) (2015). *Special Publication 800–161.* https://nvlpubs.nist.gov/nistpubs/SpecialPublications/NIST.SP.800-161.pdf

U.S. National Institute of Standards and Technology (NIST) (2018 April 16). *Framework for improving critical infrastructure cybersecurity version 1.1.* https://nvlpubs.nist.gov/nistpubs/CSWP/NIST.CSWP.04162018.pdf

U.S. National Institute of Standards and Technology (NIST) (2020a). *Special Publication 800–207. Zero trust architecture.* https://nvlpubs.nist.gov/nistpubs/SpecialPublications/NIST.SP.800-207.pdf

U.S. National Institute of Standards and Technology (NIST) (2020b). *Special Publication 800–124 Rev. 2 (Draft).* https://csrc.nist.gov/publications/detail/sp/800-124/rev-2/draft

U.S. National Institute of Standards and Technology (NIST) (2021, July 9). *Security measures for "EO-Critical Software" use.* https://www.nist.gov/itl/executive-order-improving-nations-cybersecurity/security-measures-eo-critical-software-use–2

U.S. National Institute of Standards and Technology (NIST) (n.d.). *Executive Order 14028, Improving the nation's cybersecurity.* https://www.nist.gov/itl/executive-order-improving-nations-cybersecurity

U.S. National Security Agency (NSA) (2021, February). *NIST Special Publicatin 800-207mbracing a zero trust security model.* https://media.defense.gov/2021/Feb/25/2002588479/-1/-1/0/CSI_EMBRACING_ZT_SECURITY_MODEL_UOO115131-21.PDF

Vailshery, L.S. (2021, March 08). *Internet of Things (iot) and non-iot active device connections worldwide from 2010 to 2025*. Statistica. https://www.statista.com/statistics/1101442/iot-number-of-connected-devices-worldwide/#:~:text=The%20total%20installed%20base%20of,that%20are%20expected%20in%202021

Varonis (2021). *134 Cybersecurity statistics and trends for 2021*. https://www.varonis.com/blog/cuybersecurity-statistics

Verizon (2020). *2020 Verizon data breach investigations report*. https://enterprise.verizon.com/resources/reports/2020-data-breach-investigations-report.pdf

Vinchesi, P. (2020, May 14). *After Covid-19: Is there a place for telework in local government?* ICMA. https://icma.org/articles/article/after-covid-19-there-place-telework-local-government

Walter, J. (2020, May 2) *Covid-19 news: FBI reports 300% increase in reported cybercrimes*. https://www.imcgrupo.com/covid-19-news-fbi-reports-300-increase-in-reported-cybercrimes

Warner, J. (2021, May 6). *What is zero trust security?* Crowd Strike. https://www.crowdstrike.com/cybersecurity-101/zero-trust-security

Watts, S., and Raza, M. (2019, June 15). *SaaS vs PaaS vs IaaS: What's the difference and how to choose*. BMC Blogs. https://www.bmc.com/blogs/saas-vs-paas-vs-iaas-whats-the-difference-and-how-to-choose

13

Summary and Recommendations

As seen from evidence presented throughout this book, local governments do a poor job of managing and practicing cybersecurity (see especially Chapters 5 and 6). Of course, this is not true of all local governments, but it is of too many. Many, if not most large, well-funded local governments understand the need for appropriate levels of cybersecurity and do their best to provide it by adequately budgeting and staffing this function. However, most local governments, at least in the US, are small and unlikely to meet this challenge effectively.[1]

Unfortunately, small- and even mid-sized local governments typically have greater financial constraints than their larger cousins, and they cannot or will not fund and staff cybersecurity adequately. As a result of these and other factors, too many of them experience adverse cybersecurity events that might otherwise have been preventable. This is not to say that larger local governments do not experience such events, but those governments are typically better prepared to prevent and recover from cyberattacks.

13.1 Important Highlights from This Book

Adverse cybersecurity events, typically cyberattacks, incidents, and breaches (especially the latter) often result in the loss of data (e.g., PII but data of all sorts stored by local governments), shutdowns of critical public services, loss of money (either directly from theft or indirectly through the cost of recovery), public embarrassment, and more. In some cases, these events take entire local governments or significant elements of them offline for months at a time. The examples of Atlanta and Baltimore (discussed in Chapter 1) are but two illustrations of the fate that regularly befalls unprepared local governments. As the evidence shows, too many of these governments are largely unable to effectively protect their IT systems in what is the wild, wild west of cybersecurity.

This is why cybersecurity – defined in Chapter 2 – and the protection of information technology systems is essential for local governments. Without appropriate levels of cybersecurity, bad things will certainly happen. With it, local governments will still be the targets of cyberattacks but would be better positioned to prevent them from succeeding and better equipped to recover if attacks should succeed.

Cybersecurity and Local Government, First Edition. Donald F. Norris, Laura K. Mateczun and Richard F. Forno.
© 2022 John Wiley & Sons Ltd. Published 2022 by John Wiley & Sons Ltd.

In order to develop and maintain acceptable and industry-standard levels of cybersecurity, buy-in from the very top of local governments is needed. An all-too-common finding from the academic and professional literature is that too often top officials pay lip service, if that, to cybersecurity. Instead, chief elected officials, members of local legislative bodies, and top appointed managers must have a basic understanding of cybersecurity, unequivocally support and, within budgetary constraints, adequately fund it. This book addressed what local officials should know about cybersecurity (Chapter 3) and questions they should ask themselves and their cybersecurity staff about it (Chapter 11). Local officials would do well to consider reviewing these chapters (and others) from time to time.

Policies that are either essential or desirable to local government cybersecurity were discussed in Chapter 7, which made clear that without the adoption, implementation, and regular review of *all* of the essential cybersecurity policies, local governments put themselves at unnecessary risk. Imagine, for example, a local government without an acceptable use policy (AUP). How will officials, staff, vendors, and other end users know what to do and what not to do? Intuition? Via osmosis? These are clearly not good options and inevitably will lead to problems. Hence, this chapter strongly recommends that local governments adopt a suite of policies that govern cybersecurity expectations, controls requirements, and standards of conduct for users.

Chapter 8 established that people are the "root of the problem" in local government cybersecurity. Yes, people make mistakes, don't follow rules, and can be malicious – all of which can lead to cybersecurity problems. At the same time, people can be great assets to local government cybersecurity. If properly trained and managed, they can be an important line of defense by identifying and reporting anomalies that they observe in local IT systems, emails that seem suspicious, and otherwise help foster a culture of cybersecurity awareness, if not cognizance, at all levels of local government.

The NIST Cybersecurity Framework is addressed and, hopefully, demystified in Chapter 9. This framework is important because it provides guidance to all organizations, including local governments regarding steps that should be taken to establish and maintain strong and effective cybersecurity programs. Local governments looking for a solid and industry-accepted approach toward cybersecurity program development should charge their cybersecurity leadership and teams with emulating those guidelines to implement the highest levels of cybersecurity possible.

Cybersecurity law, which is rarely covered in books providing information and guidance to organizations about cybersecurity, was addressed in Chapter 10. Laws and regulations govern how local governments must protect their information systems and sensitive data. Local government cybersecurity programs must consider compliance obligations imposed by federal law and regulations, state law, and even some international regulations like the EU's GDPR. Although the wide variety of the various laws and regulations can seem overwhelming to non-lawyers, local governments can help ensure higher levels of cybersecurity protection by following them.

In order to do their jobs effectively as leaders of local governments, top elected and appointed officials need to know questions about their governments' cybersecurity that they should ask themselves and their cybersecurity teams. Chapter 11 discussed several such questions and also made the case that asking such questions should never be a one-off activity. Rather, top officials should engage in ongoing conversations with their cybersecurity experts on a range of important cybersecurity issues facing their local government organizations.

Looking ahead, Chapter 12 suggested what the future of cybersecurity holds for local governments. Just as in the present day, both offensive and defensive cybersecurity tools, techniques, and procedures will continue to evolve, and local governments must stay informed about how this evolution affects them. Local governments must also be agile and flexible enough to respond to changes in the threat landscape presented by the constant evolution of internet technologies in order to provide the most effective cybersecurity possible to their organizations.

Throughout this book, several themes should be apparent. First, local governments are under constant or nearly constant cyberattack and the number of attacks is increasing. For example, between 2019 and 2020, ransomware attacks in the US alone increased by more than twofold (Nakashima, 2021). There is no expectation that this trend will reverse itself anytime soon.

Second, many cyberattacks succeed. As this book, and many cybersecurity practitioners routinely warn, it is not *if* your local government will be successfully attacked...it is *when*. Indeed, even the most well-defended information systems are likely to experience periodic attacks, breaches, or other cybersecurity incidents. What makes things worse, however, is that most local governments do not practice or manage cybersecurity well. As this book's third major observation, poor cybersecurity practice and management is almost certainly true, at least at this writing, of most organizations. But local government officials should take no solace here, for it is the very organizations for which their top officials are responsible that practice and manage cybersecurity poorly, not some business small or large, that makes today's cybersecurity headlines.

One of and perhaps the most important reason that local governments do not manage and practice cybersecurity well is that too often top elected and appointed officials are not sufficiently invested in cybersecurity. This is the fourth major lesson of this book. As Atlanta's mayor said after her city's ransomware attack in in 2019, cybersecurity had not been a priority. Cybersecurity does not become a priority until after a breach. Even then, the lesson does not always take, as the example of Baltimore's back-to-back breaches in 2018 and 2019 demonstrates.

Fifth, the top barrier to cybersecurity across organizations, including local governments, is lack of funding. This is not entirely unexpected: why would one expect this not to be the case considering that top officials are not sufficiently invested in it, and these officials control their local governments' purse strings? Adequate funding is essential to provide adequate cybersecurity staffing, technology, training, policies, and procedures – everything that is needed to ensure appropriate levels of cybersecurity and better cybersecurity outcomes.

The sixth and final significant lesson from this book is that too many local governments are one generation or more behind current best cybersecurity practices. Again, the 2016 survey found that just over half of local governments reported their cybersecurity technology was at the best practice. Further, as the data from Chapter 6 shows, the number of local governments reporting current best practices being used for cybersecurity policies and procedures were even worse. This places local governments at greater, often much greater, risk than necessary and that their officials and residents should tolerate.

13.2   Important Recommendations

These and other findings presented throughout this book lead to recommendations that, if adopted and implemented, can assist local governments manage and practice cybersecurity much more effectively. Many of these recommendations have been made throughout this book but are sufficiently important to warrant repeating.

Perhaps most important, top elected and appointed officials must be fully supportive of and committed to effective cybersecurity for their local governments. The evidence shows that too many top officials are not engaged in and committed to cybersecurity. As mentioned earlier, if these officials are not committed to cybersecurity, those rank-and-file employees beneath them will understandably wonder, "If they don't care, why should I?"

So what can be done to ensure buy-in from top officials? One important step is for local governments to formally elevate their top IT and cybersecurity officials (typically CIOs and CISOs) to positions within the top management team in the organization. These technology leaders should be regarded as key advisors to the city or county manager, the mayor or county executive, and other top officials, and should be tasked to brief these officials as well as local legislative bodies regularly on cybersecurity matters.

Of course, no cybersecurity program can just materialize on its own. It must be adequately funded and staffed. Regardless of a local government's budgetary situation and regardless of whether top officials *say* they support cybersecurity, if those officials do not provide adequate funding and staffing, it is more likely than not that bad cybersecurity outcomes will occur. Adequate investment in cybersecurity is essential to ensure adequate cybersecurity staffing, technology, policies, and practices. Without it, local governments are at unnecessary risk for adverse cybersecurity outcomes. So: fund it and staff it, for actions speak louder than words.

Local governments must provide cybersecurity awareness training for all parties, regardless of their rank or job title, and the training must be mandatory. Training must begin when new employees are hired and new elected officials join the local government. Training must be offered periodically throughout employees' and officials' careers in the organization. Training must also be tightly connected with accountability measures so that *when* (not if) a member of the organization, for example, violates rules set forth in the AUP, whether accidentally or intentionally, that party should face appropriate counseling. Should violations continue, more serious accountability measures should be instituted, such as loss of user privileges or, in the case of employees (though likely not elected officials), termination of employment.

The 2016 survey found that barely a third of local government cybersecurity policies reflected industry best practices. This constitutes cybersecurity malpractice and must be rectified. If local governments' cybersecurity policies are not at least representative of current best practice, once again, those government are at unnecessary risk of adverse cybersecurity events. Policies (and their enforcement within organizations) are every bit as important as cybersecurity technology and practices. Policies also establish the foundation of, and expectations for, a cybersecurity program. Best cybersecurity practices can be found in documents and advice provided by organizations such as NIST, CISA, local government membership and professional organizations, and other local governments. Wherever they are located, the important point is that local government officials should demand (and fund) the adoption of cybersecurity best practices throughout their organizations.

To confirm those policies and procedures are followed and remain effective in the face of a constantly changing cybersecurity environment, local governments should adopt a philosophy of continuous improvement. At a minimum this means that they will continuously assess and evaluate cybersecurity policies, procedures, practices, and controls for effectiveness. Inculcating a serious commitment to continuous improvement helps to ensure that cybersecurity policies and procedures are current and actually doing what management expects them to be doing. Continuous improvement activities not only help foster a cybersecurity culture, but also develop and share institutional knowledge that can keep cybersecurity policies and procedures current and relevant.

As local governments develop or enhance their cybersecurity postures in the face of nearly constant cyberattacks, they would do well to embrace the concept of resiliency. Just as they have planned to keep the critical functions of government operating during natural disasters or other emergencies, that same approach can be applied to IT systems to ensure they remain functional when under duress as well. This risk-based, systems-oriented planning process, which ideally involves stakeholders from the CIO, CISO, and facilities management teams (among others) can help minimize the impact of a cyberattack on government operations and thus keep the wheels of government turning when they're needed most.

Remember the CIA triad from Chapter 2. Ensuring and protecting the "Availability" of IT systems is a core function of cybersecurity teams.

Partnering with other local governments in the region, joining information sharing and analysis centers and building relationships with the cybersecurity experts at the FBI and CISA is essential to local governments attaining cybersecurity resiliency. MS-ISAC already has at least 10,706 local governments and local agencies as members and provides exceptional threat information and other resources to help improve local government cybersecurity such as incident response services, a 24/7 security operations center, and education materials like tabletop exercises. Similarly, the FBI and CISA also provide incident response assistance. If relationships with such organizations are established prior to an adverse cybersecurity event taking place, the built trust and familiarity will help the local government respond and recover more quickly.

Finally, all local governments should develop a culture of cybersecurity within their organizations. Among other reasons, the purpose of a culture of cybersecurity is to ensure that good cybersecurity practices (the proverbial "cyber-hygiene") are prevalent throughout the organization and among all personnel. To be most effective, a culture of cybersecurity starts from and must be maintained by those at the top of the organization. That is, top elected and appointed officials must develop and demonstrate ongoing commitment to cybersecurity through effective policies, management actions, and practice of "cyber-hygiene." Indeed, *cybersecurity is everyone's responsibility* – crafting and inculcating an appropriate awareness of and responsibility for cybersecurity by everyone in the organization can provide a solid, and most importantly, proactive, way of helping minimize potential cybersecurity problems.

13.3 Conclusion

Providing and maintaining effective cybersecurity is important for organizations of all types and sizes in the modern world. It is especially important to local governments because they are *public* organizations that serve residents, businesses, visitors and presumably others, and that provide vital public services. When local governments are successfully attacked (see the examples of Atlanta and Baltimore – and countless others), their ability to provide those services is not only compromised but can and often is rendered impossible for periods of time. Local governments (and other organizations) can take months to recover from adverse cybersecurity events, which can cost millions of dollars, damage residents and others' trust in the affected local government, and be a source of considerable embarrassment to local officials.

Consequently, the authors of *Cybersecurity and Local Government* believe that the top elected and appointed officials in local governments should take quite seriously the findings and recommendations presented in this book. They must adopt and implement the cybersecurity technologies, practices, and policies necessary to achieve the most effective levels of cybersecurity possible for their organizations. Accomplishing this requires political courage and the management chops to identify, assign, and spend the necessary resources to meet this critical local need in an era of ongoing fiscal stringency. At the same time, these officials should remember that local government does not exist in a vacuum and that plenty of free or low-cost resources exist that can help make this process easier, as will learning from, emulating, and collaborating with other government entities at the local, state, or federal levels.

The choice is a serious one for local governments. Admittedly, there are costs involved no matter what decision is taken. Nevertheless, local governments must prepare either to take proactive actions now to improve their cybersecurity, or prepare to face the inevitable technical, operational, financial, and public consequences of failing to do so.

Note

1 The Census Bureau estimates that around three-quarters of the nation's incorporated places had fewer than 5000 residents in 2020 and, among them, more than four in ten had 500 persons or less (Toukabri and Medina, 2020). Moreover, the vast majority of US municipalities (78 percent) have populations of 10,000 or less, 5866 out of 7524 (ICMA, 2013). This does not include the 12,801 municipalities with populations of less than 2500 (Miller, 2018).

References

International City/County Management Association (ICMA) (2013). *The Municipal Yearbook 2013* (pp. xii and xv).

Miller, B. (2018, December 3). *Nearly half of U.S. cities have fewer than 1,000 residents.* Government Technology. https://www.govtech.com/data/nearly-half-of-us-cities-have-fewer-than-1000-residents.html

Nakashima, E. (2021, September 18). *U.S. aims to thwart ransomware attacks by cracking down on crypto payments.* Washington Post. http://thewashingtonpost.pressreader.com/epaper/viewer.aspx

Toukabri, A. and Medina, L. 2020 (May 21). *Latest city and town population estimates of the decade show three-fourths of the nation's incorporated places have fewer than 5,000 people.* U.S. Census Bureau. https://www.census.gov/library/stories/2020/05/america-a-nation-of-small-towns.html

Index

Cybersecurity and Local Government, First Edition. Donald F. Norris, Laura K. Mateczun and
Richard F. Forno.
© 2022 John Wiley & Sons Ltd. Published 2022 by John Wiley & Sons Ltd.